T0319083

Learning to make change

Learning to make change

Developing innovation competence for recreating the African university of the 21st century

Paul Kibwika

Wageningen Academic
P u b l i s h e r s

ISBN-10: 90-8686-017-6
ISNN-13: 978-90-8686-017-3

The individual contributions in this publication and any liabilities arising from them remain the responsibility of the authors.

First published, 2006

The publisher is not responsible for possible damages, which could be a result of content derived from this publication.

Wageningen Academic Publishers
The Netherlands, 2006

Table of contents

List of tables

List of figures

List of boxes

Acronyms

ADC/IDEA	Agribusiness Development Centre of the Investment in Developing Export Agriculture
AHI	African Highlands Initiative
ARD	Agricultural Research for Development
ASARECA	Association for Strengthening Agricultural Research in Eastern and Central Africa
CAEC	Continuing Agricultural Education Centre
CGIAR	International Agricultural Research Centre
CPD	Continuing Professional Development
DLG	District Local Government
FARA	Forum for Agricultural Research in Africa
FORUM	Forum on Agricultural Resource Husbandry
HRD	Human Resource Department
I@mak.com	Innovations at Makerere Committee
IAR4D	Integrated Agricultural Research for Development
ICRA	International Centre for Research in Agriculture
INRM	Integrated Natural Resource Management
KVFGA	Kooja Vanilla and Fruits Growers Association
MAAIF	Ministry of Agriculture, Animal Industry and Fisheries
MAK	Makerere University
MIS	Management Information System
NAADS	National Agricultural Advisory Services
NARI	National Agricultural Research Institute
NARO	National Agricultural Research Organisation
NARP	National Agricultural Research Policy
NARS	National Agricultural Research Systems
NGO	Non-Governmental Organisations
NRM	Natural Resource Management
PAU	Participatory Approaches and Up-scaling
PEAP	Poverty Eradication Action Plan
PIT	Project Implementation Team
PLG	Peer Learning Group
PM/SS	Personal Mastery and Soft Skills
PMA	Plan for Modernisation of Agriculture
RF	Rockefeller Foundation
SLA	Sustainable Livelihoods Approach
T & V	Training and Visit extension system
TAD	Technology of Agrarian Development
UNESCO	United Nations Education, Scientific and Cultural Organisation
USA	United States of America

USAID	United States Agency for International Development
Win26	The 26 pioneers of the PM/SS programme
ZARI	Zonal Agricultural Research Institute

Acknowledgements

This thesis, *Learning to Make Change*, was inspired by deep reflection on my personal life history, organisational challenges and professional contribution to solving the multitudes of problems of improving the lives of the poor in Uganda. That reflection happened in a workshop on enhancing professional skills organised for the Participatory Approaches and Up-scaling (PAU) PhD programme at Boxmeer, Netherlands in 2002. The workshop facilitators, Jürgen Hagmann and Ulrike Breitschuh triggered the reflection with the question: *looking back into your personal background, organisation and the critical problems you face in your country, what would your PhD change?* This question induced deep thoughts about the value of a PhD beyond my personal interests and inspired an action research for a PhD thesis. In pursuance of this study programme, I am indebted to several organisations and individuals.

First, I thank the Rockefeller Foundation for the scholarship through the PAU programme and for funding the research. Without this scholarship, I would not have been exposed and challenged this way and consequently my thinking would be different from what is portrayed in this thesis. I am also grateful to my employer, Makerere University for granting me a study leave to pursue the PhD study. Similarly, I extend my appreciation to the PAU programme and the Technology of Agrarian Development (TAD) Group of Wageningen University for guidance throughout the study period. Specifically, I thank Conny Almekinders, the Coordinator of the PAU programme for the creativity to integrate professional skills development in the PhD programme with a view of turning out professionals capable of influencing change in their respective organisations and countries. The flexibility in management of the PAU programme to meet specific needs of candidates is highly appreciated.

Second, I remain challenged by the support, guidance and learning that I gained from my promotion team comprising of Paul Richards, Arjen Wals and Jürgen Hagmann. I am inclined to expresses my appreciation to each of them. The intellectual and often philosophical discussions with Paul Richards challenged me to explore to better understand the different dimensions of social science. Many times I got confused in the course of the discussions but I now do realise that without confusion, there cannot be clarity. It is such situations that nurture academic maturity.

I must have been lucky to work with Arjen Wals who passionately cared about me and showed great interest in what I did. At some moments, my stay in the Netherlands was stressful but his counsel, empathy and appreciative attitude were a therapy. He always challenged me to look for opportunities among challenges. From him, I learnt how to guide others through an academic programme. At a personal level, he ensured that I was comfortable enough to concentrate on writing this thesis. Proximity to his office and frequent interactions were motivating. Sometimes his advice not to work too hard just encouraged me to work harder instead. All staff of the Education and Competence Chair Group are highly appreciated for being so friendly and supportive during the time I was writing this thesis.

For Jürgen, we worked as brothers and we so addressed each other. His humility, selflessness and commitment to enabling people solve their own problems is a legacy that I will always strive for in my career. To say the least, he taught me a new profession for which a PhD alone would have been inadequate. Through him, I gained in terms of knowledge, experience, exposure and finance that supported my completion of this research. Wider exposure to the challenges and criticisms of higher education in the sub-Saharan Africa contributed to the enthusiasm for timely completion of this thesis.

Third, I recognise the support of Adipala-Ekwamu, the champion of the innovation competence development initiative at Makerere University. His humbleness and determination were inspirational to me and my colleagues ('Win26') in the learning programme. Similarly, I sincerely thank the 'Win26' for the encouragement and support extended to me in different ways. They were always willing to help in all ways possible and their social support was no mean contribution to this work. Their cooperation and honest discussions about their learning experiences form the backbone of this thesis.

Fourth, I acknowledge all the vanilla farmers who participated in this study. From them, I learnt more about vanilla and its social context. In a special way, I thank Christopher Wali, the extension staff in-charge of Ntenjeru sub-county where the vanilla case study was conducted. His sacrifice of time to introduce me to the vanilla farmers and assistance to enable me obtain the information I needed are highly appreciated. Similarly, I recognise my colleague, Vincent Kayanja for his unreserved support during data collection from farmers.

Fifth, I am grateful to the partner organisations in the IAR4D initiative *i.e.* NARO, ICRA, Makerere University, and AHI. The initiative presented an opportunity to engage with researchers in an action learning mode. Specifically, I recognise all members of the Project Implementation Team (PIT) for steering the initiative, and my co-facilitators namely: Richard Hawkins, Maria Goretti Nassuna-Musoke, Richard Miiro and Chris Opondo for their contributions. All the participants in the IAR4D initiative are acknowledged.

Lastly, I am thankful to my family for the overwhelming support and encouragement to complete this work. With optimism they endured my absence and offered me the most needed care and support. My wife Rachel was a wonderful teacher, counsellor and comforter during the stressful moments. My sons; Joshua Kibwika and Derek Kibwika, were a source of energy to complete my studies as soon as possible in order to create more time for them. Now that it is done, I am hopeful that with God's Grace, the future will be much better.

Paul Kibwika, October 2006

CHAPTER ONE
Introduction

Background

There is concern that the 19th century model of higher education with which we are most familiar is inadequate for the very different conditions and challenges of the 21st century (Sterling, 2001). These challenges include issues of poverty, sustainability and democracy arising from the complex interaction of many social, political and technological elements. We live in an essentially 'systemic world' characterised by multiple causation and complex feedback, yet the dominant educational structures are based on fragmentation rather than connection, relationship and synergy (Sterling, 2000). From an emancipatory perspective, Wals and Jickling (2000) view education as a means for people to become self-actualized members of society, seeking meaning, developing their own potential and jointly creating solutions. They argue that a sustainable world cannot be created without the full and democratic involvement of all members of society; a sustainable world without participation and democracy is improbable, and perhaps even impossible. For education to help shape a participative, democratic and sustainable world, it has to be redesigned to fit that context. As Wood (1995) puts it, the fundamentals of organisation life – thinking and interaction, roles and relationships, learning and work habits - are modelled in the way schools are organised; only deep restructuring at the level of beliefs, and the complete reinvention of educational workplaces, can hope to advance society's development.

These challenges fundamentally question the relevance of education today. Universities, expected to be champions of educational reforms, are themselves challenged concerning their relevance. Universities today often find it easier to construct buildings and increase endowments than bring about fundamental improvements in the teaching and learning processes; but to respond to the learning requirements of individuals for a world society in the twenty-first century there is need for innovation in the learning process (Boyatzis *et al.*, 1995). Innovation in learning is even more crucial for universities in the sub-Saharan Africa where the highest levels of poverty and food insecurity persist. Can African universities in their current form contribute to a reversal of the situation, or (put another way) what has been their contribution to the problem? This thesis addresses the question of relevance of universities to development challenges, particularly in sub-Saharan Africa. Bearing in mind that farming is an important element in the livelihoods of a majority of people in the region this research focuses on the agricultural context, using Uganda as a specific case.

About this thesis

This thesis describes and evaluates an experiment in transforming learning, research and consultancy in an African university, in the hope of making university research and training more innovative, and more able to influence wider processes of change in society. Current university education is oriented towards developing *"experts"* in specialised disciplines, but there is an increasing demand for the universities directly to influence change in development. Bridging a perceived gap between *"experts"* and *"change makers"* is at the core of what this thesis describes. Making change in society, it is argued, requires competences over and above technical expertise. These competences have to be learnt, and the learning starts with the university lecturers, hence the title of the thesis *"Learning to make change"*. The thesis specifically discusses a pilot programme in innovation competence development in the agriculture-related faculties of Makerere University in Uganda. This explains why the discussion in this thesis is focused on the agricultural context, but the application of the argument extends to other disciplines.

The first chapter introduces the reader to the research. It is explained that the format is that of action research, in which the author was both one of the lecturers learning to make change, while also seeking to document and critically understand the process of which he was a part. The chapter offers a statement of the research problem from which more specific objectives and a set of research questions are derived. These are justified by examining why there is need for change, starting with historical perspectives and leading up recent reforms and new demands. The conceptual framework, research methodology and methods used are also discussed. The second chapter then reviews a number of theoretical arguments providing support for a transformational approach to higher education in general, with emphasis on universities.

The third and fourth chapters aim to establish the key competences required in agricultural innovation systems. Specifically, the third chapter explores how farmers learn in their own context in a self-organised way, using vanilla as a case. This then helps to identify areas where agricultural professionals can intervene to enhance this type of learning and hence facilitate processes of change in community. These areas of intervention are used to draw out implications for the competence of professionals, to which university training needs to respond. The fourth chapter analyses the challenges professionals face in working with farmers, in order to achieve a shift to a demand-driven arrangement for agricultural research and extension services. The challenges are then used to further clarify competences required on both the demand side (farmers) and on the supply side (research and extension) in order to create an effective innovation system. These constitute the changes towards which universities need to orient themselves.

Chapters 5, 6 and 7 then look in some detail at actual attempts to implement a competence development programme aimed at making the university more innovative and responsive to current and emerging competence demands for agricultural professionals, as well as shaping university research and consultancy to have a more far-reaching influence on societal development processes. The design and implementation of such a competence development programme within a specific university setting are major features of interest in the present study. Chapter eight brings together the outcomes of the three case studies to build synergies in competences at the levels of farmers, agricultural professionals (service providers) and university. The generic meta-level competences at the university level are discussed in relation to the competences of the other two levels. From this discussion, conclusions follow.

Context of the problem

The past two decades have been characterised by major policy and structural reforms in Uganda. These include devolution of power to local governments through decentralisation, liberalisation of trade and privatisation of service delivery. The reforms were accompanied by new institutional arrangements and responsibilities in the planning and execution of development programmes. Central to the reforms is the search for more effective ways of addressing the challenge of poverty and good governance. Resulting from this new ways of doing business in the public and private sectors are required. Consequently the new ways of doing things demand new knowledge, skills and attitudes. The comprehensive and multi-sectoral government poverty eradication action plan (PEAP) is a good example of a framework requiring new functions and relationships between actors within and between the public and private sector. Academic institutions, particularly universities, are in turn challenged to produce a new type of graduate with capabilities effectively to steer the private and public sector in dealing with complex problems such as poverty.

In response to the challenge, Makerere University initiated a survey to gain better understanding of the expectations of the university from employers (particularly local government and the private sector). The survey (Asiimwe *et al.*, 2001) revealed gaps between the qualities of current graduates and what actually the market demands. While existing graduates were considered to be academically sound in their specialities, they largely lacked abilities to effectively apply their academic knowledge to influence change in society. A similar conclusion was reached in a meeting of Deans and leading researchers from seventeen Eastern and Southern African universities to discuss "Curriculum Development and Transformation in Rural Development and Natural Resource Management" in Bellagio, Italy (Patel *et al.*, 2001). Agriculture being the main source of livelihood for over 80% of the population and the main focus of the PEAP, agriculture-related faculties face an even bigger challenge. Findings of the survey commissioned by the university led to a project known as 'I@mak.com' whose aim was to stimulate innovations within the university to ensure relevance in the new economic and social context. 'I@mak.com' was coined from Innovations at Makerere Committee – the committee responsible for developing the project.

Many universities have moved quite rapidly towards improving marketable skills of their graduates by offering new credential such as graduate certificates and diplomas often drawn from existing curriculum rather than starting with a reflective exploration of the range of needs of practitioners themselves (Guiton, 1999). In view of this, the Bellagio meeting went beyond curricula and defined the profile and competences of graduates capable of addressing current and future challenges in an agrarian system, and then explored what it takes to develop such graduates. In addition to their technical skills in agricultural disciplines (hard skills) such graduates would also have to have the conceptual and management skills (so-called "soft skills") to facilitate joint learning processes, negotiate, integrate disciplines, and think critically and analytically (Patel *et al.*, 2001; Hagmann, 2002). This reflected a core competence gap within the university systems that reflected in the graduates. The University commissioned survey for example highlights that:

"University graduates were criticised for lack of practical skills, low motivation, lack of dedication, inability to solve problems, narrow focus and lack of cross-cutting, multidisciplinary and integrative knowledge....... However, training institutions in Uganda, such as Makerere University, have been blind to, or possibly, insensitve to, local governments' human resource needs. They continue to produce human resources that have more theoretical than practical knowledge that is required...." ('I@mak.com', 2001: 7-8)

Bridging such competence gaps necessitated targeting the university lecturers first. A pilot programme to build the missing skills among lecturers was therefore initiated at Makerere University, with the first phase focusing on agriculture-related faculties.

The research problem

That universities need to transform to be more innovative and relevant in the development arena is not contested in this thesis, but rather the challenge will be to explore how such transformation can be effected. Persistent levels of poverty and food insecurity in the Sub-Sahara Africa are unbearable, and yet universities in the region continue to turn out graduates every year, and generate technologies and knowledge ostensibly to deal with such development challenges, without much evident impact on poverty reduction. This is a clear reason for wanting to do things differently. Developing country universities remain an "ivory tower" for academicians far detached from the development process. The graduates from the universities parade in gowns symbolising academic achievement that has so far failed to translate into development change in society. While their academic abilities are often undoubted, the relevance of such academic achievements to national development is highly contested.

Makerere University intends through initiatives like the 'I@mak.com' to stimulate innovations to ensure that the training, research and consultancy it offers is more relevant to national development. But a key question is whether the same thinking that created and sustains the existing university can solve the problems it has created. Coleman (1984) points out that one of the limitations and obstacles that any university in a Third World country faces in trying to be developmental is the competence of the existing professorial body – its members were never trained to think, act or teach development, and so nothing is likely to change unless they retool themselves; to expect institutional change from existing competences would be the 'blind leading the blind'. The new demands for relevance imply a shift from performing purely academic functions to combining academic and developmental roles. This requires a shift in mindsets, values, and competences to challenge the very purpose of the university. As in many other countries depending largely on agriculture, the major challenge in Uganda is how to transform the agricultural sector to get the majority of the population out of the poverty trap. For this reason, Makerere University launched a pilot programme to develop innovation competence among lecturers in agriculture-related faculties, with a view to learning lessons useful in enhancing the relevance and visibility of the university on the development scene more generally.

This study is intended to establish how this pilot in innovation competence development contributed to our understanding of how to transform universities so that they are more relevant to development in an agrarian context. The study first explores how farmers themselves learn and innovate within existing local social networks, in order to help more clearly define the functions of agricultural professionals (how they can complement what farmers already do for themselves). It then synthesizes key challenges for agricultural professionals to engage with farmers in (researcher-farmer) innovations systems, from which key competences for both the professionals and farmers are distilled. With this in clear view, the relevance of the Makerere competence development programme is analysed in terms of its design, implementation and outcomes.

Objectives

The overall objective of this research was to establish how the innovation competence development programme for university lecturers could be set-up and implemented to increase the relevance of universities to national development in Uganda. From the point of view of relevance with respect to development in an agricultural context, the specific objectives were to:
1. Identify the main functions of agricultural professionals in enhancing farmer innovations.
2. Identify the key competence challenges for agricultural professionals to engage with farmers in an innovation system.
3. Describe how an innovation competence development programme for university lecturers can be designed and implemented to respond to the challenges of agricultural development.
4. Assess what a competence development programme contributes to addressing the challenge of making universities relevant to development.

Research questions

The objectives listed above were pursued via the following research questions:
1. How do farmers learn and innovate in their own context?
2. What can agricultural professionals do to enhance farmer learning and innovation?
3. What are the key competence challenges that agricultural professionals face in working with farmers to enhance learning and innovation for development?
4. How can a comprehensive competence development programme for lecturers in university be designed and implemented to respond to the competence requirements of agricultural professionals working with farmers?
5. What does such a competence programme contribute, more broadly, to the transformation of university training, research and consultancy aimed at poverty alleviation and development?

Justification

Historical aspects of education in Uganda

We cannot question the relevance of higher education today without looking into the history of education itself. Formal education in Uganda was introduced by European missionaries with the aim of turning the supposedly "ignorant savage" into a good Christian and eventually a good tool for the colonial government (Opio-Odong, 1993: 11). At one level, Christian missionaries were concerned with conversion of the indigenous people, but a critical examination of their activities in Uganda and other African countries reveals that missionaries were often highly meshed with European colonial projects in Africa (Tiberondwa, 1998). Tiberondwa goes on to suggest that the indigenous or traditional education aimed at equipping young members of society with essential skills to enable young people to play a full role as members of their community was replaced with a type of instruction prerequisite to social, political and economic advancement. Education was looked at as skills to be used in the white man's employment, and thus strongly connected with office work (Ssekamwa, 2000: 84). Ssekamwa quotes a son of Sir Apollo Kaggwa, one of the first Ugandans to 'benefit' from Western education as having said (in the 1930s):

> "Parents sent their boys to high school not to learn to drive bullock wagons and to look after cattle, but to learn to be fitted for posts of high standing".

The purpose of education then was to get people out of the community, cleanse them of their traditional values, indoctrinate them with Christian values, and give them formal education fitted for "white collar" jobs.

African universities were established by colonial regimes to create locally educated collaborating elites, and prevent the African youths from going abroad for higher education where they might be exposed to ideas questioning the basis of colonialism. Universities often thrive on respect for tradition, so until now a number of the older (colonially-created) universities, such as Makerere, have been slow to shed traditions of practice and thinking rooted in the colonial period (Kasozi, 2003: xv, xvi). After independence, governments developed five-year development plans and undertook manpower surveys, on the basis of which ministers advised universities about numbers of graduates required in a particular discipline for each planning cycle (Ssebuwufu, 2005). Even in the late 1970s the strategy for enrolment of undergraduates at Makerere University was to keep the levels of intake in the Arts and Social Sciences stable in order to avoid fuelling unemployment (Opio-Odong, 1993: 14). One reason the form and purpose of university education did not change much, even after independence, is probably a degree of mental colonisation, as referred to by Tiberondwa (1998: vi):

> "In order to make a critical evaluation of the missionary education for the African, we must not stop at the surface. We must be able to appreciate the fact that colonialism can be economic, political, cultural and, worst of all, mental".

The inherited system served colonial government's need for trained bureaucrats, and this demand remained after independence. It is now challenged by the down-sizing of African governments required by donor agencies led by the World Bank and IMF. Training for commercial and developmental relevance is thus a requirement of a new style of international neo-liberal thinking. But the challenge is not actually a new one. Ssekamwa (*ibid.*: 60) quotes the Phelps-Stroke commission (1924-25) criticising missionary education in the following terms:

> "The missionaries have failed to relate their educational activities to the community needs of the people. The type of education has been too exclusively literary. In a country with unusually fertile soil, they have made practically no provision for agricultural education".

Ssekamwa further explains that even when agricultural education was introduced, the curriculum was oriented towards making school leavers look for employment in other establishments rather than setting up their own farm enterprises. Disgusted by this type of education, some Ugandan teachers in 1969 left their employment to start private schools determined to teach practical skills combined with better agricultural knowledge. However, the pioneer private schools failed since pupils preferred education that would give them white-collar jobs.

The debate about universities in Uganda as cogs in an education system preparing people for jobs in offices and not the community continues (Opio-Odong, 1993: 17). While sharing his experience in a workshop in 2005, Professor Ssebuwufu, the former Vice-Chancellor of Makerere University (1993-2004) stated that:

> "Post independent African universities continued to offer same type of curriculum which in essence emphasized "heart and mind" and largely ignored the "hand". As long as every graduate they churned out found one or more awaiting jobs, African universities had little incentive to reform their curricula".

Ssebuwufu explained that at the time, government was the major employer of university graduates and could absorb all graduates coming out of universities regardless of quality. Africa of that era hardly had any organised larger scale private sector enterprises advocating for relevance and hands-on skills. So what is it that has changed to warrant major reforms in university education?

What has changed?

Complexity of development challenges
The development challenge now is much more complex than before. Elements include population explosion, degraded natural resource base, collapse of international markets for traditional cash crops, environmental degradation, and political and economic struggles. The interaction of these factors culminates in poverty. For example, the Ugandan population has more than doubled since 1980, rising from 12.6 million in 1980 to an (estimated) 26.8 million in 2005 (www.ubos.org/stpopulation.html). This means more people earning a living on increasingly sub-divided plots of often degraded land. The collapse of the market for traditional cash crops has exacerbated poverty, especially among smallholders. Political upheavals and crises only make a bad situation worse.

In the agricultural sector, for example, the challenge is no longer to improve production and productivity but to enhance the livelihoods of the poor. Poverty is a multi-dimensional challenge that cannot be solved by merely increasing production and productivity. Wals and Bawden (2000) contend that agriculture today presents a complex of social, political, economic, ecological, aesthetic and ethical aspects. They argue that dealing with complexity, uncertainty, conflicting norms, values and interests in a globalising world, requires a radical transformation of agricultural practices and thus an equally fundamental transformation in the competences required to be gained by students of agriculture and rural development. New approaches to contend with complex problems such as innovation systems, not only require a new set of competences but also reorientation of mindsets by all actors, including members of the farming community. Cognisant of these challenges, governments have begun to undertake structural and policy reforms to confront this new complexity and break with the state-led developmentalism of the past. The universities resisted the challenge of practical relevance in an earlier period because an expanding independent state required bureaucrats even more than the colonial state. Now – in an age of burgeoning formal-sector unemployment - it requires entrepreneurs and facilitators, capable of making useful work for themselves, and in assisting others to find such useful work. Educational frameworks must change accordingly, and nowhere more so than in farming.

Policy reforms
Structural adjustment policy reforms such as decentralisation, privatisation and liberalisation of trade and services have set a platform for new functional arrangement and responsibilities in both the public and private sector. Privatisation, for example, has thinned job opportunities in the public sector, making the private sector the major employer. Further, in 1997, government introduced a decentralisation policy which devolved the responsibility for service delivery from the central government to the local governments, making the local governments the major employers within the public sector. Both private sector and local governments are more interested in satisfying the needs of their clients or constituents than maintaining bureaucratic structures. In this kind of situation, an education aimed at mainly creating white-collar job

seekers does not fit. What the private sector and local governments want now are change makers not scholars.

Secondly, government programmes for addressing poverty, such as the Plan for Modernisation of Agriculture (PMA), are designed to be multi-sectoral, integrated and participatory. Government looks for university graduates to champion these programmes, as exemplified by the government directive of 1999 that local governments recruit university graduates at the sub-county level to work directly with the community. This call was made without recognition that the training in universities is not oriented to this type of development approach (see Asiimwe *et al.*, 2001). To comply with the PMA, the national agricultural extension and research systems have transformed from the linear top-down to demand-driven approaches. This demands new competences and orientation as discussed in Chapter Four.

Thirdly, liberalisation and privatisation policies have also opened up the higher education sector to competition. As a result university enrolment has tremendously increased and many new private and public universities have emerged (see Makerere University, 2003; Kasozi, 2003). Preparing graduates for jobs whether in the public or the private sector cannot any longer be left to tradition. Universities need to do more and prepare their graduates to be entrepreneurs in their own right, because existing jobs (in public and private sectors combined) are simply too few compared to the number of people graduating every year.

Based on the history of education in Uganda and the changes that have taken place over time, it is convincing to argue that if universities are to be relevant to the new development challenges, they have to change. Many students of education (see Guiton, 1999), including those of Ugandan education more specifically (Ssebuwufu, 2005; Kasozi, 2003; Kajubi[1], 1992), tend to assume that reshaping university education is basically a matter of curriculum reform, but the problem (it will be argued here) is much deeper than curricula. Even before considering curriculum review, it is critical to address the need, for example, to change mindsets, build a new vision of purpose, and inculcate new competences for training and research among the academic staff. If it was just a matter of the curriculum, the numerous privately sponsored programmes started recently in both public and private universities would have led to a qualitative difference in the graduates emerging. What has happened is simply a proliferation of programmes to offer wider choice to students, rather than a fundamental change in the quality of education. In fact, as Kasozi (*ibid.*: xvi) sadly notes, even the new universities in Uganda are imitating the inherited (colonial) traditions.

A problem is that those who are expected to reform and implement curricula are products of the system they need to change. Thus the danger is that curriculum reform is pursued using the same mindset sustaining the ivory tower, *i.e.* there is no qualitative change. Given the propensity to build on inherited structures and practices it will be argued that a critical requirement for fundamental change in quality of education in Africa is "mental decolonisation", to build new mindsets capable of grasping changed realities and new perspectives, thus fostering systemic

---

[1] Referenced as GoU (1992) The Uganda Government White Paper on implementation of the recommendations of the report of the education Policy Review Commission. Kajubi was the chair of the commission and the views expressed therein represent his opinion.

skills that will eventually lead to competence-based curriculum reforms. In short, the key to policy reform in the African university of the 21st century is to change the change-makers.

Conceptual framework

Conceptualising transformation for innovations

The complexity of the development challenges discussed above requires systemic education ensuring adaptive capacity for current challenges and future uncertainties. As Harvey and Knight (1996) put it, higher education is about more than just producing skilled acolytes, important though these undoubtedly are; it is also about producing people who can lead, who can produce new knowledge, who can see new problems and imagine new ways of approaching old problems. To do that, individuals and institutions have to continuously engage in learning processes with other actors. This capacity for co-learning is the core fabric of innovation systems. Universities as champions of learning need to engage with other stakeholders to become joint learning organisations. For this to happen, universities need to abandon a linear, hierarchical, model suited to the factory age (where they simply produce graduates as "input" to organisations providing community services) towards interfacing with the service providers and community to learn how better to contribute to real development challenges. The required shift is pictured in Figure 1.

For simplicity, the figure illustrates interfaces between the university, agricultural service providers (extension and research) and the community. In this model, the university interfaces with service providers through joint research, consultancy and student internships.

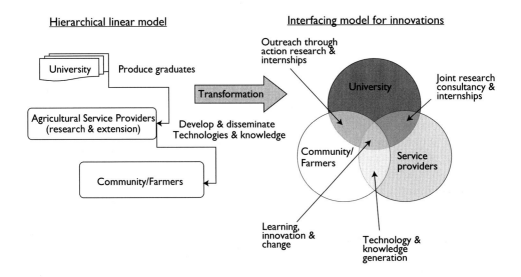

Figure 1: Towards innovation systems.

For their part, internships expose students to the dynamics of work where they are likely to apply their professional knowledge and skills. The university can also interface with the community through outreach, including action research, internships and consultancy, in which the university staff and their students engage with community to deal with real-life problems. Internships in this part expose students to social realities of technology and knowledge generation/dissemination. Service providers and the community interface through participatory technology and knowledge generation and exchange. The outcome of all these interfaces is learning, innovation and change for all parties. This is the basic conceptual model towards which the reforms described and analysed in this thesis are directed.

Designing the research

With the above conceptual framework in mind, research was designed around three case studies, each one targeted on specific research issues as laid out in Figure 2. While the overall intention is to influence innovations in university training, research and consultancy, this influence has to operate in context. Case studies 1 and 2 provide the context which determines

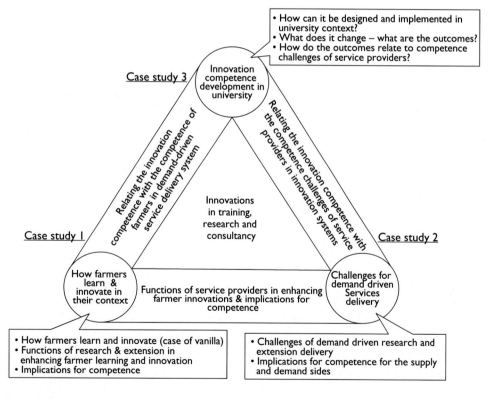

Figure 2: Research design.

the relevance of the competences developed at the university. The goal is to be able to influence development change at the community level. For this reason case study 1 (Chapter 3) explores the context of the farmer learning and innovation, using vanilla as an entry point. Based on the understanding of farmer learning and innovation processes, the functions of research and extension are articulated as outlined in the later part of Chapter 3. The second case study explores challenges faced by research and extension in demand-driven service delivery systems. These challenges are used to identify competence gaps relevant to functions graduates are expected to perform in an innovation system (as explained in Chapter 4). The competence gaps reflect what universities hope to provide in terms of capacity building for service providers, but such competences must exist in the university in the first place. Case study 3 focuses on how these required competences are first developed in the university, and in university staff. Outcomes are analysed in relation to findings from case studies 1 and 2.

The conceptual framework and research design are based on the thinking that the shift towards innovation systems requires competences at all levels: community, service provider and the university. But the required competences have to be congruent; otherwise they cannot function in a systems perspective. The research design, therefore, is intended to take account of the inter-relationship of competences found in the university, among service providers and at community level.

The case study design fits this type of research to permit in-depth and holistic inquiry into how factors interact in context. Given the systemic nature of the inquiry, the case study approach helps to avoid the *tunnel vision syndrome,* which Verschuren (2003) describes as a tendency to look at an object, (a) at one single point in time, (b) detached from its physical, social and political context, (c) without taking into account its relations with other objects in the case; and (d) without looking at functions fulfilled in relation to the larger whole (*i.e.* the case) of which it is a part.

Creating common understanding concerning some terminologies

For purposes of coherence, it is important to explain some of the terminology used in this thesis. The terms in question include competence, innovation systems, innovation competence, personal mastery and "soft skills".

Competence
Mulder (2001) demonstrated the difficulty of defining the term 'competence' because of variation in perspectives. He grouped various definitions in four major categories: (1) competence as a core competence, or competence of the organisation (2) job or task oriented competence (3) competence as a capability of employees or learners and (4) competence as an integral cluster of knowledge, skill and attitudinal aspects. These four categories indicate different levels, from organisation down to individual capabilities. Liles and Mustian (2004) look at core competence generically to encompass all levels. They define core competence as "the basic knowledge, attitudes, skills, and observable behaviours that lead to excellence in the workplace." The notion of competence puts emphasis on practice, *i.e.* 'knowing how' rather

than 'knowing that' (Gibb, 2000). Competence is desired for organisational performance but organisations are made up of individuals who perform specific jobs/tasks. So the very basis of competence lies in the capabilities of individuals not only to do the job in their organisations but also to be aware of and to respond effectively to wider societal expectations, even these are often multidimensional and contested. The issue is not conformity to a single set of societal norms, but recognition of the contested nature of societal claims, and the need to take this contestation into account in designing effective organizational responses.

There is a collective interest at stake. Society as a whole needs, through educational systems, to nurture competences – capabilities through which there can be rapid adaptation to changing and challenging circumstances (Raven, 2001). This implies that competence goes beyond job performance, and also involves the development of societal responsibilities and obligations. Epstein and Hundert (2002: 226) provide a comprehensive definition of competence in context of the medical profession as follows:

> "Professional competence is the habitual and judicious use of communication, knowledge, technical skills, clinical reasoning, emotions, values, and reflection in daily practice for the benefit of the individual and community being served".

This definition is comprehensive in that it takes into account several dimensions: cognitive, technical, integrative, context, relationship, affective/moral and habits of mind. In a nutshell, the purpose of competence is to shape desirable change in society. As summarised by Barnett (1994), competence is reflected in the abilities of individuals to perform better in a changing environment, and to stimulate beneficial change.

Innovation systems

The terms "innovation" and "innovation systems" are increasingly used in the literature on research and development, but their interpretation remains a source of some confusion. There is a tendency to use "innovation" and "technology" synonymously. Consequently there is a tendency to think that innovation systems are equivalent to research systems (since "technology" generally is taken to mean "new technology", or even more specifically "new machine or device"). But here something broader is intended. For a start, the Technology & Agrarian Development group in Wageningen University defines technology as (any kind) of human instrumentality. This instrumentality always has organizational dimensions. Edquist (1997: 3) defines innovations as new creations of economic significance, incorporating technological and organisational aspects. He explains that the emergence of innovations is by no means a linear path from basic research to applied research but instead is characterised by complicated feedback mechanisms and interactive relations involving science, technology, learning, production policy and demand. There is recognition that innovation increasingly takes place at the interface of formal research and economic activity, thus denying the primacy of either knowledge creation or validation institutions, including universities, or knowledge application institutes; rather innovation involves partnership between these types of actors (Hall *et al.*, 2000).

Innovation systems, therefore, refer to institutional arrangements and networks that lead to creation and application of economically useful knowledge and innovations for improving the wellbeing of society (see Hall *et al.,* 2000; Mowery and Sampat, 2004; Lundvall *et al.,* 2002; Galli and Teubal, 1998). Lundvall and colleagues argue that innovation systems work through the introduction of knowledge into the economy (and into the society at large) and that the most important elements in innovation systems have to do with the learning capability of individuals, organisations and regions. The trend of increasing complexity influenced by globalisation, liberalisation, dematerialisation, and a broad-based technology revolution, has widened the concept of research and development (R&D) to that of innovation system, reflecting the need to link the generation of scientific and technological knowledge with the diffusion, transfer and application of R&D results. This reasoning informs the conceptual model in Figure 1.

Innovation competence, personal mastery and soft skills
Innovation competence as used in this thesis, therefore, refers to capacity to influence patterns of thinking (mindsets), to develop visions for personal and group/community development, to explore new grounds for learning to foster desirable change in individuals and community, and to enable individuals, organisations and groups to develop adaptive capacity in relation to changing contexts and demands. Personal mastery and soft skills are then seen as indispensable components of innovation competence, empowering change in the face of resistance by addressing personal weaknesses and social tensions. In a nutshell, innovation competence is the capability to influence change in individuals, organisations and communities through reflective learning processes guided by a clear development vision. The purpose of innovation competence in a university is to stimulate creativity in training, research and consultancy of relevance to national development needs and to enable the graduates to stimulate desirable change in complex environments throughout their future careers. Ability to perform well in these tasks requires a high level of personal mastery and soft skills, among other things.

Personal mastery is a discipline of personal growth and learning as advocated by (Senge, 1990: 141) in a well-known book, *The Fifth Discipline*. As a discipline, it embodies two underlying movements. The first is continually to seek to clarify what is important to us. The second is continually to learn how to see current reality more clearly. Among other characteristics, Senge says, people with high levels of personal mastery are acutely aware of their ignorance, their incompetence, and their growth areas; they are more committed to, and have a broader and deeper sense of responsibility in, their work. The aim of personal mastery therefore is continually to clarify and deepen personal vision. Senge explains that personal vision means keying into what you want while resisting being taken over by what you do not want – in other words, it is an ability to converge on ultimate intrinsic desires and to do positive things towards achieving them. But it is termed "soft," to flag that the notion diverges from normal social science concepts, in being based in part on unquantifiable concepts such as intuition and personal vision. In this regard, it owes more to the arts and humanities, where unorthodox means are often considered valid, so long as creativity is fostered, than to the analytical traditions of applied social science.

Soft skills in this sense also refer to cross-cutting management skills necessary for every professional to be effective in an organizational context. These are the skills that enhance communicative, interactive and facilitative abilities to influence change in society. Discussing a programme for teaching interaction skills to engineers, Seat and Lord (1998) note that while teamwork is an integral part of modern engineering practice successful team interaction depends on individuals possessing skills that allow them to communicate and interact with other people in an adaptive, contributory manner. Simply putting people in teams does not teach them to work together effectively. This means that beyond the technical aspects of engineering (hard skills), engineers need additional cross-cutting social skills to make them effective in their professional performance. Senge's approach is but one of many (the work of Mary Douglas on *How institutions think* [1986] might be cited as a classic from the analytical, sociological tradition) but it is one that has had specific influence on the Makerere pilot project, and so requires to be introduced here.

Methodology and methods

Distinction between methodology and methods in social research remains blurred. Other terminologies such as approach and tools only add to the confusion. It is not the intention of this research – nor is the author capable – to distinguish these terminologies. For purposes of clarity in this study, I am inclined to use the distinctions made by Dillon and Wals (2006) that "methodological considerations involve examining positions and tensions in research ontologies, epistemologies and axiologies", where "ontology looks at what we're dealing with (*the what*) – the nature of reality; epistemology refers to how we make knowledge (*the how*) – or at how we make knowledge ourselves; while axiology relates to ethical considerations and our own philosophical viewpoints (*the why*)." These two scholars regard methods as the tools or instruments used for data generation or collection. Alvesson and Sköldberg (2000) are of the view that it is not methods but ontology and epistemology which are the determinants of good social science. My view is different; the two are probably equally important. Methods must be appropriate to the nature of objects we study and the purpose and expectations of our inquiry, though the relationships between them are sometimes slack rather than tight (Sayer, 1992: 4). Good research should also be based on clearly defined methods. Research cannot be more credible than the methods used to collect or generate data; and hence there is a need to be clear on methodology and methods used in any particular research.

Methodology

The research questions posed in this study require an understanding of people's knowledge about vanilla and how that knowledge is generated and disseminated, perceptions of professional challenges in a demand-driven service delivery context, and analysis of learning and how that learning shapes the lecturers' thinking and practice. Behind these phenomena are underlying social structural mechanisms influencing action and practice. Unearthing these mechanisms, as they exist in context, is a prior requirement to understand change dynamics, which is the ultimate focus of this engagement. This type of inquiry resonates in a space between constructivist and realist epistemologies. I have tried to make a "marriage" of the two, but first I will introduce them separately, before illustrating their convergence and application in the present study.

Constructivism

Piaget's work in 1930s challenged the notion that the mind apprehends reality directly, thus attacking received notions of 'what knowledge is' and 'how we come to have it' (see Glasersfeld, 1995). Influenced by Kant's arguments about space and time as stemming from the mind, Piaget showed how children "made" their conceptual worlds through the age-specific explorations in which they engaged. According to Staver (1998, *cf.* Segal 1986), constructivism challenges objectivist (or positivist) claims that (a) reality exists independently of us, (b) we can discover the secrets of reality, (c) these secrets are lawful, thereby permitting us to explain, predict, and control reality, and (d) our discoveries about reality are true and thus certain. On the whole, knowledge, our criteria and methods for attaining it, and bodies of public knowledge (the disciplines) to which our knowledge activities contribute are all 'constructed' (Phillips, 1995; Light and Cox, 2001). The mind organises the world by organising itself (Piaget, 1937 quoted in Glasersfeld, *ibid.*). Glasersfeld explains that the cognitive organism shapes and coordinates its experience and, in so doing, transforms it into a structured world. Hence Piaget's view is that 'knowledge is a higher form of adaptation', which Glasersfeld interprets as referring to a mental and not biological mechanism, as in the ordinary use of the term. Constructivists maintain that social reality is not something outside the discourse of (social) science but is partly constituted by scientific activity (Delanty, 1997). Delanty argues that clearly, the object - social reality - exists independently of what social scientists do, but there is a sense in which social science itself plays a role in the shaping of knowledge. A simple example would be where informants adapt their answers to what they presume to be the purpose of a questionnaire. Another is the performative, a typical behaviour of contestants in television "reality" shows, where they "act up for the camera".

Within the constructivist paradigms, several strands exist. Geelan (1997) distinguishes six strands based on literature: personal constructivism (Kelly and Piaget); radical constructivism (Glasersfeld); social constructivism according to Solomon; social constructivism according to Gergen; critical constructivism (Taylor); and contextual constructivism (Cobern). I limit this study to two forms of constructivism; radical constructivism and social constructivism; although in some instances my usage will appear to go beyond these two. In radical constructivism, the focus is on cognition and the individual; in social constructivism, the focus is language and group dynamics (Staver, 1998). Staver helps to distinguish the two forms of constructivism, and also draws similarities between them. For radical constructivists, social interactions between and among learners are central to the building of knowledge by individuals in which cognition is fundamental and adaptive. He strengthens the argument with Glasersfeld's assertion that cognition's purpose is to serve the individual's organisation of his or her experiential world and not the discovery of an objective ontological reality.

For social constructivists, knowledge is created and legitimised by means of social interchange in its many forms. Radical and social constructivism share much in common. First, knowledge is actively built up from within by each member of the community and by a community as an interactive group. Second, social interactions between and among individuals in a variety of community, societal, and cultural settings are central to the building of knowledge by individuals as well as building of knowledge by communities, societies and cultures. Third, the character of cognition and language employed to express cognition is functional and adaptive. Fourth, the purpose of cognition and language is to bring coherence to an individual's world of experience and a community's knowledge base respectively. Delanty (1997) says that except for extreme constructivism, constructivists do not deny the existence of social reality as an objective entity, but he remains in doubt as to what is actually constructed. He argues that in constructivism it is generally unclear whether reality is something constructed or whether there is an underlying reality that is constructed by the social actors (*i.e.* they build only what can stand, according to the laws of nature or society). Constructivism therefore seems to fall short in explanatory power in regard to underlying mechanisms, which in the context of change are critical for scaling up. Realism puts more emphasis on digging deeper into social reality to expose underlying structural mechanisms.

Realism

Realism is a philosophy not a substantive social theory (Sayer, 1992). The history of realism is associated with the works of Karl Marx and Sigmund Freud on understanding economic and political systems (see May, 1997: 11) and was tailored more to social science by Bhaskar and others (see Delanty, 1997: 130). Realism argues that the knowledge people have of their social world affects their behaviour; the social world does not simply 'exist' independently of this knowledge. Thus there are underlying mechanisms which structure people's actions and prevent their choices from reaching fruition (May, *ibid.*). Delanty expounds more on the parallels between constructivism and realism and attempts to reconcile the two. He argues that realism stands for the separation of the sciences both in terms of their subject matter and method, and that as a philosophy of social science attempts to integrate three methodologies. Firstly, it defends the possibility of causal explanation. Second, it accepts the hermeneutic notion of social reality as being communicatively constructed. Thirdly, most varieties of realism - although not necessarily all - involve a critical dimension. Some prefer to call the new realism critical realism.

Delanty explains that the central ideas in Bhaskar's approach is that social reality is composed of 'generative mechanisms' and these mechanisms generate 'events'. His model of scientific progress is one of science digging deeper into the hidden structures of social reality, identifying the generative mechanisms. The primary difference between critical realism and constructivism lies in the former's concern with discovering generative mechanisms within an objectively existing social reality. This has major implications for how we regard the role of knowledge in relation to social change. Realists would be doubtful about how much could be achieved by "personal mastery" alone. Senge's commitment to intuition, for example, seems a typical constructivist move, but makes little sense (on its own) to a realist, who would want to know precisely how the mechanism of intuition worked, and in what it might be grounded. However, there are also similarities and complementarities between critical realism and constructivism which make a combination of the two a more powerful methodology for the present study, as will be explained shortly. But first, I rely on Delanty's reconciliation to explain the integration of constructivism and realism.

Integrating constructivism and realism

In finding a common ground for constructivism and realism, Delanty observes that on one side, only extreme constructivists, such as Woolgar and Latour (cf. *Laboratory Life* 1986) would deny the existence of underlying structures. On the other side, the realists, while advocating the objectivity of the social and the possibility that science can provide knowledge of things other than science; do not deny a dimension of constructivism in knowledge. His conclusion, in principle, is that the constructivist-realist divide is in fact a false dichotomy and that the two sides can be interpreted in a reconcilable fashion.

Constructivists and realists are both united in the rejection of correspondence theories of truth – even realists acknowledge the importance of hermeneutic issues, for example; both sides are united in their support for an emancipatory critique; and both embrace the principle of reflexivity (See Delanty, *ibid.*: 131-134). On the basis of this common ground, Delanty clearly puts it that those who advocate a critical constructivism are closer to critical realism, but he also challenges that realism will have to undergo reappraisal of its commitments to critique, which occupies an unclear status in realist philosophies. Constructivists, on the other hand, will have to forego the pleasures of post-modernism, in which any story – any invention or reinvention of the self - is as good as any other. This is especially implausible in relation to poverty alleviation, where clearly some stories are much better than others, and the ability to construct a desired future is so obviously a product of wealth and opportunity. Combining constructivism and realism, therefore, provides the power for breadth and depth of inquiry into social phenomena. For this reason, I explain how this combination was applied to the respective case studies.

Application of integrated methodology to the study

As explained above, both constructivism and realism embrace reflexivity and hermeneutic aspects as common ground. Reflexivity refers to the complex relationships between processes of knowledge production and the various contexts of such processes as well as the involvement of the knowledge producer (Alvesson and Sköldberg, 2000). A realist conception of social science would not necessarily assume that we can 'know' the world out there independently of the ways in which we describe it (May, *ibid.*). Science cannot escape its own historicity, but it can make its situation reflective in order to distinguish between the realms of freedom and necessity (Delanty, *ibid.*). I cannot claim neutrality in this research. In particular, my involvement in case studies 2 and 3 as facilitator and learner respectively in an action research mode obviously had influence on the interpretation of data and probably in the framing of questions asked in the interviews. For constructivists, observations, objects, events, data, laws, and theory do not exist independently of the observers (Staver, 1998; Geelan, 1997). No one can escape this fundamental subjectivity of experience, and the philosophers who purport to have access to a 'God's eye view' are no exception (Glasersfeld, 1995: 72). The strategy therefore was to subject my own interpretation of observations and recordings to validation by participants in those processes through feedback and reflection, as later described in the respective case studies. By doing so, the constructive dimension is subject to a radical process of critique. It is more than just my own construction.

Hermeneutics refers to the theory and practice of interpretation (May, *ibid.*; Glasersfeld, *ibid.*). Through engagement with practice and theory and other elements of pre-understanding it is inevitable that our assumptions and blind-spots influence our interpretation based on how we construct our social reality. Unravelling underlying meaning was possible by soliciting and allowing alternative interpretations of other participants through feedback. In this situation, and as Alvesson and Sköldberg (2000) say, hermeneutics is an important form of reflection leading to primacy of interpretation. Misconceptions are clarified through dialogue, and it is here that Eger (1992) emphasises that hermeneutic categories and ideas prove their value most explicitly. Iterative processes of reflection, dialogue and synthesis in the learning processes and feedback aided interpretation of my interpretations for clarification of issues. The study largely utilises interpretive data, hence the centrality of hermeneutics.

Relating the integration of constructivism and realism to the study, it is my belief that in the first case study farmers' knowledge about vanilla has independent validity, though it does not exist independently of them. The choice of this case study is based on assumption that farmers are able to generate knowledge and innovations without external intervention from either research or extension. Farmers' knowledge, therefore, is constructed through interactions between farmers and through farmers' interactions with the crop and the environment, including markets. This knowledge is shaped through experience into new practices or innovations, shared through communicative processes. Individuals seek what they consider to be new knowledge relative to what they know; in a way, they are creating coherence in their world of experience. Also, since the knowledge generated is shared and spreads, it means that there must be underlying social structures serving as mechanisms for communication. Going beyond knowledge as it is perceived by farmers to unravelling what it is that enhances its generation and dissemination is a cardinal issue discussed in this case study.

In the second case study, the perceptions of challenges of agricultural professionals in the context of demand-driven service delivery are articulated with respect to what they know and do. The case study is based, therefore, on an analysis of interactions with the community the professionals serve, and what they perceive to be their functions in such processes. Given a different context, the challenges could be quite different. The search for new knowledge and skills is driven by what they want to achieve as individuals, as well as what their employers and a wider society expects them to deliver. The ultimate aim of the search for new knowledge and skills is to adapt effectively to specific circumstances.

In the third case study, the entry point is the mental re-orientation which represents a higher form of adaptation. The lecturers themselves are active participants in their learning process, exchanging knowledge and experiences and integrating new knowledge into their existing knowledge and cultural frames. This integration is bound to bring about different interpretations and reactions to new knowledge and experience. All this is influenced by the context of the organisation and participants' personal goals. Change - if it is to happen at all - requires new meaning to be forged, offering to make coherent an individual's existing knowledge base and world of experience. In this case, mindsets appear to be the central structural mechanism to be addressed if change is to be achieved. The design of the learning process programme (Chapter 5) relies a lot on a realist approach, with emphasis on finding the right mechanism to motivate and enhance learning in a particular context to arrive at desired outcomes (cf. Pawson & Tilley, 1997). Similarly, evaluation of the programme (Chapter 6) goes into depth on determining what brings about change (or a specified outcome) by identifying relevant triggers.

The choice for a combination of constructivism and realism as a methodology is to take the stance that social reality does not exist independent of the social actors, but at the same time to embrace the possibility of causal explanations of how that reality is shaped by the actors. In this view, then, constructivism and realism reinforce each other through their complementary interpretive and explanatory strengths. At this point I turn to the question of methods used to generate data.

Methods

The generic methods used to gather data included interviewing, workshops, documentary reviews, participant observation, and self assessment. Triangulation is a key principle, as explained in the specific case studies. Application of these methods in each case is only partly covered in this section. More detailed explanation is to be found in the respective empirical chapters. Given the variation in contexts of the cases, it is appropriate that the methods are described in detail on a case by case basis.

Case study 1: Farmer learning and innovation

Extended conversational interviewing was applied to this case study guided by open ended questions to allow respondents to explain their views within context. In this case, vanilla was used as an entry point to understand how farmers learn and innovate on their own initiative. Histories of vanilla and associated knowledge flows were the conceptual guide for the questions asked. To put the farmers (respondents) in charge of the conversation, it was important that, as a researcher, I disclosed my ignorance about the subject. This was even more critical because of my institutional affiliation, the university, which is most often mistakenly perceived to be the centre of all forms of knowledge. Disclosure of total ignorance about vanilla put farmers in a position of confidence to narrate the history of vanilla, in so far as they knew it, and to explain their experiences with the crop over time. From the position of an inquisitive learner, it was possible to appreciate innovations in farmer practices, and understand knowledge flows leading on to these innovations. Extended interaction with farmers in their gardens put them at ease and increased their confidence to explain issues to show practically what they did and how they did it.

Though I was guided by a checklist of issues, unstructured conversational interviews like those described by Bernard (1988) were preferred. Such interviews put the respondent at ease, to tell their stories. Probing questions (some elicited by observations in the field) were used to seek more information and clarification, to help in interpretation and ensure completeness of data. A voice recorder was used to take record of the interviews but field notes were also taken in notebooks. A research assistant helped in taking these notes during the interview, as the principle researcher's attention was more on interacting with the farmers. At the end of each day, a full account of each farmer's interview was written up, structured around thematic issues in the checklist. The field notes were used to cross-check accuracy of transcription of the voice records. Some farmers were visited more than once to follow-up on incomplete or unclear information. Also, in many cases, discussions were held in presence of other members of the family, mainly spouses and children, who also chipped in with information to enrich the discussions. Data were subsequently synthesized according to themes, as laid out in Chapter 3.

Case study 2: Challenges of demand-driven service delivery

This case study had two parts; the first part was focused on challenges of demand-driven research and the second part on challenges of demand-driven extension services. For the first part, challenges were identified through a synthesis of processes and activities in a capacity building programme for researchers, academicians and other partners engaged in Integrated Agricultural Research for Development (IAR4D). The initiative is explained in more detail in Chapter 4. Workshops and participant observation were the main methods for data generation. Five workshops were conducted as a sequence over a period of nine months (Figure 8). In each workshop the participants brainstormed in their zonal teams, to articulate the challenges they faced or envisaged with regard to IAR4D. The results were clustered and synthesized to bring out the generic challenges for IAR4D. Subsequent workshops reviewed previous challenges with a view to further clarify them, but also to monitor the extent to which the learning programme was addressing the pertinent challenges.

The researcher engaged in this initiative as one of the facilitators of the learning workshops and as field mentor for one of the research teams. This means that the researcher was not in the normal position of neutral observer, but a participant who actually manipulated the phenomena being studied. Manipulation in this sense was through facilitation to stimulate deep thinking, reflection and consensus on the challenges faced. It should be borne in mind, therefore, that the data I present are products of an action research process in which my responsibilities was to stimulate certain kinds of discussion. If I had not been present, or had handled my responsibilities differently (e.g. treated them less conscientiously) the data sets would have been different. More challenges emerged through reflections on the field practice of IAR4D. Further observation of participants during field mentoring clarified some challenges with concrete examples and also generated more challenges. This type of action research engagement is characterised by cycles of action and reflection. In this case two loops of action and reflection are distinguished. One loop is related to learning workshops and the other is related to field practice (see Figure 3).

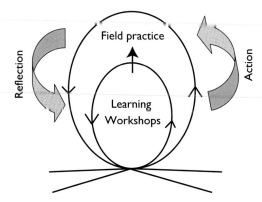

Figure 3: Action research loops.

Experiences of field practice were reflected upon during the learning workshop to generate consensus on the generic challenges of IAR4D. These reflections provided opportunity for reinterpretations to come to a shared understanding. Aware of Punch's (2000: 59) caution that participant observation in such situations has potential problems, such as the tendency of the researcher to assume an advocacy role or to provide support for the group being studied, synthesis of the challenges relied more on outputs of the five workshops. It is important to note here that the subsequent workshops incorporated previous field experiences and individual observations including those of the mentors. Therefore the workshops outputs largely represent a negotiated consensus on the key challenges of IAR4D. Implications for competence were derived from analysis of these challenges.

The second part of the case study (challenges of demand driven extension) relied largely on documentary review of the National Agricultural Advisory Services (NAADS) programme. The NAADS programme is described in more detail in Chapter 4. In the five years since NAADS was first implemented several reviews and needs assessment studies had been conducted highlighting the major challenges of a demand driven extension service approach. Synthesis of challenges was based on these studies, complemented by observation of some field activities associated with NAADS implementation. Like in IAR4D, implications for competence were derived from the synthesis of challenges, drawing on review of documentation.

Case study 3: innovation competence development in university

This case study was based entirely on an action research process, where the researcher was a participant (learner) in the competence development programme. Being a staff of the university, this fitted very well. The case study set-up and its assessment form chapters 5 and 6 respectively. The researcher's involvement here represents complete participation, according to Spradley's categorisation of participation (Table 1). Complete participation enables deep extraction of information and interpretation.

Table 1: Levels of participation (Adapted with modifications from Spradley, 1980: 58).

Degree of involvement	Type of participation	Description
High	Complete	Researcher is an ordinary participant. This is the highest level of participation
	Active	Researcher does what other people are doing, not merely to gain acceptance, but to more fully learn the cultural rules for behaviour
	Moderate	The researcher seeks to balance being an insider and an outsider. May participate for the sake of gaining acceptance
Low	Passive	Researcher present at the scene but does not participate or interact with other people to any great extent. The role is that of bystander, spectator or loiterer
	Non-participant	No involvement with the people or activities

Participant observation, face-to-face interviews and self-assessment were the main methods for generating data in this case study. These are further elaborated in Chapter 6. A relationship between participant observation and action research is highlighted here. Without engaging in debates about different interpretations and applications of action research, I agree with the broadly-formulated view of Reason and Bradbury (2001) that action research is about working towards creating new forms of understanding, since action without reflection and understanding is blind, just as theory without action is meaningless. The practice of action research in the context of this study is discussed in more detail in Chapter 2. Involvement is a property of action research, whose rationale rests initially on three pillars: first, that naturalistic settings are best studied and researched by those participants experiencing the problem; second, that behaviour is highly influenced by naturalistic surrounding in which it occurs; and third, that qualitative methodologies are perhaps best suited for researching naturalistic settings (McKernan, 1991). These three pillars suggest a rationale in the form of a critical participant observation mode of practitioner inquiry. In this sense, the researcher was also a practitioner by virtue of his being a lecturer in the university.

Participant observation is a special mode of observation in which the investigator is not merely a passive observer but may take a variety of roles within a case study situation and may actually participate in the events being studied (Yin, 1984). Participant observation allows the researcher to experience activities directly to get a feel of what events are like and to observe activities, people and physical aspects of the situation (Spradley, *ibid.*). This type of engagement was necessary for the researcher to understand processes, attitudes, behaviours in a context in which the learning programme was implemented. It also provided the basis for framing relevant questions for interviews.

The three case studies are linked by their implications for innovation competences. Ultimately the aim is to understand the competences that universities need to be able to induce, in order to influence developmental changes in society through their primary mandates of training, research and outreach (or consultancy). Having discussed the context and nature of the study in general, the next chapter (Chapter 2) focuses on opportunities and challenges for universities in the 21st century from a broader perspective. Emphasis is on change that delivers greater relevance to the surrounding society. This is context bound. Makerere University is therefore used as an example to put the discussion in context. Opportunities and constraints discussed illuminate the competence gaps for African universities, to steer their own change towards relevance.

CHAPTER TWO

The mixed-grill: a review of challenges and opportunities for a university of the 21st century

This chapter presents a critical review of challenges and opportunities for universities and higher education in general to meet changed conditions at the beginning of the 21st century. Though the overall focus is on universities in the sub-Saharan Africa, it was difficult to locate literature (if it exists at all) on reforms in higher education in the region, or in Africa in general. Higher education as it exists today in Africa, however, is to a considerable degree a reflection of higher education in the North (*i.e.* Europe and USA). Therefore, although much of the literature reviewed is from the North it is also applicable to Africa, albeit the challenges are often much bigger in Africa. To put the discussion in context, I first present some historical aspects of the African university, as encapsulated in the story of Makerere University.

Makerere University as shaped by the past

Colonial education and establishment of the University

Makerere University is the oldest university in East Africa. In her book, *"A Chronicle of Makerere University College 1922-1962"*, Macpherson (1964) gives a detailed historical account of its establishment. With the approval of the then Secretary of State for the Colonies, Winston Churchill, in 1920, Makerere opened as a technical college in 1922. In 1929, a meeting of Directors of Education of the former East African British colonies in Dar es Salaam agreed that higher education for Africans from the Eastern African territories should be centred at Makerere, and thereafter the college started to admit students from Kenya and Tanzania besides those from Uganda. As elsewhere in British colonial Africa, such colleges of higher learning later affiliated with and sometimes became constituent colleges of metropolitan universities, to provide "native" white collar workers for the colonial administration (Ssebuwufu, 2005). Following the recommendations of the De La Warr Commission in 1937, Makerere College became a university college supervised by the federal University of London. The De La Warr Commission was sent to the region by the colonial office in London on the suggestion of Sir Phillip Mitchell, governor of Uganda 1935-1940, to examine the state of higher education in East Africa.

Transformation to a university college also meant that practical courses such as carpentry, building and mechanics, previously offered under the technical college, were replaced by more academic programmes. In other words, emphasis on the "hand" was replaced by emphasis on the "mind". As a consequence of its establishment, governments and missionaries endeavoured to increase the number of secondary schools with the orientation to produce candidates for Makerere College, which affected their quality and orientation as well (Ssekamwa, 2000).

Colonial education was intended to groom Englishmen in black skins, who shunned rural life in preference for the urban, who looked down on practical education and crafts as inferior to academic pursuits, and who in some cases rejected local languages in favour of English (Kyeyune, 2002). The term "ivory tower" is appropriately applied to African universities offering this type of elitist education (Ssebuwufu, *ibid.*).

In a way, colonial education enforced patronage to the colonial masters rather than equipping Africans with the capacity to develop themselves. For example, to counter the influence of the Verona Fathers, who attempted to recruit Italian peasant priests to teach small-scale agriculture to African boys after the second World War, the Director of Education spelled out in new terms quite clearly 'that those Europeans engaged in education should be capable of giving to Africans a proper understanding of British ways of life and thought and of training Africans of such ways' (Hansen, 2002). This was intended to give dominance in education to British missionaries, who often collaborated with the colonial government closely. Notwithstanding the fact that most African countries had vast potential for agriculture, universities established in the British colonies had very little role in agricultural research (generation of agricultural technologies), Opio-Odong (1992) notes.

African universities have been among the major instruments and vehicles of cultural westernisation on the continent, and an initial problem, still today largely uncorrected, lay precisely in the model of the university itself, viz. the paradigm within academia of a distrust of direct problem-solving in the wider society (Mazrui, 2003). De-linking university training from potential resources for national development and wider African social values might be considered as corrupting the minds of Africans. Colonial education shaped the thinking of many Africans de-Africanised by the influence of colonial life (Dumbutshena, 2002). Those who follow this line argue that instead of providing freedom for Africans, colonial education undermined it (Tiberondwa, 1998). Tiberondwa, in fact, suggests that many educated Africans act as colonial puppets – when the colonialist wound up the springs, the African puppet danced to the colonialist tune. Mazrui (2003) adds that the original colonial university was uncompromisingly foreign in an African context; its impact was more culturally alienating than it need have been, and a whole generation of African graduates grew up despising their own ancestry and scrambling to imitate the West.

Not everywhere was the African university shaped entirely by colonial impulses. In Nkrumah's Ghana, for instance, the university at Legon (near Accra) experienced more radical anti-colonial influences from the political left. But to build a credible institution Nkrumah had to rely upon inputs the European left, and again it can be argued that the curriculum, in effect, oriented students towards an internationalist vision of development issues, rather than starting with local problems and building on local intellectual agenda. Did independence change this mentality of intellectual dependence on the metropolis?

The immediate post-independence era: the Africanisation of the University

Governments of newly independent African countries did not dismantle the colonial administrative structures but inherited them as if a birthright, and even reinforced the ideologies upon which they were based (Ssebuwufu, *ibid.*). The colonisation of the mind alluded to by Tiberondwa was very successful, even if we might also want to introduce the point made by Douglas (1986) that it is the administrative structures themselves that require certain forms and styles of thought to be maintained. After independence, the Europeans who manned the civil service were leaving and had to be replaced by local technocrats. Moreover, African leaders wanted to see rapid Africanisation of their government functions. The immediate independence era was characterised by rapid expansion of education in general, and universities in particular, to produce the required numbers of local bureaucrats and technocrats. For example, the University college of Nairobi (evolving from the Royal Technical College of Nairobi) and the University College, Dar es Salaam were established in 1956 and 1961 respectively to cope with these new national demands. Incidentally, all these colleges were grouped under the supervision of the University of London until 1963, when they became independent as constituent colleges of the University of East Africa centred at Makerere. The three constituent colleges, *i.e.* Makerere University College, University College of Nairobi and University College of Dar es Salaam, then became independent universities in 1970, and the University of East Africa ceased to exist.

Except for the attempts of the University of Dar es Salaam to realign to Julius Nyerere's vision of a socialist Tanzania, the independent universities continued largely to offer a type of education based on European models. They pursued rapid post-graduate training at home and abroad to create East African academics to teach in universities, conduct research and manage key positions in the civil service. With the support of donors – including the Rockefeller and Ford Foundations - expansion of post-graduate programmes was undertaken to fill the vacuum created by departing European experts, resulting in the rapid Africanisation of the university and civil service. By the 1967/68 adademic year, Makerere had achieved 20 per cent East Africanisation of its staff (Opio-Odong, 1993). Once the East African University had ceased to exist in 1970, the next challenge was to Ugandanise the staff.

In addition to the shortfall of technocrats created by departing Europeans, the post-colonial civil service was expanded, to take account of new developmental and social welfare functions. Governments employed all the university graduates they could find to staff various sectors of the civil service. In the agricultural sector, government strategy was to intensify and expand export crops such as coffee and cotton, to sustain government revenue and gain economic independence. The university's role, therefore, was to build the human resource capacity to implement the government strategy through research and extension, basically using a colonial service delivery set-up. The University then produced technocrats who basically performed administrative duties. Up to this date, university training was still modelled around principles of hierarchy and bureaucracy unchanged from colonial times. As argued by Byamungu (2002) the African academy in the post-colony, by-and-large, was expanded without much or any attention to the quality improvements needed to suit it to new African needs and challenges. He sums up the situation in the following terms:

> "The African University does not as yet help to produce competent people to tackle state problems or to manage state resources. Right from the primary level, pupils are not taught to think so as to

be critical of the environment situation, which would lead to relevant researches and therefore to solutions adequate to the local problems. The syllabus does not include the transmission of skills to take care of these cracks in the system. Put differently, education remains foreign to the people's aspirations and is impotent to solve people's problems. What is needed is a reform, a change of pattern, so that pupils are taught to use their imagination and to translate them into action. This would give to the African Nations a breed of leaders with a vision to change the fate of their people" (Byamungu, 2002: 23).

Byamungu suggest total overhaul of the educational system right from the primary level (see also Mazrui, 2003), because we should remember that the type of education offered at the university influences the lower levels of education. Primary and secondary education continues to prepare candidates for the university from an early age, as it is the dominant wish of all pupils and their parents to gain access to a well-paid and influential government job. But this means that reform at the university has high potential to influence changes lower in the educational system. An opportunity to break away from the colonial stereotype was presented in the 1970s and 80s – a period characterised by economic crisis, political turmoil and the disruption of colonial influence. This was an opportunity to find new pathways to development, but the sad reality was that the crisis seemingly overwhelmed any capacity to think differently and to innovate on an institutional level. Need for reform has not been lessened by the passage of time.

Political turmoil and economic crisis era: unutilised opportunities within a crisis

For over a decade (1971 to the early 1980s), Uganda experienced acute economic crisis and political instability. Government infrastructure and services broke down due to mismanagement, markets for primary export commodities such as coffee and cotton collapsed, and the economy went through crisis after crisis. The dictatorial regime of Idi Amin (1971-1979) set the pace of social strife and economic failure. During this period nearly all the foreign experts in public institutions left the country; Makerere University lost more than half its teaching staff. It was a period of "brain drain", with many Ugandan professionals also leaving the country in search of "greener pastures", due to social unrest, economic hardship and human rights abuse. To cope with the staffing crisis, fresh graduates recruited as teaching assistants were given full teaching responsibilities for some courses. At the same time, there were limited opportunities for staff development, particularly for post-graduate training. Up to this day, Makerere University is yet fully to regain its desired staffing capacity and quality of staff. The University largely relies on retaining some of its best graduates (academically) to take on teaching positions. This way, the university tends to reproduce itself. Fresh graduates with little experience outside Makerere tend only to teach what they were taught and in the same manner they were taught it.

Because of mismanagement of state institutions, the civil service sector also shrank, and university graduates could no longer find ready employment in government departments. The 1972 expulsion of Asians who dominated the private sector, purportedly to Ugandanise the economy, strangled the emerging private sector, that might otherwise have provided alternative employment opportunities. The Ugandans who took over the private sector lacked managerial and entrepreneurial skills and experience to survive in private business. Collapse of the market for traditional export commodities, and the Ugandanisation of the private sector, were again just the right moments to rethink and transform education to support alternative "home grown" approaches to national development. But the crisis simply overwhelmed rational thinking, and with the best brains having already left the country, those who remained found themselves severely demoralised and rendered incapable of changing anything. The opportunity to reform education could not be seized. There was need; first, to recover from this depression and to build an environment allowing critical thinking and dialogue, before a new vision for education could emerge.

The recovery period: coming to terms with challenges

The past two decades of relative peace and stability have witnessed some economic recovery and the revitalisation of the public and private sector. With population increase over the years, demand for higher education has increased tremendously. Government - the sole provider of scholarships to the university - was overwhelmed, and Makerere, the only University in Uganda until the late 1980s, could no longer satisfy the demand. A (private) Islamic University in Uganda and Mbarara University of Science and Technology (a public-sector institution) opened in 1988 and 1989 respectively, to offer increased opportunities for university education to an ever increasing number of qualified candidates. Private expansion has continued in the period since. To date, there are over thirteen licensed universities, with only four belonging to the public sector.

Emergence of private universities is part of the overall growth of the private sector to provide vital services previously provided by government. This was enhanced by government policy to divest itself from managing enterprises and providing services that can be more efficiently provided by the private sector. Due to rising demand, and inadequate funding from government, public universities admitted privately sponsored students as a means to generate funds to expand university facilities and programmes. By the 1995/96 academic year, nearly half of the total Makerere University intake of 4,801 students was privately sponsored; the following year, intake was 7,904 and 71 per cent were private (see Kasozi, 2003: 4). Alongside privatisation went a decentralisation of public services to the District Local Governments. Ssebuwufu - the Vice-Chancellor of Makerere University at this point - then narrates that in this era, many African Universities began, through fora such as the Association of African Universities, UNESCO, and Donors to African Education, to re-examine their role in society. Standards, relevance, access and equity, never before discussed in academic boards, suddenly became serious issues for debate. The public, particularly private sector and local government stakeholders, became more concerned about and critical of theory-oriented education, programmes with little or no perceived relevance to society, falling standards and the low quality of graduates. The private sector is interested in people who can do things, not those who can talk about things.

Despite many difficulties, Makerere University built its own reputation for teaching and research, even during the difficult years, but without shedding the European model of education.

It was still moulded around British academic standards first set by the supervisory link with the University of London. But with outside criticism mounting, the time had come to change course; "the old good days were over", as Ssebuwufu put it. Makerere University responded in 2000/2001 by commissioning a study to identify the new training needs demanded by private sector and local governments. The findings of this study led to the development of a university strategic plan, 2000/2005, which emphasized three pillars: teaching, research and outreach or community service. To implement the strategic plan, a committee of 14 members ("C14"), comprising of seven members from government and private sector and seven from the university, initiated negotiations with donors, and particularly with the Rockefeller Foundation and the World Bank, and secured a $17 million Learning and Innovation Loan (LIL). It also set-up the 'I@mak.com'. This project aimed at stimulating innovations in the university to build capacity for decentralised districts and the private sector. Makerere can now claim to be at the leading age of the search among African universities to meet the challenge of relevance posed by national development agendas in an era of privatisation and decentralization.

The above account is not intended to be a full summary of the rise of the African University, nor even of developments at Makerere University in particular; but what has been said so far provides a background and basis for the conceptual and theoretical discussions to follow, and a framework for understanding the subsequent empirical chapters relating to on-going change processes in Ugandan higher education. I begin with a discussion on the relationship between universities, society and development.

Are universities accountable to society?

Thinking of reforming universities for whatever reason compels us to seek to understand what universities actually are in the broader context of society and development. There is no single generic definition of the term 'university' that encompasses the wide range of institutions sharing this name and the national contexts in which they are located (Galbraith, 1999; Barnett, 2000). Allen (1988), for example, defines British universities as institutions with the power to award their own degrees, and pre-eminent in their fields of research. Universities under the former British colonies fit well in this definition. Implicitly, the definition spells out the functions of universities as to train (*i.e.* to award degrees) and to conduct research. Allen, however, does not state in whose interest pre-eminence in research is attained. Power to award their own degrees probably also indicates some degree of freedom to determine whom the British university will serve.

Nyerere (1971), in inaugurating the University of Dar es Salaam in 1970, provided a function-based definition of a university as an institution of higher learning, a place where people's minds are trained for clear and independent thinking, for analysis, and for problem solving at the highest level. He further explained that a university has three major social functions. First is to transmit advanced knowledge from one generation to the next, so that this can serve as either a basis for action or springboard for further research. Second, it is a centre for the attempt to advance the frontiers of knowledge by concentrating in one place some of the most intellectually gifted minds. And third, through its teaching it provides for the high-level manpower needs of society. Nyerere makes it clear that the importance of these three functions at any particular university may vary from time to time, according to resources which the community is able to allocate to it, the pressures which society exerts on it, and the accident of personalities and abilities among its members. Nyerere's view challenges universities to provide intellectual and practical leadership to advance society, and that the university should be able to adjust to the changing needs of society and be accountable to it as well. He later puts it very bluntly that knowledge which remains isolated from the people, or which is used by a few to exploit others, is a betrayal – a particularly vicious kind of theft by false pretence.

Vavakova (1998) talks of the old and new social contracts between universities and society, but in the context of industrialised countries. The argument is basically about the relationship between universities and industry with regard to research. She says the old contract is an exchange in which government promises to fund the basic science that peer reviewers find most worthy of support, and scientists promise that the research will be performed well and honestly and will provide a steady stream of discoveries to be translated into new products, medicine or weapons. She recognises that this contract ignores the fact that translation of research results into new products, medicines or weapons is a complicated process, often leading to "alleged scientific fraud" and loss of public confidence in the capacity of academic science to regulate itself. The claim for the new contract is therefore a "moralistic" discourse, but Vavakova also cautions that to understand the terms of the new contract between university and the larger society, greater transparency is needed about who is determining which knowledge should be produced by public research – in universities and other institutions – and for whose benefit this knowledge is destined.

It is increasingly becoming clear that universities cannot continue to claim independence to do only what pleases them. They have a moral responsibility to address immediate development challenges of society, since their existence is supported by public resources. Smith (2003) argues that new relationships between creative subjects and technology require new thinking about the nature and purpose of universities, in particular with regard to the growing involvement of the private sector in higher education. In the developing or less industrialised countries the social contract extends beyond industry to the larger society and attempts to deal with real-life challenges such as poverty. In his book, *University Education in Uganda*, Kasozi (2003: xiii) articulates the public expectations of universities as:

> "Ugandans have eagerly participated in paying for the costs of higher education because they have higher expectations of the benefits of this commodity. They expect higher education to facilitate improvement of the quality of their lives. They count on higher education to contribute to the economic development of the individual and the state".

The investment that society puts into the university should translate into relevant services offered to society, as Nyerere (*ibid.*: 109) emphasizes:

"The peasants and workers of a nation feed, clothe, and house both the students and their teachers; they also provide all the educational facilities used – the books, test-tubes, machines, and so on. The community provides these things because it expects to benefit – it is making an investment in people. The community investment will, however, have been a bad one if the student is ill-equipped to do any of the jobs required when he is called upon to make this contribution. In such a case, the university will have failed in its task".

Nyerere is here using the language of a failed socialist experiment. The new debate centres much more on ideas of value-for-money and cost-effectiveness of knowledge producing institutions, which need to pay their way by the added value they contribute, but the thought is, at root, much the same. Societal expectations cannot be met if universities remain "ivory towers". Those at universities whose job includes working with the public are usually separated from the rest of the system (Levin and Greenwood, 2001: 106). We live in a dynamic world and universities, too, need to maintain dynamism to address new problems and meet new demands from society and government. But what is remarkable about the university is how much of its form and character has remained the same over many centuries and in many different cultures (Ross, 1976: 254). As Ross puts it; "the university has survived". It is however, unlikely, that universities will survive the same way in the 21st century if it cuts itself off from challenges posed by public demands. As government funding to universities continues to decline, survival depends more and more on support from the private sector and on sponsorship of students, notably by parents (also see Boyatzis *et al.*, 1995). Given growing concern to extract value for money, by way of development impact, even support from government is likely to be conditional upon service to society. Sustaining public support requires that universities engage in forging a new social contract with society and government. This trend is already reflected in university vision and mission statements. For example Makerere University envisages itself as becoming:

"a center of academic excellence, providing world-class teaching, research and service relevant to sustainable development needs of society".

Its mission statement, accordingly, is:

"to provide quality teaching, carry out research and offer professional services to meet the changing needs of society by utilizing world-wide and internally generated human resources, information and technology to enhance the University's leading position in Uganda and beyond".

Articulation of societal responsibilities in vision and mission statements has to be accompanied by processes and mechanisms for bringing universities nearer to society and the challenges of poverty alleviation – *i.e.* the new social contract has to be operationalised, and not just a dream on paper. This is where the discussion ought to focus now. It is no longer in debate whether the African university should change; it is rather a question of "how".

Bringing universities closer to society and development

The conceptual framework presented in the previous chapter proposes an interaction between universities, community and service providers as part of a learning process. We know the prime functions of universities to be as training and research, and for some universities like Makerere another function of outreach/or service to community has recently been added. The outreach part attempts to depict the university's social responsibility to community, but is the least understood of the three functions. It can mean anything from merely participating in village meetings to engagement with community in solving development problems. While sharing his personal experiences as former Vice-Chancellor, Ssebuwufu (2005) narrated the difficulty that the university management had in defining outreach: to some it meant consultancy, to others it meant industrial attachment or school practice. If such an important societal function is interpreted in so many different ways, then it cannot be readily implemented, as everything fits the claim of being outreach or service to community. As suggested in the framework, outreach can be operationalised through action research and action learning. Student internship in this sense is a form of action learning. Although action research and action learning are closely related, they are not exactly the same. The two are discussed separately with respect to their application in bringing universities nearer to community and to development.

Action research as a link between university and society

According to Levin and Greenwood (2001) universities as institutions responsible for the generation and transmission of knowledge have created a variety of conditions inimical to the practice of action research, thereby producing poor-quality knowledge and isolating themselves unproductively from the societies they claim to serve. These authors argue that it is vitally important to reconstruct universities, converting them into engaged social institutions, functioning as critical and reflective training centres for new generations of social actors. For this they suggest utilising action research as one avenue for the recreation of universities serving an effective social role. Action research is fed by philosophical traditions of pragmatism. Two things stand out: knowledge generation through action and experimentation, and emphasis on participative democracy. Levin and Greenwood justify their claims (p. 106) by challenging universities as follows; if, as academics and university administrators often claim, one of the aims of the university is to discover how things work, to teach others to learn these things, and to guide research and teaching according to what society at large most wants and/or needs, then pragmatic action research would dominate all aspects of university operations, including administrative activities.

Action learning is a mechanism for enabling university lecturers to interface and participate in development with the community in order to gain experiences that would make university training more relevant. Harvey and Knight (1996: 170) describe action research as a continuing cycle of inquiry, reflection, planning and action: it is a stance towards practice, whereas development work is often an event. Action research starts with the view that research should lead to change, and change should be incorporated in the research itself (Thorpe *et al.,*

1997). Action research is part of the new scholarship, in which it is recognised that knowledge generation is a creative practice evolving through dialogue, and that knowledge is not only an outcome of cognitive activity but a set of embodied skills (*i.e.* mind and body are not regarded as separate entities but are seen as integral entities, McNiff *et al.,* 2003: 17). McNiff and colleagues differentiate action research from other kinds of research with the following characteristics (*cf* Levin and Greenwood, 2001: 105):

- **It is practitioner based**. Action research is also called action inquiry. It involves making public an explanatory account of practice. The practitioner base to action research means that all people in all contexts who are investigating a situation can become researchers, regardless of age, status, social setting, or social or professional positioning. The researcher is therefore inside the situation and will inevitably influence what is happening.
- **It focuses on learning**. Action research is concerned with how individuals' learn in company with other people. Different from social scientific research, which aims to understand and describe an external situation (whether in terms of adequacy as objective explanation or as an established interpretation in the eyes of participants), action research is a process aimed at helping a practitioner to develop a deeper understanding of what s/he does as a researcher inside a research process (*i.e.* it aims at developing new interpretations). It has both personal and social aim. The personal aim is improvement of one's own learning, while the social aim is improvement of the situation the learners find themselves in.
- **It embodies good professional practice, and goes beyond**. Action research is more than problem solving, and involves identifying reasons for the action, related to the researcher's values, and gathering and interpreting data to show that the reasons and values were justified and fulfilled. Good professional practice emphasises action but does not often question motives. To count as action research there must be an element of praxis. Praxis in this context is informed, committed action giving rise to knowledge as well as to successful actions.
- **It can lead to personal and social improvement**. People commit to evaluating their own work and finding ways of improving it with a view to influencing others. Self-evaluation helps people to hold themselves accountable for what they think and do. The idea of social change is embodied in the processes of groups of individuals committed to changing the way they think and act. Individual practitioners become dynamic change agents generating wide-scale social change by working together.
- **It is responsive to social situations**. The researchers do not only observe and describe the situation; they also take action to improve the situation. They try to understand how they might improve what they are doing, on the assumption that the decision to improve the situation, beginning with their own activities and interactions, will enable them to influence others in context, and in accordance with their values.
- **It demands high order questioning**. Action research may not be problem-solving (*i.e.* bring an investigation to closure), but it does imply problem posing (or problematising); that is, there is an orientation towards not accepting things at face value. This involves questioning at first, second and third order learning levels (also see Sterling, 2000, 2004). First-order learning refers to learning about the situation (simple or basic learning). Second

order learning what has been learnt (this is learning about learning, or meta-learning); and third order learning is asking why the situation is as it is, and why one might need to change the way one thinks about it (epistemic learning, or learning about learning about learning).

- **It is intentionally political.** Deciding to take action is itself a political act, because what one person does invariably has consequences for someone else. When researchers question phenomena that, for example, reveal injustices, they have to make a decision whether they wish to follow their own value commitments and try to improve the situation according to what they believe in, or whether they will go along with the status quo (and be explicit about the reasons).

- **The focus is on change and the self as a locus of change.** Situations do not change themselves, people change and they change their situations. Change begins in people's minds, which then translates into social change. Traditional research usually stops at describing the situation and sometimes at suggesting ways to change situation. Action research takes action towards the desired change process through a process involving reflection and self-analysis by all participants.

- **Practitioners accept responsibility for their own actions.** In traditional research, researchers usually carry out what is required by someone else, such as policy makers or funders. Action researchers make their own decisions about what is important and what they should do. This is a massive responsibility, because they invoke their own values as a basis for their actions. Because of this responsibility, they need to always check whether their values are justifiable and justified, whether they are living in accordance with their values, and whether their influence is benefiting other people in ways that those other people also feel are good. This involves rigorous evaluation checks and restraints, to ensure action researchers can justify, and do not abuse, their position of potential influence.

- **It emphasises the value base of practice.** Action research is value laden, which differs from the stance of neutrality claimed by (some) other types of research. It begins with practitioners becoming aware of what is important to them – their values – and how they might act in the direction of those values.

Action research in this sense can be seen as a potential vehicle for building a new relationship between university, development agents and society at large. It is also a platform for a new mode of learning to understand the real needs of society. The aim is to use the dynamics of change as a basis for self-examination to influence training and research that benefits society. This is not to suggest that all research in the university should be action research. It is not a replacement for other types of research, such as the basic research on which the universities set such pride. But what is argued here is that action research could be an effective instrument for intellectual re-orientation, and so universities interested in becoming relevant to the needs of societies which historically have emerged in very different conditions from those sustained on campuses ought to allocate a prominent place to action research.

Action learning as a link between universities and society

Action learning has for long been simply defined as *learning by doing*. Revans (1997) explains that this is based on the common knowledge that lectures and bookwork alone are not sufficient for educating people who have to take decisions in the "real world"; as the old saying puts it, practice alone makes perfect. Revans argues that action learning is not what a person already knows and tells that sharpens the countenance of a friend, but what that person and the friend together do not know – it is recognising ignorance and not programmed knowledge that is key to action learning. University teachers are commonly known as lecturers and so they lecture. Revans' argument is that this is not sufficient to develop people who are expected to take decisions in the real world. This is probably part of the reason society's expectations from universities are far from reality. What society expects cannot be delivered by universities in their current form.

Another point in Revans' argument is the exposure of ignorance as part of the learning process, which challenges universities to quit the teaching paradigm for learning and to begin learning from the realities of life. Boyatzis, *et al.* (1995: 10) give the epistemological differences between teaching-centred and learning-centred approaches (See Table 2; *cf.* Thorpe *et al.*, 1997)). But as Ison (1990) says, universities reinforce the teaching paradigm by describing their purpose and function as "custodians" and "preservers" of knowledge – which creates the image of knowledge as a "commodity" to be "stored" or "warehoused" and then dispensed (by lecturer) to recipients (students). Moving to the learning paradigm is only possible if universities begin to engage in activities of real-life problem solving in pursuance of their

Table 2: Contrast between teaching-centred and learning-centred approaches.

Focus on teaching	Focus on learning
Input orientation – staff* controls input and determines and evaluates how much material is sufficient to teach	*Output orientation* – attention to relationship between staff and student
Discipline – defined knowledge – focus on narrowly defined, specialised knowledge	*Problem centred* – or contextually defined knowledge. Greater focus on learning rather than teaching
Staff's way of knowing – staff viewed as the expert and unique source of knowledge	*Student's way of knowing* – pace and flow of understanding, logic, and way of knowing centred on student's capabilities
Stakeholders – staff and specialised field	*Stakeholders* – staff, students, employers, alumni, and so on

*I use "staff" instead of "faculty" to avoid confusion. Faculty in this thesis refers to a university unit (in the British sense) and not to the complement of lecturers and researchers (as in American usage).

Learning to make change

functions. Dreyfus and Wals (2000) emphasize that we may never understand the problem until we start to implement some potential solutions and that without ability and willingness to act, it is impossible to participate in, or rather to contribute to, a democratic society. For universities to understand the problems they are expected to assist in solving they have to take part in implementing possible solutions to those problems.

Action learning is a continuous process of learning and reflection, supported by colleagues, with the intention of getting things done (McGill and Beaty, 1995: 21). McGill and Beaty add the dimension of collective or joint engagement. Reflecting with colleagues to get things done is based on mutual relationships, common goals and complementary efforts. This working together has to be nurtured through training of professionals. On the contrary, universities, by their functioning, tend to "breed" and promote individualism, and yet they expect their graduates to cooperate and work productively with others. The dominance of the lecture format in university teaching, and assessment of student learning based examination of the individual, tends to promote excellence of individuals, while in the world of government or business "excellence" is often only possible through collective action. Allen (1988) argues that one of the effects of teaching in university is to identify talent by filtering out the more able students from the average. The British First Class Degree, for example, once led to an automatic invitation to apply for a post as a member of the top administrative grade in the civil service. Probably the need to recruit top civil servants was once a justification to focus on individuals, but talent should also take into account abilities to work with others, if individual "excellence" is ever to be of value in a systemic and systems-led society.

Pedler (1997: 63) asserts that the shift from regarding learning as an individual phenomenon to seeing it as something which results from people-in-relationship seems particularly relevant today. He considers this a generative view of learning reaching beyond the individual making sense of the world in isolation to one in which people jointly engage in collective social processes of sense making and meaning creation. Pedler and Aspinwall (1996) view learning as:

1. ...being about things (knowledge).
2. ...doing things (acquire skills, abilities, competences).
3. ...becoming ourselves, to achieve our full potential (personal development).
4. ...achieving things together (collaborative enquiry).

University training tends to limit itself to the first two levels. Ideally, universities as the highest institutions of learning should strive to achieve the highest levels of learning, and thus need to include personal development and collaborative inquiry. These two levels, however, demand collective engagement, which has to be mainstreamed in university training. In this regard, action learning is here advocated as a method to build on and reinforce the academic tradition, and not (as some seem to fear) as a populist and simplistic attempt to confront that tradition (Revans, 1997). It fulfils the deepest aspirations of the academic tradition to seek to provide learning for fundamental change. In agriculture, for example, Ison (1990: 7) proposes that to meet the needs of a changing, sustainable agriculture, radical thinking about agricultural education is urgently required; perhaps the most fundamental challenge is to re-establish universities as communities of learners. Ison says academics must become involved in learning, learning about learning, facilitating the development of learners, and exploring new ways of understanding their own and others' realities. Dreyfus and Wals (2000) clarify that a learning experience becomes fundamental when the whole person becomes part of the learning experience (*i.e.* head, heart and hands are engaged).

Based on the discussion above, the prerequisites for action learning in university are that there must be action in real-life situation, reflection, and group openness to learning. As suggested in the conceptual model in the first chapter, action learning can to a great extent be achieved through a well-designed programme of student internships. In addition to offering interactive learning approaches towards fostering creativity, critical thinking, and competence, student internships provide the opportunity to deal with actual problems as an extension of learning. It is the platform where students, lecturers, other development actors and the community engage to learn from solving real-life problems. With support from 'I@ mak.com' and other development agencies, Makerere University, for example, is attempting to institutionalise student internship in several faculties. At present internship is treated mainly as an opportunity for students (alone) to gain exposure and "hands-on" experience. The lecturers exclude themselves from this learning process, and thus cut themselves off from practical experiences that might influence their own performance and that of the university system as a whole.

Action learning has been used as a process to reform organisations and to liberate new human visions within organisations (Garratt, 1997). Garratt elaborates that action learning attempts to achieve the blend of logic and emotional engagement necessary to transcend organisational difficulties by giving rigour and pace to the cycle of learning, and, through drawing on the positive powers of groups, to sustain discipline and rhythm. Boyatzis and colleagues (1995: xi) introduce their book, *Innovations on professional education,* with a warning that driven by people from within educational institutions as well as by stakeholders such as prospective students, parents, employers and funding agents this process of transformation is likely to leave few areas of the academic world untouched. We might conclude that universities are unlikely to be able to resist change along these lines; the only option may be to find the best ways to manage such changes.

Learning and change

Learning changes you, and equally, change requires learning – people change behaviour because of new learning that requires them to adapt (Allen *et al.*, 2002). Learning can be interpreted in so many ways, and it is also found at various levels, as explained earlier. Learning aimed at developing a person only happens when the world begins to look different to that person (*cf.* McGill and Beaty, 1995: 175). Gaining a new world view requires a mental shift, sometimes induced by personal experiences or reflections, and sometimes (as Douglas, 1986 argues) through organizational re-orientation. Sterling (2000, 2004) suggests the shift of mind that many commentators require in university work involves not just simple learning but learning of a higher order (*i.e.* 2nd and 3rd levels), and the relevant accompanying organizational changes to support such learning. It is therefore at these levels that we can influence change or development.

Kanter (1995) suggests that change is always a threat when it is done to people, but it is an opportunity when it is done by people. Senge (1990: 155) adds that people don't resist change, but rather that they resist being changed. This means that change agents have to be aware of and address an inherent fear of being changed. For that reason, Kanter suggests that the ultimate key to creating pleasure in the hard work of change in a challenging and demanding environment is to give people the tools and the autonomy to make their own contributions to change. Whether the future holds breakdown or breakthrough scenarios, people will require flexibility, resilience, creativity, participative skills, competence, material restraint and a sense of responsibility and transpersonal ethics to handle transitions and to provide mutual support (Sterling, 2001). Such tools to cope with unpredictable future are embedded in the second and third levels of learning. This is the basic justification for the argument made earlier that universities need to shift from teaching-centred to learning-centred approaches, in order to negotiate a shift to higher levels of learning.

From and individual staff perspective, the problems associated with learner-centred approach include the loss or devaluing of skills, fear of not being an expert any more, need for new skills, and far-reaching and destabilising changes in student/client expectations (Thorpe et al., 1997). Getting staff to change from, say, the (self-contained) lecture method to a more open, interactive style of instruction always meets with considerable resistance (Knapper and Cropley, 1985; Harvey and Knight, 1996: , Chiang, 2005). Changing the role of the teacher to become a mentor rather and facilitator of learning is one of the characteristics embedded within flexible learning (Moran and Myringer, 1999). However, as Wheatley (1999) suggests, change in behaviour is a gradual outcome of iterative reflections on an individual's actions, and support from colleagues to enact new values and develop new patterns of behaviour.

This view raises several issues. First, changing the way we do things is not a linear stepwise process; it is an iterative process that will likely involve steps backward, and the need for critical reflection to find a new way forward. Secondly, the learning process is collegial, and demands exposure of our ignorance and a willingness to learn from others. Thirdly, it involves making decisions to take action; otherwise we cannot change from the status quo. Taking action also means overcoming fear to making mistakes, and developing confidence in the social support around us. Fourthly, it is not a random or incidental activity, but an entire process, that has to be designed and pursued with a clear vision of what we want to achieve. Managing change processes, therefore, implies having optimism in the future while at the same time avoiding acting naively. By being optimistic here, I mean focusing on what we can possibly do rather than what we cannot. The approach involves exploiting our potential and/or developing our hidden potential, as opposed to falling victim to circumstances.

In his argument for 'Preferred Futuring' as a paradigm shift from focusing on deficiencies to focusing on potential, Lippitt (1999) puts forward what he thinks makes change successful, in terms of a seemingly simple model as follows:

$$C - D \times V \times F \times R$$

$C = Change$, which is moving from one stage to another, becoming different from what was.

$D = Dissatisfaction$. Dissatisfaction with the current situation is a change lever often expressed as complaints and the belief that nothing can be done. Dissatisfaction must be transformed into motivation for change.

$V = Vision$. Vision is a clear, detailed, and agreed-upon picture of the future. It is a collective picture of a future all stakeholders deeply and passionately want.

$F = First step$. Action plans – concrete, agreed-upon steps – move the system from vision to implementation and specific results.

$R = Resistance to change$. When people let go of the dissatisfaction, decide what they want (vision) and take the first step, the product is greater than resistance (R).

He concludes that if any of the factors D, V or F is missing in the model, the product is zero. Resistance remains greater than the desired change. V is an special source of difficulty, because institutions – not least those afflicted by poverty – typically harbour deep disagreements about ways forward, and specific conflict resolution activity may be needed to arrive at a clear, agreed vision. Thus we might conclude that the model is too simple to explain all the complex dynamics of change, but nevertheless it emphasizes the fact that we can enhance our influence on change by maximising D, V and F. These are therefore key entry points for "change agents". We can increase dissatisfaction with the status quo by creating awareness of *what could be*. "What could be" then has to be made compatible with what in our overall imagination we want to achieve, and where we want to go as individuals as well as within an organisation/community. In turn getting where we want to go requires us to develop strategic action. Strategic action is driven by levels of dissatisfaction, how compelling the vision is, and (most important) by the realisation of our potential to get where we want to be. Our ability to influence change, therefore, depends on how well we can facilitate processes that increase dissatisfaction with the status quo, create a compelling and shared vision, and generate motivation sufficient to overcome fear of taking action.

I am aware that putting things this way might provoke the question from researchers "how can one measure C, D, V, F and R?" Wals (1993) addressed this question by challenging that what we can't measure still exists; aside from learning about people, research should also aim to understand reality with people as it challenges them. And to emphasise the importance of the intangible systemic processes, Galbraith (1999) adds that when dealing with systems, processes must be included because of their existence in the real world, and not on the basis of availability of data, and that a process deemed important must be included, for to 'omit' such a process on the grounds of insufficient data is not to omit it at all, but to include it with an assigned weight of zero. Knowing people's reality means learning with them so that they are able to change themselves. Kanter (1995) and Senge (1990) refer to people's fears of being changed. But the reality is that we cannot change people; we can only help them to change themselves through learning. Organisations learn and change through individuals who learn; hence we arrive at the important concept of a learning organisation.

Can universities become learning organisations?

In the view of Senge (1990) learning organisations are organisations where people continually expand their capacity to increase the results they truly desire, where new expansive patterns of thinking are nurtured, where collective aspiration is set free, and where people are continually learning how to learn together. This description ought to describe universities, at the helm of learning; unfortunately the concept of the learning organisation is not closely associated with the university (cf. Franklin et al., 1998). It is more associated with private sector business organisations striving to make money in a changing and competitive environment (also see Sterling, 2004). While universities are expected to turn out more independent citizens, they themselves have remained too dependent on the public resources guaranteeing their existence. For that reason, university dissatisfaction with the status quo remains low. While they continue to enjoy the comfort of public resources the motivation to learn and change is low. But in a country like Uganda this situation is unlikely to continue for long, as public funding to universities continues to diminish and competition for students in a market with several private players hots up. In the corporate sector, the advantage of being the first to capture customers with new products on the market is what drives innovations in competing organisations (Kanter, 1995).

Similarly, in a market-driven competitive education environment today's universities cannot deny that they operate in a climate of change (Cullen, 1999; Williams, 1993). Even for developing country institutions competition is not only within the country or region but is global. Universities worldwide have recently been confronted with a new raft of changes and demands, and some of these are difficult to respond to adequately on the basis of existing organisational and governance structures (Kovac et al., 2003; Srikanthan, 2000; Lysons, 1999) and cultures. Galbraith (1999) has comprehensively discussed some areas of weakness including:

- *artificial internal structures* – variously described as faculties, groups, or divisions, themselves comprised of smaller cells called departments, schools or centres;
- *false dichotomies* – arguments based on the splitting of cause-effect chains that deny the existence of system feedback; funding formulae based on student load and research effort;
- *the tragedy of commons* – proportional policies used to distribute funds in situations where no constraints (natural or imposed) act to curb competition for scarce resources such as funding based on research productivity;
- *weights and parameters* – weights assigned to various entities, e.g. staff levels versus government funding, funding loading for research versus undergraduate students or disciplinary weights;
- *interaction effects* – dual emphases on the need to balance budgets and to maintain or increase research efforts;
- *research traditions* – tendency to ignore impending impact of management decisions aided by entrenched views, and encouraged by traditional research training involving use of linear statistical models and predictions; and

- *significance of time scales* – e.g. cyclical patterns of debts and surplus, cyclical patterns of staff numbers and rates of adjustment to changing enrolment conditions.

Universities now operate in a complex, turbulent and competitive education environment characterised by resource constraints and demands for accountability from a range of different entities. To do more and better with fewer resources is the challenge for universities in the 21st century (UNESCO, 2003). Universities of the future will require creativity and innovation (Gunkel, 1994 quoted by Srikanthan, 2000); they will need strong and effective leaders able to cope with new quality demands and public accountability but also willing to develop new values and a 'new' culture at all levels of the university (Kovac *et al.*, 2003). In order to cope with complexity and turbulence, corporate management practices have been embraced by universities around the world (Lysons, 1999), but the presence of delayed feedback means that outcomes have been problematic (Galbraith, 1999; Williams, 1993). To manage this Brave New World faced by the University of the Future, Srikanthan (2000) suggests the following organisational characteristics to be cultivated:
- an ability to operate at the depth of a disciplinary speciality, at the same time be involved in a course team to make the learner experience meaningful;
- an ability to manage extreme complexity;
- a collaborative approach to develop integrated and interactive programs; and
- a capacity to manage and plan technology applications, with a view to using them as tools.

The current trend implies that universities that succeed to become learning organisations are likely to go through the 21st century more successfully than those that do not. As Senge (1990) puts it, organisations learn only through individuals who learn; individual learning does not guarantee organisational learning, but without it no organisational learning occurs. Senge suggests mastery of five basic disciplines necessary for a successful learning organisation:
- *systems thinking* - interconnected actions;
- *personal mastery* - the discipline of continually clarifying and deepening personal vision, of focusing energies, of developing patience, and of seeing reality objectively;
- *mental models* - assumptions, generalisations or images that influence how we understand the world and how we take action;
- *building shared vision* - involves the skill of unearthing shared 'pictures of the future' that foster genuine commitment and enrolment rather than compliance; and
- *team learning* - teams not individuals are the fundamental learning units in modern organisations.

Srikanthan draws a comparison of Senge's five disciplines of a *'learning organisation'* and Bowden and Marton's *'university of learning'* models and to these I add Galbraith's *'dark'* version of the five disciplines in Table 3.

Galbraith's "dark" version illustrates the current situation in universities versus the ideal situation for learning organisations. Higher education for the 21st century must be open to innovation and willing to learn (Lysons, 1999; Laurillard, 1999). Universities indeed can

Table 3: Comparison of the ideal situations for learning organisation and current situation in universities (Adapted with modification from Srikanthan, 2000).

Learning organisation (Senge, 1990)	University of learning (Bawden and Marton, 1998)	The "dark" version of learning organisation disciplines (Galbraith, 1999)
Personal mastery: Each person has a clear vision and understands the current reality. As a result there is creative tension which is directed to exploration of alternatives	Academics commit themselves to a deep exploration of the subject matter from a learner's perspective to develop alternative patterns of understanding.	**Personal mystery:** The insensitivity and inflexibility of funding formula allocation is a continuing de-stabilising agent for managers in charge of academic centres. Far from developing confidence and feelings of mastery, mystery, or perhaps misery, emerge, as responsible leaders begin to doubt their efforts.
Systems thinking: The group develops a holistic view of the situation and explores the interconnections and interactions. They visualise patterns of cause and effects	The academics develop a holistic view of the competences created by the course experience in students. They explore the potential for 'discerning variation'.	**Systems tinkering:** On the contrary, purposes and goals of higher education have been set by government authorities with all the cultural inheritance associated with linear, non-systemic thinking. Surface 'tinkering' has pre-dominated over incisive systems thinking
Team learning: Synergistic involvement in the work groups by each one. Use of 'dialogue' and 'skilful discussions'.	Synergistic involvement in a course/research team. Developing, along with colleagues, a holistic view of student competences.	**Team lurching:** In universities, the substantial rewards accruing on the basis of individual academic effort, means private time is guarded jealously, and commitment required for genuine team learning may be resented. In some areas, lurching from issue to issue remains more accurate description than learning.
Shared vision: Alignment of objectives of all members of the group.	A collective consciousness of what is common and what is complementary.	**Shared fission:** As long as the bottom line remains individual survival and 'the devil takes the hindmost', 'fission' rather than vision will characterise interchanges between individual and groups, and the benefits of productive sharing will remain tantalisingly beyond reach.
Mental models: A balanced advocacy with inquiry, in clarifying intentions and assumptions. Awareness of 'leap of abstraction'.	Differences and complementarities brought into the open to get a clear view of each one's position. Uninhibited communication.	**Mental muddles:** Managerial concerns appear to be triggered by 'amplitudes of variations' while policies enacted relate to 'time-scales' determining rates of change. Pre-occupation with magnitudes rather than rates of change is like addressing a problem of a broken shock absorber by driving slowly over potholes.

learn – they must become vibrant organisational learning entities, to play their rightful role in social development (Srikanthan, 2000), though the rate of change is liable to be slow (Ison, 1990). Given their more privileged position, universities have a unique opportunity to lead development of the concept in practice as well as theory (Franklin *et al.*, 1998). Perhaps the biggest single challenge to the application of learning organisation principles is the identification and use of leverage points (Galbraith, 1999). However Galbraith cautions that if the reaction is to shoot the messenger bringing unwelcome news, then as with other organisations universities will miss the opportunity to push the boundaries of their potential.

The central message of the five disciplines is that organisations work the way they work because of how their members think and interact (Douglas, 1986; Retna, 2005). Like any other organisation, universities are systems, and they too seek to influence change in other systems they are part of. But as Wood (1995) emphasizes, regardless of the amount of change, unless the thinking involved in the system is developed or evolved, the underlying structures (laws and principles, including those of the mind) remain unchanged. Therefore, understanding change in a systems perspective can help to guide reforms in universities.

Systems thinking: a mechanism for transforming universities

Senge (1990) describes systems thinking as a discipline for seeing wholes - a sensibility for subtle interconnectedness that gives living systems their unique character - and that the essence of systems thinking discipline lies in a shift of the mind to see interrelationships rather than linear cause-effect chains, and thus seeing change as a set of processes rather than in terms of snapshots. Broadly, Kreutzer (1995) sees the goal of systems thinking and systems dynamics as providing tools to transform perspectives and mental models so that actions lead to real sustainable long-term improvements Systems thinking gives rise to a qualitatively different epistemology and worldview, beyond the reductionist, linear and objectivist approaches associated with theories of modernity, but which remain dominant in educational theory and practice (Sterling, 2000). A whole systems approach means every necessary sub-system within the organisation is created, modified, or redesigned and then integrated and aligned (Cindy and Bill Adams, 1999). The Adams' further argue that the approach is grounded in practicality, *i.e.* where practitioners have to learn what works and what cannot work inside organisations. They spell-out that a whole systems approach is particularly valuable when:

- there is a need fundamentally to change what exists;
- a system or process is not running effectively or optimally;
- creating a new possibility adds significant value; and
- current efforts are not on track – they lack speed, results, or broad ownership.

These conditions perfectly fit the situation under investigation. The shift from teaching to learning in higher education that many authors advocate is a fundamental change. The fact that change is suggested means that the system is not running effectively in terms of producing the graduates we expect to confront complex problems in society.

A systemic perspective on education starts by questioning what the whole system is for and whom it is meant to serve, before any systemic analysis can be undertaken on how well it serves its purposes and what to do about shortfalls (Brown, 1999). The first part – the "whom" universities are meant to serve - has already been discussed under whether universities are accountable to society. Here, I intend to focus more on how well the university serves its purpose, and on the shortfall, already partly discussed under the heading of whether universities can become learning organisations.

Considering how universities serve their purpose, Banathy (1995, 1999) complains that we have entered the 21st century with education systems designed for the 19th century and an industrial machinery no longer suited to the era of post-industrial knowledge. He suggests that only radical and fundamental change of educational perspectives and purposes, and the reconceptualization and redesign of our educational institutions, will satisfy emergent new realities. Universities have traditionally been conceived and functioned as loosely coupled networks of academics, with coupling and accountability usually maintained not through managerial control or accountability to government, but through allegiances to disciplines and academic communities (Weil, 1999; Brewer, 1999). This can be related to their design. Banathy (1999) describes the technical approach of organisation of higher education institutions at three levels: 1) the institutional/governance level makes system-wide decisions and manages resources that support the instructional level, 2) the instructional level educates students, and 3) students receive instructions at the learning level. Banathy says the application of systems suggests that if we wish to shift the focus from instruction to learning we have to redesign higher education around the learning experience.

Problems faced at all levels in the world today tend to resist unilateral solutions. The web of global interdependencies tightens, but our capacity for thinking in terms of dynamic interdependencies has not kept pace (Richmond, 1993). Richmond suggests that systems thinking and systems dynamics are important in developing strategies for closing the gap. Therefore there is a need to re-establish universities as communities of learners. Lecturers must become involved in learning about learning, in facilitating the development of learners, and in exploring new ways of understanding their own and others' realities (Ison, 1990; Weil, 1999).

Based on his wide experience of teaching and facilitating systems thinking in universities and business organisations Richmond (1993) puts forward seven inter-related thinking strata for good systems thinking, and illustrates how they can be developed. I summarise them here as:
1. *Dynamic thinking* – the ability to see and deduce behaviour patterns rather than focusing on, and seeking to predict, events.
2. *Closed loop thinking* – seeing the world as a set of ongoing, interdependent processes rather than as a laundry list of one-way relations between a group of factors and a phenomenon that these factors are causing.
3. *Generic thinking* – avoiding thinking in terms of specifics and shift to generic thinking taking into account processes and their feedback mechanisms.
4. *Structural thinking* – thinking in terms of units of measure, or dimensions. The distinction between stock and flow is emphasized.

5. *Operational thinking* – thinking in terms of how things really work, not how they theoretically work, or how one might fashion a bit of algebra capable of generating realistic-looking output.
6. *Continuum thinking* – ability to recognise the familiar in what appears diverse or distinct – finding common ground. It is the ability to see connections and interdependencies rather than sharp boundaries and disconnections.
7. *Scientific thinking* – being rigorous about testing hypotheses. It has more to do with quantification than measurement. Establishing a scale, for example, does not mean one can specify what exactly these values are in the real system; it means only that one has established a rigorous convention for thinking about the dynamics of the variable.

Simultaneous development of these strata of thinking seems to offer a pathway to higher order (2nd and 3rd) learning levels to govern change in higher education for the 21st century (*cf.* Ison, 1999). The dynamics of higher education and increasing prospects of its globalisation mean that all academic groups have to scan the environment with a view to identifying actions that maintain the quality of their systems-environment relationships (Ison, 2001). The institutionalisation of systems thinking and practice within the academy is perhaps now more precarious than at any other time in the last fifty years (Maiteny and Ison, 2000). If we take seriously the idea of both a learning society and a learning organisation then it is reasonable to expect them both to exhibit the form and function of a system capable of learning (Laurillard, 1999). Universities need to enter into dynamically different forms of partnership that become knowledge generating, rigorous and transformative – otherwise complex tensions will render universities valueless and visionless (Wel, 1999; Maiteny and Ison, 2000). Barnett (2000) says the visions of the university for the 21st century expressed as 'the entrepreneurial university'; 'the service university'; 'the corporate university'; 'the virtual university'; a 'university for the learning society'; a 'university characterised by excellence' all imply a greater set of linkages between the university and its wider environment, but share a common weakness, in that they address sets of issues and offer a narrow view of the university. He summarises the task of a university for the 21st century as:

> "The university has the responsibility to inject further uncertainty into an already uncertain world; and it has itself to comprehend that role and itself to take on the conditions of uncertainty of the wider world. Universities have for long been safe havens. In an age of uncertainty, the universities have to abandon the idea of knowledge as an emblem. Instead they should help us to revel in uncertainty for that is the condition of our age." (Barnett, 2000: 128)

In effect this is to advocate a kind of open systems approach which welcomes uncertainty and change. In this age, the concept of universities as collections of individual faculties will not work any more – more attention should be given to creating mechanisms of integration and coordination among faculties (Kovac *et al.,* 2003) to make universities function in a systemic way, but as open rather than closed systems. This is not an easy task, but there are many examples around the world that have been encouraging. The Hawkesbury experiences documented by Bawden and colleagues and the work of Ison and colleagues at the Open University suggest some light at the end of the tunnel. Given the complexities of the 21st century in education, research and development, universities have no choice but to transform in this direction. Education and society must change together in a mutually affirming way, towards more sustainably adaptive patterns (Sterling, 2004). Systems understanding is at the cutting edge of societal learning in an age acknowledged to be more interactive, in almost every way, than any other (Maiteny and Ison, 2000). What is critical now is to explore new institutional forms for capacity building for systems practice (Ison, 2001). The capacity required in this case is that of transformative learning to facilitate fundamental recognition of the new paradigm and to enable paradigmatic reconstruction (cf. Sterling, 2004). In this light, I now turn to discussing transformative theory in university learning.

Transformative learning and universities

Transformative learning theory was first advocated over thirty years ago, by Jack Mezirow. Over time, it has been widely debated, revised and applied in different ways. Transformative learning refers to the process by which we transform our taken-for-granted frames of reference (meaning perspectives, habits of mind, mindsets) to make them more inclusive, discriminating, open, emotionally capable of change, and reflective, so that they generate beliefs and opinions that are true and/or justified guides to action (Mezirow, 2000: 7, 1997). The frames of reference are the structures of assumptions through which we understand our experiences, and a frame of reference encompasses cognitive, connotative, and emotional components, and is composed of a habit of mind and a point of view (Mezirow, 1997). Transformative learning is a social rather than solitary process, with the person at the centre – the values of the imagination and the power of emotion exist within a rational notion of transformation (Grabove, 1997). Transformative learning is similar to action learning on the basis that both aspire to locate fundamental principles of learning for change through critical reflection upon actions. Applications are diverse. But not all change is transformative, and not all critical reflection leads to transformative learning (ibid.). The centrality of transformative learning is to empower individuals to think as autonomous agents in a collaborative context rather than to act uncritically on received ideas and the judgements of others (Mezirow, 1997). Recognizing that the educational experience is never neutral (Taylor, 2006), the uniqueness of transformative learning is its focus on epistemological change rather than merely change in behaviour – it is a way of knowing (Kegan, 2000). In meaning-making processes, it is not *what* we know but *how* we know that is important (Baumgartner, 2001).

Transformation may simply mean a change from one form into another. If there is no form, there is no transformation (ibid.), but Harvey and Knight explain what transformation means in education as follows:

> "Transformation is not just about adding to a student's stock of knowledge or set of skills and abilities. At its core, transformation, in an educational sense, refers to the evolution of the way students approach the acquisition of knowledge and skills and relate them to wider context... A prime goal

should be to transform the learners so that they are able to take initiative, work with independence, to choose appropriate frames of reference, while being able to see the limitations of those frameworks and to stand outside them when necessary" (Harvey and Knight, 1996: viii, 12).

Transformation is not only for students, the educators, managers and practitioners too transform when they critically examine their view, open themselves to alternatives, and consequently change the way they see things or make meaning out of the world (*cf.* Cranton, 2002). Indeed education itself can be transformed by design (Banathy, 1995).

There is no particular teaching method that guarantees transformative learning (Cranton, 2002; Grabove, 1997). From her experience, Cranton recognizes that transformative learning is enhanced by creating a safe environment to challenge our beliefs, assumptions, and perspectives (also see Taylor, 2006). Grabove notes that facilitating and engaging in the process of transformative learning requires a great deal of effort, courage and authenticity on the part of both the educator and the learner, because it involves considerable risks, and the effort may or may not result in reward. This is one of the uncertainties of the age that Barnett suggests universities must plunge themselves into. Taylor (2006) however presents a more optimistic picture of the rewards of transformative learning, though he still cautions that it is not easy. He says that becoming a transformative educator should not be taken lightly as it requires and demands a great deal of work, skill and courage.

The sceptics of the possibility for current education system to become transformative suggest a redesign of the entire system. Banathy (1995) says there is no more important task than transforming education by design. He uses metaphors to illustrate his point. The first metaphor is that "you can't remake a horse-and-buggy into a spacecraft". Thereby, Banathy portrays the message that the design of current education is outdated and we cannot just improve it, but that it has to be utterly redesigned. From a technical perspective, he suggests that a system cannot do anything else but what it was designed for – the existing system of education was not designed for the 21st century. It is unfit for purpose. To illustrate his point he says:

> "Our schools perform today so badly precisely because they used to perform so well in the industrial society. But the world in which our schools must operate today has changed beyond their capacity to adjust. Their basic organisational principles are obsolete" (Banathy, 1995: 260).

Banathy's second metaphor is "improvement does not produce a butterfly, only a faster caterpillar". By this, he emphasizes that education must go through a complete metamorphosis. From the cocoon of fundamental re-design a beautiful butterfly - the new system – will emerge; peace-meal improvement does not give us a butterfly, only a faster caterpillar. In other words, Banathy calls for re-engineering the entire education system. Similar sentiments were raised by the Carnegie Forum on Education and the Economy (1986). As a society, and in higher education sector, we can choose either to strive towards deep learning and reorientation by conscious design, or have it thrust upon us by default, through the effect of mounting crisis (Sterling, 2004). The most plausible option is for universities to begin through their own transformative processes to rebuild relevance amidst the complexities of the 21st century.

This chapter discussed challenges and opportunities for universities from a theoretical and conceptual perspective. These challenges and opportunities have now to be put into a national context. As earlier explained, arguments in this thesis are anchored in an agrarian context. Specifically, Uganda is largely an agrarian society with smallholder farmers comprising over 80% of the population. In this case, the phrase "relevance to society" has a strong orientation towards smallholder farmers who also form the largest proportion of the poor. It is therefore critical to explore opportunities and related challenges for improving the well-being of smallholder farmers. Farmers operate in a very dynamic socio-political, ecological and market environment which requires a high level of adaptation and hence innovation. The next chapter will explore in rather specific terms how smallholder farmers respond to opportunities in their context, and what the function of agricultural professionals actually is in enhancing farmer capacities to cope and benefit from such opportunities. Based on a clear appreciation of these functions, it is then possible to identify the key competences that universities need to integrate into their training to make agricultural professionals more effective in working with farmers. The chapter (Chapter 3) will seek, therefore, to create a better understanding of the context and mechanisms through which smallholder farmers learn and innovate, so as to suggest ways in which the professionals can enhance this local learning process. Enhancing the learning and innovation opportunities of the scattered masses in an impoverished agrarian society is not only a problem for research and extension but also one of the biggest outreach challenges faced by the African university of the 21st century.

CHAPTER THREE

Professional ignorance and non-professional experts: experiences of how small scale vanilla farmers in Uganda learned to produce for export

Introduction

Falling World market prices for agricultural commodities is likely to sustain poverty in developing countries that rely on traditional agricultural exports (Figure 4). In Uganda, small scale agriculture employs over 80% of the population (PMA, 2000), but the proportion directly depending on agriculture for livelihood is even higher in rural communities (Abdalla and Egesa, 2004). With shocks due to price falls for agricultural commodities producers are likely to become poorer, even relative to the country's average income (Page and Hewitt, 2001). Indeed according to PEAP (2004), crop producers are among the poorest, even among farmers.

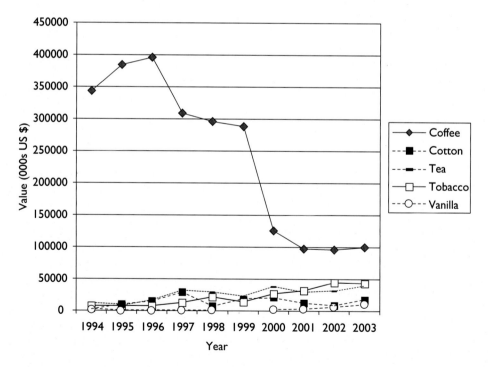

Figure 4: Performance of selected export crops, 1994-2003 (Data source: Uganda Bureau of Statistics).

Dependence on traditional exports such as coffee, cotton and tobacco for income will only worsen the poverty situation among small-scale farmers. Bahiigwa, et. al., (2005) for example, shows that producer prices as a ratio of world prices steadily increased from 12% in 1987 to 79% in 1998, but these positive developments for coffee producers were subsequently undermined by declining prices, with the 1999-2000 price falling to 36% of the 1994-95 price.

Recently, several African countries have gone into production of non-traditional fruits and vegetables to diversify their exports and increase hard cash earnings (Singh, 2002). In Uganda, small scale farmers are exploring new opportunities for niche market crops such as vanilla and cardamom as alternatives to traditional cash crops. Tamale and Namuwoza (2004: 767) emphasize Uganda's comparative advantage, in vanilla production, by for example, noting that: "Uganda is the only country on the mainland of African continent which grows vanilla and it is the only one in the world which harvests vanilla twice a year".

The shift to new crops is accompanied by demand for new knowledge and technologies, but research and extension, for many reasons, including a continued focus on traditional crops in training, institutional priorities and bureaucracy, are unable to adjust quickly enough to offer the support needed. An alternative is to open new windows of opportunity for farmers to engage in their own group learning processes to generate their own knowledge and technologies (this I refer to as social learning). This chapter describes a case of how small scale farmers self-organised to learn and share knowledge and innovations on vanilla without the intervention of research and extension. Farmers then became the "experts" in vanilla production while the professionals (researchers and extensionists) remained largely ignorant about the crop. Ignorance can be defined "as absence of knowledge in a particular arena that might fairly be expected to be overcome" (Chambers, 1995). In this case, absence of knowledge about vanilla among the professionals expected to support farmers with technical knowledge and skills is thus properly described as a state of ignorance. Ignorance is 'not just to know' but may suggest decay and dismantling of complex structure, or 'something more primordial the cognitive term of moral evil' (Vitebsky, 1992 quoted in Hobart, 1993). Gibb (2000) says a major manifestation of the growth of ignorance is the emergence of outstanding 'mythical concepts' and 'myths', an example of which I refer to later in this chapter.

In agriculture, the process of social learning requires that farmers become experts, instead of users of other specialists' wisdom and technologies (King and Jiggins, 2002); this challenges professional relevance to such processes. What then is the role of research and extension in the social learning process? The chapter also highlights "new" or additional functions for research and extension that warrant a new breed of professionals. The case study is based on vanilla farmers in Ntenjeru sub-county in Mukono district, Uganda. Specifically vanilla was of interest to the researcher because it is a new crop; it is largely produced by smallholder farmers, and has gained prominence as an export crop in the recent past. Despite its prominence as a high income crop, it has not had any intervention from research and extension. This case, therefore, presents a good example of what farmers can learn for themselves, and thus how research and extension organisations often fail to respond to the dynamic needs of smallholder farmers to take advantage of opportunities that exist. The system failure reported here is treated as an indication of decay in professional relevance – in other words it challenges professionals to address their state of ignorance.

Objectives

The objective of this case study was to understand how the smallholder farmers came to see vanilla as an opportunity, the innovation process through which they adopted and produced the crop, and what learning this entailed. Specific objectives were to understand:
1. the history of vanilla in Uganda and among the smallholder farmers; and
2. the social organisation and mechanisms for learning and innovation among the smallholder vanilla farmers.

This case is later used to raise discussion about the roles and functions of research and extension in such circumstances. Analysis of these functions provides a basis for articulating the competences that agricultural professionals require to enhance farmer learning processes, and thereby provides useful information about the ways in which higher education might have to be redesigned in Uganda if agricultural professionals are to retain their role and relevance.

Methods

As explained in Chapter 1, data for this case study were generated through extended interviews that allowed the farmers to tell their story and experiences, starting from how they came to know about vanilla, why they chose to grow it and their subsequent experiences. The stories and experiences were enriched by illustrations provided by the farmers and observations made by the researcher as they together walked through the farmers' gardens during the conversations. Observations in the gardens elicited probing questions for further clarification. Follow-up visits were made to some farmers, where gaps were identified in the information provided or if additional lines of enquiry were needed. Farmers' stories about vanilla enabled an understanding of the crop's history, cultivation practices, processes of knowledge generation and spread, experiences including innovations since the crop was adopted and perceptions of the vanilla business in general.

Ntenjeru was purposively selected because it was the pioneer sub-county for vanilla production in Uganda, and therefore ideal for understanding farmer learning mechanisms. To trace these mechanisms, 31 farmers were selected from the four parishes of the sub-county according to three periods when vanilla growing was taken up, *i.e.* before 1990; 1990-1995; and 1996-2000+. Table 4 presents the characteristics of the farmers involved (farmers identified by a coded rather than by name).

Farmer selection was based on key informants in each parish. The key informants were among the pioneer vanilla farmers in their respective parishes. The choice of these periods was to understand the mechanisms for knowledge flows. However, priority was given to the pioneer farmers and those referred to by other farmers as being resourceful in terms of knowledge on vanilla production. Their privileged knowledge on this crop was of great interest for this study.

Table 1: Farmer characteristics

Parish	Farmer	Sex	Year of vanilla uptake	Vanilla acreage	Age	Years of schooling
Bugoyo	A1	M	2001	1.5	48	-
	A2	M	1995	2	65	10
	A3	M	2001	1.5		-
	A4	F	1987	1.5	70	0
	A5	M	1990	1	62	6
	A6	M	2001			-
	A7	F	1988	2	30	6
	A8	M	1991	2	29	11
	A9 (Mr & Mrs)	M&F	1984	-	81 & 74	-
Bunakijja	B1	M	1990	1.5	60	4
	B2	M	1991	1	65	6
	B3	M	1991	<1	37	6
	B4	M	1994	2	31	7
	B5	M	2000	2.5	30	8
	B6	M	1995	0.5	33	11
Mpunge	C1	M	1982	0.5	50	11
	C2	M	1981	-	71	8
	C3	M	1990	5	39	8
	C4	M	1990	-	65	3
	C5	M	1984	2	46	11
	C6	M	1993	1.5	43	14
	C7	M	1984	0.25	71	8
Nsanja	D1	F	1986	4	44	9
	D2	M	1995	1	30	10
	D3	M	2000	1.5	59	6
	D4	M	1993	0.5	37	15
	D5	M	1997	3	78	5
	D6	F	2002	1.5	36	6
	D7	M	1985	6	53	8
	D8	M	1990	1	34	7
	D9	M	1994	2	26	11

History of vanilla in Uganda

How it was introduced in Uganda

Vanilla planifolia, a fruit of the Orchid family, is not an indigenous crop to Uganda. It is a native of Mexico and Central America now grown in parts of the tropics including Madagascar, Indonesia, Reunion, Seychelles, Comoro Islands and Uganda (Tamale and Namuwoza, *ibid.*). Its fruits (beans) are harvested before they are fully ripe, fermented and cured as flavouring and spice for food and for use in the pharmaceutical industry (Purseglove, 1972).

Pioneer farmers who well know its history say vanilla was introduced in Uganda during the colonial period by British farmers as far back as the 1940s. Salama estate farm in Ntenjeru sub-county in Mukono district was one of three farms owned by British farmers where vanilla was grown. It was exclusively protected as a "white" farmer crop and Ugandans employed on the estate as labourers were routinely checked before leaving the farm to ensure that none escaped with planting materials (vines). This type of control aroused the curiosity of some labourers who stealthily manoeuvred to take away some vines. They planted it in the middle of coffee gardens, secretly, for fear of losing their jobs (or possible arrest) if the British farmers found out that they were growing vanilla. In the late 1960s however, the British farmers experimented with an out-grower scheme involving a few farmers in the neighbouring Kooja parish as a strategy to increase production. Kooja parish later became the pioneer and nucleus for vanilla production in Uganda, after the British farmers abandoned their farms and left the country due to unfavourable political conditions.

When dictatorship released vanilla to smallholder farmers

The "economic war" declared by the military regime of Idi Amin (1971-79) made the economic and political environment unfavourable for foreigners; so the British farmers abandoned their farms around 1972 and left. Their departure halted commercial vanilla production due to difficulties in marketing. Those who had vanilla only used it to spice tea and local brew. The most vibrant economic activity then was smuggling, in which many youths engaged directly or as brokers.

In 1980 some business men deployed brokers in Mukono district to search for vanilla, allegedly wanting to use it to conceal drugs like marijuana which they trafficked abroad. Kooja parish was the target since it was the place where it was suspected vanilla could be found. The price offered (USh. 300/= per Kg) by the brokers was very attractive compared to other crops, and this stimulated interest to grow vanilla. Due to demand the price had more than doubled to USh. 800/= per Kg by 1983. Many farmers obtained planting material (vines) from the former Salama estate where vanilla was by that time growing wild. At the time only former labourers at Salama estate, some of whom were also the experimental out-grower farmers, had knowledge of vanilla production. Because vanilla differs from other crops in many ways these farmers were the main resource persons in knowledge and practice of vanilla production.

What is unique about vanilla?

Vanilla is peculiar in that:
- it requires shading to provide two-thirds to one half of normal sunshine (ADC/IDEA Project, 2000). For this reason, vanilla is intercropped with banana and coffee; however, through experience, farmers have also identified appropriate shade trees. Small leaved trees like *Glyiricidia* are preferred to broad leaf trees like mangoes. Small leaves decompose faster, allow better water infiltration and reduce incidence of soil related fungal diseases, compared to broad leaves;
- the climbing vines are staked and looped to control plant height and ease pollination. At the point of contact with the ground the looped vines are buried to increase root establishment for higher nutrient uptake. A local shrub (kirowa in local language), commonly used as a boundary landmark, has been found to be the most appropriate way to stake vanilla because it establishes well even under dry conditions, provides shade, and is strong and flexible enough to support the weight of a big cluster of vines;
- weeding with a hand hoe has to be minimised since the crop is a surface feeder and hoeing would affect the root system; at the same time roots have to be protected from the heat of the sun, especially during the dry season. In this regard, a variety of weed management options have been experimented;
- flowering is naturally induced by the dry season. This is not adequate for cultivation. The plant has to be induced by cutting some of the looped vines (pruning), to stimulate flowering;
- pollination is done by hand. Unlike other crops, vanilla is not naturally pollinated by wind or insects; the flower is opened and the male (anthers) and female (stigma) parts are joined physically. Timing is important here as the flower is viable only for 12 hours, according to the farmers. This is probably the most technically demanding practice that farmers can be expected to do successfully.

The uniqueness of these production practices compared to other crops in the farming system incited my curiosity to understand how farmers learn about vanilla. It was clear that successful production was not the adaptation of indigenous knowledge to a new crop but involved generating new knowledge and practices, yet all this happened amongst farmers without intervention of research and extension.

Farmer exploration and experimentation was deployed in a search for effective ways to produce the crop. It transpired that non-involvement of research and extension to provide knowledge and technological support enhanced farmer experience sharing and mutual learning. This self-directed learning turned farmers into "non-professional experts", while researchers and extensionists, in keeping away from the learning process retained their "professional ignorance" about vanilla. I call them *non-professional experts* because they are self-made. I also consciously use the phrase *"professional ignorance" to* depict the rather arrogant notion that what is not taught during career training is less valued knowledge, an attitude that bars professionals from making use of an important social learning opportunity. Often this is defended in terms of reference to "national" priorities that may have little relevance to farmers' real needs and aspirations. The case will illustrate processes of social learning that rapidly spread vanilla as an export crop in Uganda. By 2002, vanilla had spread to over 18 districts (Tamale and Namuwoza, *ibid.*). As is usually common in social learning, the process was characterised by conflict and other social dynamic factors, to which I will now turn.

The role of conflict and competition in social learning

Conflict as a trigger for learning

While farmers exchanged materials and knowledge, real self-organisation for learning was triggered by conflict (see Dewey, 1922; Eshuis and Stuiver, 2005; Heymann and Wals, 2002). Two major conflicts influenced social learning; the first was a conflict between brokers and farmers and the second was between the Ministry of Agriculture, Animal Industry and Fisheries (MAAIF) and farmers.

Until 1990, farmers did not have direct contact with vanilla exporters. They dealt with brokers who bought the produce at less than the prevailing price and sometimes purchased on credit, but often faulted on making payments. Farmers realised they had a problem. The challenge for farmers was how to deal with dishonest brokers.

Through sharing of the challenge, the idea of forming a farmer cooperative society emerged. This idea came as advice from a visiting son of one of the farmers in 1988. In January 1989, Kooja Vanilla and Fruits Growers Association (KVFGA) was started to promote marketing of vanilla and other fruits produced in the area. Using their subscription fees, they advertised on radio advising the vanilla exporters to deal with KVFGA directly. Soon, two exporters visited them to verify their existence and to clarify the quality of vanilla they wished to buy. As a farmer association, KVFGA negotiated the price and devised a system for bulk sale of vanilla in two neighbouring parishes of Mpunge and Nsanja.

In 1990, a prominent business man, Agha Sekalala, with links to an American firm, McCormicks Ltd, seeking to procure vanilla, contacted KVFGA with the aim of promoting vanilla production for export. He provided credit to farmers on the understanding that they would supply him all their produce. For technical support Sekalala, in conjunction with McCormicks Ltd, secured support from USAID, through a project on Investment in Developing Export Agriculture (IDEA project), to hire an expert, Steve Caiger, to work with farmers for about three years. Having had experience under different climatic conditions, Caiger's expertise was not directly transferable. Instead, he engaged with contact farmers in a learning process to generate context specific knowledge and practices (*cf.* Eshuis and Stuiver, 2005) which he then compiled into a production manual (also translated into a local language, *Luganda*). For language translations he was assisted by the area extension worker (an agricultural assistant). Basically, Caiger's main function was to scale up learning through experimentation and sharing of experiences.

Shared knowledge flows in the farming community through informal (oral) networks. It is therefore not surprising that only two farmers still had copies of the manual at the time of fieldwork, retained more as a souvenir than as a source of information. In addition to marketing,

KVFGA became a network for learning. It secured funds from Sekalala and the IDEA project to support a regular radio programme, called *vanilla buggaga* (interpreted as "vanilla is wealth"), to increase awareness and disseminate knowledge about vanilla. The thirty-minute programme was presented once a week by a farmer, John Nviiri, who had vast experience on vanilla (from production to primary processing), having been an employee of one of the British farmers. The name of the programme conveyed the shared goal of wealth creation, which also inspired learning. The resultant awareness created overwhelming demand (from within and outside Mukono district) for planting material. The vanilla farmers then reaped profits from selling vanilla beans and vines. But beyond wealth creation, sustainability came into contention. This was the basis for the second conflict (that between farmers and MAAIF).

The conflict between MAAIF and farmers involved different perception concerning the impact of vanilla on soil fertility, and whether the crop was sustainable. When institutions and mechanisms of governance seem increasingly archaic they usually respond with pessimism to unfamiliar circumstances (Woodhill, 2003) to conceal their inabilities. MAAIF discouraged farmers from growing vanilla on the pretext that it would lead to rapid soil degradation. This was based on an untested assumption that the shrub used to support vanilla (*kirowa*) took up nutrients that could otherwise be utilised by crops; hence nutrient mining of the soil was alleged. But farmers saw it as an opportunity, and it was difficult to dissuade them from growing vanilla anyway. On the contrary, farmers argued that vanilla cultivation practices (namely planting shade trees, minimal weeding, and non-use of chemicals) offered a more sustainable environment than other crops. Given this conflict of ideas, farmers could hardly expect support from research and extension, departments falling directly under MAAIF. This pushed them towards greater interdependence; it was clear that farmers would need to learn through their own initiatives.

KVFGA was an outcome of a conflict between farmers and brokers. The conflict between farmers and MAAIF likewise served to strengthen farmer learning and self-reliant innovation capacities. The case illustrate how conflict is beneficial to social learning when it is turned into a shared challenge for which solutions are jointly sought. Articulation of a shared challenge is a social phenomenon anchored in a common goal (in this case the desire to be wealthy). But harnessing conflict into opportunity for joint learning is easier when stakeholders pursue complementary objectives than when they compete. Competition can be a barrier to social learning.

Competition as barrier to social learning

Because social learning is a move from multiple individualised perspectives to shared or distributed cognition (Röling, 2002) competition can prove counterproductive. Röling (*ibid.*) emphasizes that parties involved in social learning must develop overlapping - or at least complementary – goals, insights, interests and starting points. In other words it is only when the process offers sustainable mutual benefit that the parties will engage to learn together for better living. The attitude of competition among smallholder farmers is often self-defeating since none of them can influence the market unless they work together. Instead it reduces exchange of knowledge which would otherwise be beneficial to all (see Box 1 for a typical example).

> *Box 1: How competition prevents knowledge exchange.*
>
>
>
> Stressing the vanilla plant to induce flowering is normally done by pruning (cutting some of the looped vines) to reduce nutrient uptake. Through experience, farmers have realized that by cutting the vines, the plant does not survive for many seasons. I met a farmer who had developed an alternative to cutting the vines. He instead pierced the vine with a small stick, as shown in the picture. The idea is to to interfere with the flow of the nutrients but without completely cutting off the nutrient supply. This gives the plant a shock and it flowers. He explained that with this method, the plant lasts longer than when the vines are cut. I thought this was an innovation based on a sound understanding of plant physiology.
>
> I went to another farmer in the next parish. As we walked through his garden, he explained how he prunes to stimulate flowering, but I could not see many vines cut like other farmers. I asked him if he had an alternative to cutting the vines and he said, "no". Then I told him about the innovation of the stick. He laughed and said: "Oh yes, I use that too. I call it the 'pin' method. I have used it for sometime and it works very well, but I keep that to myself. It is my secret and I do not disclose that to anybody else". He then showed me several 'pins' with which he had pierced into the vines.

The case of pinning vines to induce flowering is an example where farmers conceal knowledge because of an attitude of competition. It might have been beneficial if all farmers used the same technique to maximise productivity. But something is needed in addition. Often, greater abundance of supply means poorer prices. Ugandan vanilla producers were expanding into an international market. But probably they would only gain sustainable high prices if they stood together against brokers anxious to cream off profits. To enhance social learning concerning technique farmers would also need to become aware that as smallholder farmers their strength rests upon a strategic capacity for collective action in areas of marketing as well as technique. It is the role of professionals to facilitate such joint processes, dissolving social barriers and creating platforms for interaction and open sharing of knowledge and innovations. Shared learning across the spectrum of technique and marketing might then create openings for inflows of new knowledge from extension and research further to enhance learning and innovation.

But in fact the necessary collective action proved hard to maintain. As vanilla demand increased, it attracted many buyers competing to raise export volumes, and in the process, quality was compromised. Competition eroded cohesion in KVFGA and its collective bargain diminished as individual farmers struggled to attract the highest price, creating opportunity for brokers again. Due to disastrous storms in Madagascar -the world's leading vanilla producer - the price to Ugandan producers sky-rocketed, reaching over USh. 100,000/= per Kg in 2004. Vanilla began to appear to be a kind of gold for farmers, and a gold rush began. Envy, jealousy and a mentality of quick gain began to become manifest in the rampant theft of vanilla, forcing farmers to hire gunmen to guard their gardens at night. This created suspicion and mistrust among members of the rural community, and capacity of farmers to continue to learn from each other declined. Only farmers sharing high levels of social trust dared to visit each others' gardens for purposes of exchanging knowledge and innovations.

The radio programme also stopped, since buyers were engaged in rampant competition, and no longer had the will to cooperate in educational programmes. Social learning is a cooperative process. To gain its benefits in a market environment ground rules are needed; appropriate levels of competition and cooperation have to be clearly defined. Resumption of production in Madagascar, coupled with neglect of quality, have recently plunged prices below USh. 1,500/= per Kg. The "gold" has simply melted away. The issue is in part about what level to allow competition to have full sway, and where to introduce cooperation. If for example the level of competition had been conceived to be between producer countries, the buyers would probably have cooperated to keep the Ugandan quality high, to sustain its favourable price on the world market.

Farmer learning mechanisms and platforms

The capacity for farmers to innovate and share knowledge, and their rationale for doing so was best articulated by one informant in the following terms:

> "We as farmers, when we face a problem or opportunity, we become creative, we explore, discover and share this amongst ourselves. For example, I was the first one in this parish to demonstrate that you can transplant a mature vanilla plant but I also learnt it from my friend in another parish. When there is a good price you can become creative in many things because everyone wants to get more from what they have" (Nsonera).

Exchange of knowledge and experiences from experimentation were largely based on personalised interactions among farmers. The motivation for experimentation is sometimes to be well-known and highly regarded in the community. This was clearly stated by another farmer who started growing vanilla at the age of 15:

> "I was motivated to discover more by producing more but I also strategically located my garden by the roadside to make it an example/demonstration for others to learn from. I do my own research to be outstanding and because of this, I have hosted many farmers from other districts. They come to learn and I also get orders to supply them with planting materials" (Kiyaga).

It is not the case that farmers learn from all farmers in the village. Information flows through an interpersonal social network (Conley and Udry, 2001). Social intimacy and values of inclusiveness are fundamental to social learning of the kind just described.

Interpersonal relationship as a vehicle for social learning

Learning is an interactive process that takes place on a platform for exchanging of knowledge and experiences. Here a platform is defined as *a forum for interaction to learn, negotiate and/or resolve a conflict* (*cf.* Röling 2002: 39). In learning about vanilla, four platforms were prominent: source of planting materials, radio programme, farmer experimentation and exchange visits, and informal sharing of ideas through conversation and casual contacts (See Figure 5). Interpersonal relationships based on friendship and trust were key factors in all four areas, as I will elaborate:

Source of planting material
Source of planting materials was a platform for exchange of knowledge and experiences about vanilla. Out of the 31 farmers involved in this case study, 24 (77.4%) obtained their first planting materials from other farmers they had prior contact with, and often their first batch of materials was offered free, an indication of a friendly relationship (Figure 6). Only 3 (9.7%) purchased their first planting materials from other farmers while 4 (12.9%) obtained the materials from the estates that the 'white' farmers had abandoned. The attractive market for vanilla created a passionate environment for unreserved sharing of personal experiences.

Radio programme
Generally, all farmers regardless of gender or wealth categories have access to and use radio as source of information (Bagnall *et al.*, 2004). In the present case, farmers acknowledged they learnt a lot from the radio programme presented by an experienced farmer who also used experiences of other farmers to explain constraints and possible solutions. While all farmers gained knowledge about vanilla from more than one source, overall, the radio programme

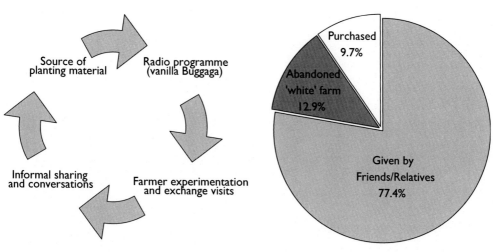

Figure 5: Platforms for learning about vanilla.   Figure 6: Sources of first planting materials.

was only second to farmer-farmer interactions (Figure 7). Farmers tended to listen to the programme in small groups and after the programme they discussed the content with respect to their own experiences. Choice of who to listen with was based on social networks, and the discussions that followed were also a means of mobilizing social energy to experiment.

Farmer experimentation and exchange visits

The absence of "blue-print" recommendations from research and extension provided the space and freedom for farmers to experiment widely, for example, on spacing, weed management options, appropriate shading trees and different ways of inducing flowering. Exchange visits were a platform for sharing successes and failures from farmer experimentation. Since these visits were informal, they were again based on interpersonal connections. As illustrated by Kiyaga's quote above, successful experiments were also learning sites for farmers from within and outside the area. Eleven (35.5%) of the farmers interviewed had hosted groups of farmers from other districts who came to learn from them how to grow vanilla. These were usually identified by leaders of their various farmer associations on the basis of their innovations and management practices. Through such opportunities, they were also able to sell vines to the visiting farmers. Kiyaga for example, claimed he had so far hosted over two hundred farmers from different parts of the country since.

Informal sharing

Vanilla as "gold" became a subject of everyday conversation at all social fora. These conversations permitted exchange of experiences, identification of best practices and creating linkages for learning. The pride of recognition for innovation was an incentive for enlarging social linkages to share individual discoveries with others. Such pride is apparent in Nsonera's quote above.

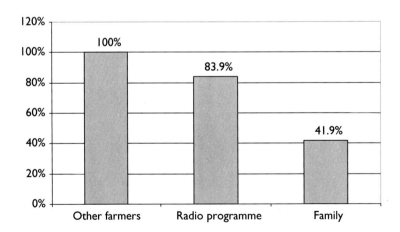

Figure 7: Sources of knowledge about vanilla.

Inclusive shared learning

The core value of participation is inclusiveness of all stakeholders in whatever affects them collectively. I look at inclusiveness beyond just involvement to building platforms for intergenerational exchange. This case presents an intriguing example of gender inclusiveness and more so the intergenerational exchanges in the learning process. In discussing inclusiveness, emphasis is on the learning process. Equity issues are beyond the present scope.

Inclusiveness of women and children

Based on interactions with farmers, there was no indication that the women were any less knowledgeable about vanilla than men and vice-versa. During the interviews, it was common for men to refer some questions to their spouses to explain because they regarded them to be more familiar with the aspects asked. What is rather more apparent is the recognition of specific expertise for men, women and children, signifying a distributed knowledge system. It was commonly said in interviews that women are better than men at pollination but children are even better. This, however, should not be misunderstood as exploitation of child labour. Children engage in some farm activities as a means to contextualise their education and translate it into life skills. This is essential for sustainability of rural life, as many young people drop out of school early without any gainful skills (Kibwika and Tibezinda, 1998).

Contrary to a common assumption in many studies that cash crops are dominated by men, here the entire family tended to work together as a social unit. It was also common that women and in many cases children had control over some plots of vanilla from which they derived income to meet their individual needs. Of the 27 men in the sample, 18 acknowledged that their spouses had separate gardens for income to meet their specific needs. Similarly, nine (29%) of the sample said that even children under their care had small plots or a few plants they managed and controlled income from those plots. It is probably this broad base of participation that facilitated complementary use of knowledge and expertise within the family.

Intergenerational exchange

Due to limited experience, children are rarely recognized as key players in community knowledge system, and for that reason they are often left out of adult learning processes. This poses a serious concern for intergenerational sustainability. In this case, children are recognized for their expertise in pollination, which can in part be attributed to science lessons acquired in school. Their understanding of the morphology of the flower puts them at an advantage to carry out more successful pollination. But what is interesting is how this knowledge/expertise is solicited from the children in a learning context. As one farmer explained:

> "I have learnt to pollinate from children. I used to invite children from homes that grow vanilla to come and pollinate for me. I would give them sugarcane in return and they would demonstrate to me as I watched carefully. This is how I learnt" (Luwalira).

These intergenerational platforms for learning also integrate local and "scientific" knowledge thereby enhancing sustainability of social learning processes. Intergenerational exchange is enhanced by targeting schools for social learning, as an old lady, a former contact farmer, reported:

> "While promoting vanilla we set-up demonstrations at schools to train the children so that they could train their parents. The children are much easier to train and they grasp the principles much more easily than adults" (Lusulire).

This is a timely reminder that schools are not only institutions for teaching children but could also be institutions for community learning.

Functions for research and extension in social learning

In the above case study I have described a social learning situation where farmers have generated relevant knowledge and technologies without intervention from research and extension. The main point is to establish that farmers may be quicker to adjust to external challenges and opportunities than government bureaucracy, and that training new professionals for life beyond the university needs to respond to this world "out there". But it is certainly not being argued that there is no place for research and extension, and professional support. The challenges of social learning call for more professional engagement than before, but in a way that is different from the "expert" prescriptive approach. Fundamentally, what needs to be done is to redefine the roles and functions of research and extension within a social learning context, otherwise the relevance of professional knowledge is liable to be contested. My objective is to use experiences from this case-study to bring to light some of the core roles and functions for research and extension to support sustainable social learning processes. These include market and market information brokerage, farmer organisational development, facilitating joint learning and innovations, facilitating multi-stakeholder dialogues, and developing entrepreneurial skills and attitudes.

Markets and market information brokerage

Learning is motivated by its economic and or social value to the learners in a sustainable environment. It has a cost in terms of time and effort; it is therefore unlikely that farmers – any more than other stakeholders - will engage in learning processes simply for their own sake. In this case, the major motivation for learning was an attractive market initially linked by brokers as earlier discussed. Therefore one catalytic role for research and extension on the social learning landscape relates to market skills and market information brokerage. This requires helping farmers to understand market dynamics - demand and price trends, quality standards, business linkages, and environmental requirements to sustain the business activity.

For example, there were wide price fluctuation between 1992 and 2005, mainly due to Madagascar's supply position on the world market. Most spectacular was the price rise to a climax of USh. 100,000/= per Kg in 2004/5, when Madagascar was affected by the disastrous storms; however, recent recovery plunged the vanilla prices in Uganda to below USh. 1,500/= in late 2005. Perhaps surprisingly, nearly all farmers interviewed lacked any adequate understanding of these reasons for price fluctuations, so as to make informed strategic decisions. To survive in global competition farmers need to be more proactive than reactive to the market opportunities; this is why smallholder farmers need to organised, in order to make effective use of information and to develop strategic responses. This is certainly a relevant opportunity for professionals to offer training support.

Farmer organizational development

One of the great appeals of market systems is their self-organising nature (Woodhill, 2002). The survival of small scale farmers lies in strong farmer organizations that allow pooling of resources and products to access reliable markets, increase bargaining power, strengthen demand for services and to protect rights. KVFGA was a good start in this direction but it was overwhelmed by the competing interests of market agents.

Through strong organisations, farmers can collectively pursue a common goal, avoid manipulation, and demand services from various providers including government agencies and politicians in a coordinated manner. With regard to learning, farmer organisations are fora for expanding social networks for learning. Even though African societies are often described as having inherent capacities for collective action, they are not organised enough to demand and influence services for improvement of their welfare. The emergent trends towards demand driven professional service delivery will hardly succeed unless deliberate efforts are focused on strengthening the demand side through farmer organisations. A key unanswered question is who is responsible for organising farmers? Private business agencies are profit driven; it would be unrealistic to expect them to invest in organizing farmers, especially where they do not have a monopoly of services. Organising farmers, therefore, is a prime responsibility of extension and research organised to supply public goods. Universities will have to teach their students the basic principles of collective action, and help form relevant organizational skills in these areas.

Facilitating joint learning and promoting innovations

Effective social learning as interactive dialogue and decision making does not just happen, but needs to be consciously and proactively facilitated (Woodhill, 2003). Facilitating such interactive learning processes requires investment in social skills to build mutual confidence and trust, opening up opportunities to share knowledge and experience around mutually agreed goals, attempts collectively to define beneficial levels for cooperation and competition, and work on developing shared values and guidelines for engagement. Moreover, innovations need to be encouraged through continuous experimentation and sharing, only possible when there is mutual recognition of contributions from the side of both farmers and professionals.

In the case-study above, for example, farmers pointed out one of the critical areas of engagement with research and extension was nutrients and soil-borne disease management in the vanilla farming system. They are willing to experiment with the professionals because they realise the need for technical knowledge, but they do not know how to initiate such an arrangement. Given their mandate, training and neutral interest in farmer learning platforms, researchers and extensionists are best placed to initiate and facilitate joint engagement for experimentation. But to do so, they need new skills (in, for example, the design of on-farm participatory trials and experiments), mindsets oriented towards knowledge as a joint product of stakeholder activity, and the ability to manage new kinds of "decentralised" power relations

Facilitating multi-stakeholder dialogues

Indeed not all stakeholders would engage in mutual learning processes. In addition to learning, there is need to focus on market services, input supply, infrastructure improvement, and better communications. All these improvements require negotiations and lobbying. A requisite overarching skill set, therefore, is the ability to handle tensions arising from conflicting interests.

Some farmers in the case-study reported above recognised that competition between buyers greatly compromised quality standards, and that this was a factor in the drastic price fall when Madagascar returned to the world market place with high quality vanilla. One farmer narrated that in the 1990s Ugandan vanilla producers ensured quality by picking only the mature beans over a period of about two months per season. But now, he reported, all the vanilla for a season is harvested within only two weeks, which definitely affected the quality. Resolving such issues for the long-term benefit of all parties requires dialogue. In a situation where farmers are less informed about market dynamics it is the responsibility of the professionals to create this awareness. They need to be able to bring the critical stakeholders together and to facilitate dialogues that safeguard the collective interest. But the professionals themselves must have the skills for this takes – *i.e.* they must know how to mobilize, facilitate and negotiate. But at present these all-important skills and orientations are not part of the career development of agricultural professionals in Uganda.

Developing entrepreneurial skills and attitudes

One of the major challenges of small scale farming in Africa is how to develop an entrepreneurial spirit and attitude among farmers who apparently treat farming as a way of life. Success or failure is often attributed to good or bad luck, rather than to deliberate or poor planning. This attitude only creates self pity and a feeling that not much can be done to change the situation. The contrary view is that learning is enhanced by confronting challenges with deliberate actions/plans, continuously reviewed in the light of clearly defined targets. The drive to achieve targets derives from an entrepreneurial attitude, which provides the momentum for adaptive confrontation of challenges for better living.

Entrepreneurial attitudes do not just happen; they have to be developed, and this is a major challenge for professional intervention. The culture of saving and investment is not part of the normal thinking among smallholder farmers in Uganda. The common argument is that they have nothing to save, but even when they get something (as in the case of vanilla) they still save nothing.

During the vanilla boom farmers earned money they never imagined receiving, but this was taken for granted, and many assumed temporary lifestyles of luxury, rather than investing in ventures that might guarantee regular income. The recent drastic price fall will push many back into the poverty levels they experienced several years back. The "gold" has melted in their hands.

Professionals will have to focus attention of farmers on this attitude of taking sudden windfalls for granted. Without major efforts to shift attitudes even the environment itself may melt away in our hands. Inculcating an entrepreneurial attitude for Africa is not a matter of teaching people to desire sudden riches at all costs. It will involve explicit emphasis on the need to ensure sustainability, including the not so obvious environmental aspects. University education for Africa in the 21st century will need to develop frameworks for professional education intended to encompass this all important mental shift.

Conclusions

The traditional linear model which suggests that innovations are developed by scientists, disseminated by extension and put into practice by users has proven ineffective in Africa, and more generally (Kline and Rosenberg, 1986; Rip, 1995; Woodhill, 2002). This chapter has argued – on the basis of a case-study – that social learning is both an opportunity and essential requirement for sustainable livelihood in agriculture. It has also been shown that, given the right market incentives, farmers learn and innovate effectively through their social networks (*cf.* Park, 2001: 82). On the other hand, it has also been suggested that social learning is far from perfect, and that sustainable innovation pathways still require research and extension support, provided this is based on appropriate intervention strategies. As farmers engage with more stakeholders - e.g. when they enter upon the uncertain terrain of the global market - the situation becomes much more complex than they can handle from their own resources, without a systematic approach to continued learning. Research and extension have the social obligation to enhance social learning by playing a facilitative role and also bring to consciousness other critical considerations such as environmental sustainability. However, professional training is still skewed towards the linear model characterised by hierarchical power relations. As a result, research and extension react rather defensively when confronted with situations requiring or liable to benefit from joint learning and discovery, because the professionals are supposed to be the "experts" who provide solutions. Clearly, this defensiveness can, in some circumstances, serve as a cover-up for the inability to engage productively in such complex processes. As observed by King and Jiggins (2002), the process of social learning requires farmers to become experts, instead of users of other specialists' wisdom and technologies.

This expertise cannot be spoon-fed. Sustainable livelihood is not something that can be offered to people on a plate. It is rather the adaptive capacity of people to respond to challenges with creativity in a solution-oriented manner. Social learning therefore contributes to sustaining the adaptive capacity to cope in changing environments by providing the impetus and confidence to take collective action. Aside from knowledge and skills exchange, social learning also has to address embedded moral values that instil social responsibility for sustainable living.

If research and extension are to meaningfully contribute to social learning in agriculture, their roles and functions have to be re-examined. They have to take on new functions such as brokerage, organisational development, facilitation of joint learning and multi-stakeholder dialogues, and responsibility for the development of entrepreneurial skills and attitudes. This means that professionals in research and extension have to be prepared for these functions with new competences, identified by the kind of case-specific analysis offered above, and integrated into career training. Attendant to this are mindsets oriented towards recognition of different bodies of knowledge and expertise that can be shared. In short, a new breed of professionals is needed to advance social learning in agriculture. At present, extension and research may be being unjustifiably blamed for not effectively playing a societal role that its professionals have not been properly prepared for. It is therefore imperative that these competence challenges are identified and addressed appropriately.

The next chapter precisely focuses on the challenges that research and extension currently face in a demand-driven service delivery context. These challenges are then used to identify new competences for effective service delivery in a social learning and innovation systems context.

CHAPTER FOUR

Challenges of demand-driven research and extension services in Uganda: implications for competence

Introduction

The last chapter suggested additional or new functions for research and extension to strengthen the demand side of social learning processes. In the struggle to increase efficiency of agricultural research and extension, the trend is to shift from top-down supply-driven to bottom-up demand-driven service delivery approaches. In Uganda, the National Agricultural Advisory Services (NAADS) and the National Agricultural Research Organisation (NARO) have recently moved in this direction. The Parliamentary Act that established NAADS (GoU, 2001: 5) stipulates one of its objectives as to: "empower all farmers to access and utilise contracted agricultural advisory services". The new National Agricultural Research Policy (NARP) of 2003 is even more explicit on the demand-driven approach. It for example partly states:

> "The farmers (particularly the poor and women) are to be empowered to demand and control agricultural research processes and services, within the wider Government policies of decentralisation, liberalisation, privatisation and increased participation of the people in the decision-making ..." (MAAIF, 2003: v).

For such a shift to become effective, however, new competences are required on both supply and demand sides. This chapter uses the experiences of NARO and NAADS to highlight the competence challenges for making a demand driven research and extension service delivery systems more effective. The implications of these challenges will provide us with a picture of the kind of competences universities training agricultural professionals to work in research and extension will need to develop.

It is important to note that this account is not a critique of research and extension but a pointer to some of the critical competence issues for improving the system. The chapter builds a case for transforming university training to address new challenges in the real-life development context. To put the reforms in perspective, I first present a brief outline of the national context before describing specific cases in research and extension.

National context for reforms in research and extension

The majority of people in sub-Saharan Africa where high levels of poverty have persisted live in the rural areas and depend on agriculture. Because of high population growth, the number of absolute poor in the region almost doubled from 164 million to 316 million between 1981 and 2001 (Bhorat, 2005). In Uganda the Poverty Eradication Action Plan (PEAP, 2004) shows that while the national poverty level increased from 34% to 38% between 2000 and 2003, the increase in rural areas was from 37% to 41%; and among crop farmers it increased from 39% to 50%. These patterns agree with the assertion of Dorward et.al., (2004) that poverty is largely a rural phenomenon *and in Uganda it is more associated with crop farmers than other rural dwellers* (my italics). Improvement of the livelihood of the majority of the poor will, therefore, depend to large extent on the state of agriculture.

This situation poses enormous challenge for organisations engaged in agricultural service delivery, and for donors supporting the agricultural sector. As stipulated in the master document for the Plan for Modernisation of Agriculture (PMA, 2000), poverty is not just the lack of income; it is also the lack of means to satisfy basic social needs, as well as a feeling of powerlessness to break out of the cycle of poverty and insecurity of persons and property. PMA is a comprehensive framework for development of the agricultural sector as a strategy for poverty alleviation. Within the PMA framework, reforms were introduced in public agricultural service delivery. These reforms targeted improvement in services in seven areas, namely (1) research and technology development, (2) national agricultural advisory services, (3) agricultural education, (4) improving access to rural finance, (5) agro-processing and marketing, (6) sustainable natural resource utilisation, and (7) improvement in physical infrastructure.

Outcomes of these reforms included the creation of NAADS in 2000 to replace the public extension system. NAADS was to provide a decentralised, farmer-owned, and private sector-serviced extension system. A year later the Uganda Government commissioned a task force to analyse and evaluate the National Agricultural Research System (NARS) with a view to enhance the contribution of agricultural research to sustainable agricultural productivity, sustained competitiveness, economic growth, food security and poverty eradication. This led to the development of a new NARP which has considerably changed the way research is to be conducted and managed in NARO. To be able to draw parallels, this chapter will discuss the challenges faced by research and extension separately. But first a brief background to the NARO reforms will be presented, before going into the details of a specific initiative for putting the reforms into practice.

Background to reforms in NARO

The new strategic direction for agricultural research is articulated in the NARP vision and mission. The vision statement is;

> "A market responsive, client-oriented and demand-driven national agricultural research system comprising of public an private institutions working in tandem for sustainable economic growth in Uganda".

The mission statement is:

> "To generate and disseminate appropriate, safe and cost-effective technologies, while enhancing the natural resource base".

To comply with the NARP and realign with the PMA principles, NARO initiated its own reform process. The process mainstreamed research into five themes (NARO's realigned strategy and plan, 2003) namely:
1. understanding people, their livelihood systems, demands, impact and innovations;
2. enhancing innovation processes and partnerships;
3. developing technological options responding to demands and opportunities;
4. enhancing integrated management of natural resources; and
5. linking producers, market opportunities and policies.

This new orientation created challenges in the management and operation of NARO, including:
- staff redeployment, to have more researchers to interface with the community and to respond to farmers' needs;
- staff retention, as the NARS had opened up competition for resources between public and private institutions in agricultural research;
- development of partnerships for effective delivery of research outputs given that the expected impacts required collective effort with other stakeholders;
- responsiveness to demand, which implies working with farmers in a collaborative manner, based on new mindsets, approaches and skills. Critical among such skills was to facilitate multi-stakeholder platforms to get insights of problems and opportunities;
- ensuring coherence of research institutes, since the NARP gives them some degree of autonomy.

To deliver effectively relevant demand-driven research services NARO had to do things differently. Consultations on how to do that identified thirteen action points (Box 2) to guide the new way of engagement. In effect, these become the new performance criteria for NARO.

These criteria imply a transformation in several aspects of doing research. In operational terms, the new policy implies a shift:
- From doing research per se to doing research for development. Responding to demand implies satisfying the needs of beneficiaries rather than the interests of the researcher, as has been characteristic of the research system hitherto. Researchers can no longer formulate research problems based only on their perceptions but are required to interact with farmers and other stakeholders in platforms to negotiate and clarify researchable issues. This type of analysis has to be put in context of current and future constraints and opportunities. Satisfying demand also implies working in partnership with stakeholders throughout the research process, thus going beyond mere consultation.
- From disciplinary and commodity-based research to an innovation systems approach. The ultimate goal of research is now placed beyond influencing production or productivity to influencing improvement in people's wellbeing, thus in addressing poverty. It requires the entire value addition chain to be addressed, involving many players who must coordinate and synchronise their activities. In such a situation, understanding issues from different perspectives and their interrelationship calls for a multidisciplinary approach. Basically,

---

Box 2: New performance criteria for NARO

1. Researchers together with farmers and other stakeholders continuously assess and prioritize needs, opportunities and demands for high quality research.
2. Researchers proactively seek to strengthen partnerships, collaboration and networking to increase plurality in research implementation
3. Researchers develop flexible and dynamic research agenda responding to stakeholder demands while integrally incorporating market-focused, sustainable natural resource management and food security, inter-disciplinarity and social differentiation.
4. Researchers engage with farmers and other stakeholders in participatory research processes, as a major approach responding to demand, and in order to build joint ownership and accountability to clients and local authorities.
5. Researchers engage with farmers and other stakeholders in integrated sustainable natural resource management as a foundation for market-orientated agriculture.
6. Researchers integrate market research with a focus on market chain integration into all research work.
7. Researchers engage in policy research in the contexts of market integration, natural resource management and food and nutrition security.
8. Researchers ensure the availability of technologies to a wider array of stakeholders.
9. Researchers support the private sector and other clients.
10. Researchers continuously improve their strategies and approaches to enhance commercialisation of agriculture.
11. Researchers monitor the impact of their own interventions and those of others.
12. Researchers and research managers regularly assess and improve their own competence.
13. Research managers develop and implement strategies for attracting and retaining high quality and high performing staff.

---

this implies adopting the innovation systems perspective, in which markets, infrastructure, commercial capacities, etc all play an equally important role to that of research, and crucially affect the outcomes and relevance of research-based knowledge interventions (Also see Hall *et al.*, 2001).

- From doing research independently to creating strategic partnerships that enhance relevant research outputs, leading to desired impact. Multi-stakeholder engagement brings new complexities, e.g. requirements for negotiation skills, forging consensus and managing conflicts arising from the differences in interests and personalities. Sustaining relevance also implies continuous adaptation in methods of work, skills and management, including performance appraisals and reward systems.

NARO's realigned strategy and plan (2003) sums it up as follows;

"In the context of the new agricultural research policy, there is need to create an integrated innovation process for generating technologies that support commercialisation of agriculture. This implies that several players and processes have to be taken into consideration as critical elements that make the system work. Consequently, the focus has to shift from commodity to dynamic innovation systems approach".

A new way of doing research necessitates new competences for the researchers and their partners. In this regard, a learning initiative was conceived to enable the NARO scientists and some partners to gain the knowledge and skills effectively to engage in Integrated Agricultural Research for Development (IAR4D).

Initiative for learning to do IAR4D

Background to the IAR4D learning initiative

IAR4D is a relatively new concept in agricultural research. There were no concrete examples elsewhere from which to learn. For this reason, the learning initiative in Uganda had to start by understanding what actually IAR4D aims to achieve, and how to set about it. IAR4D terminology emerged out of a conceptualisation of alternative approaches for effective research for Africa, as elaborated below in the ICRA-NATURA workshop documentation in 2003.

"The acronym IAR4D was first used in March 2003 by a multi-stakeholder group at the Forum for Agricultural Research in Africa (FARA) involved in the formulation of its Challenge Programme for sub-Saharan Africa. By embracing IAR4D as a new paradigm for research for development, FARA wants to mainstream a new way of doing business that ensures that research does not only lead to knowledge and publications, but also and first of all contributes to change and innovation for the betterment of people, while also preserving the natural resource base for future generations" (ICRA-NATURA, 2003: iii).

The acronym was soon after adopted by the ICRA-NATURA project on "mobilising partnership for capacity building in IAR4D". IAR4D presented a holistic approach to research, with similarities in process to other approaches such as the Sustainable Livelihoods Approach (SLA, see Farrington *et al.*, 1999; Ellis and Biggs, 2001; Carney, 2003), Integrated Natural Resource Management (INRM, see Douthwaite *et al.*, 2004) and Agricultural Research for Development (ARD, see Mettrick, 1993; Reij and Waters-Bayer, 2001).

With NARO taking the first step, the learning initiative was conceived as a partnership between NARO, Makerere University and ICRA in the Netherlands for capacity building in IAR4D. The intention was to utilise shared experiences, capacities and resources for approaching IAR4D in an action oriented way. The initiative then was called *"Learning together for change in IAR4D in Uganda: NARO-MAK-ICRA collaborative initiative"* (MoU, 2004). To enrich the learning process with practical experiences, Jürgen Hagmann, a process consultant, and the African Highlands Initiative (AHI), a CGIAR programme, were invited to join the initiative.

Hagmann's brief was to strengthen facilitation capacity, and also bring in experiences from his involvement in various reforms in agricultural research in other parts of Africa. AHI was to enrich the initiative with experiences in INRM which they were championing in National Agricultural Research Systems (NARS) in East Africa.

Objectives of the initiative

The general objective of the initiative was to strengthen human and institutional capacity to undertake IAR4D, as a new way of approaching research, initially in Uganda, and later on at sub-regional level in collaboration with the Association for Strengthening Agricultural Research in Eastern and Central Africa (ASARECA). The specific objectives were:
- To enhance and mainstream within NARO the capacity of teams to apply IAR4D approaches.
- To strengthen and institutionalise the ability of Makerere University to provide capacity-enhancing opportunities in IAR4D for a range of stakeholders at various levels.

It was hoped that these broad objectives would satisfy the different but convergent interests of the various partners. The following is a brief description of the partners and their interests in the initiative.

About the partners

National Agricultural Research Organisation (NARO)
Established by an Act of Parliament in 1992, NARO is the largest public research organisation in agriculture. Because of its mandate, it is the main recipient of public resources for agricultural research. For example, in 2000, NARO accounted for three quarters of both total research spending and numbers of agricultural researchers (Nienke and Tizikara, 2002). Consequently it is responsible for the state of agricultural research. Therefore NARO's response to the PMA and NARP was intended to make agricultural research more relevant to the national development needs. NARO sought to enhance the impact of its research by strengthening the capacity of its Zonal Agricultural Research Institutes (ZARIs) which directly interface with the community. For that reason the learning initiative involved larger numbers of ZARI staff, and fewer from the National Agricultural Research Institutes (NARIs) and District Local Government (DLG) partners. Although involvement of more partners, e.g. NGOs and NAADS was necessary, emphasis in the first phase, due to resource constraints, was placed on strengthening partnership with the DLGs.

Makerere University (MAK)
Given the paradigm shift in agricultural research, reorienting researchers in NARO and other agricultural research organisations will likely prove a continuous and expensive process. As the main university training agricultural scientists, Makerere University intended to mainstream the IAR4D concept in its training. This would make it relevant in addressing the capacity

development needs of research and development institutions. But first it also needed to enhance its understanding of and capacity in IAR4D. Experiences from this learning exercise would form the basis for curriculum review, leading to new teaching approaches to turn out scientists fitting the requirements of the new research system.

From the university, lecturers from the Agriculture, Veterinary Medicine, Forestry and Nature Conservation faculties, and the Continuing Agricultural Education Centre (CAEC) participated in the learning initiative. To link this with similar ongoing initiatives within the university, most of the participants were selected from among those involved in the innovation competence development programme (PM/SS learning programme) to be described in subsequent chapters. This was intended to advance capabilities for innovation within the perspective of IAR4D. Indeed, three of these participants, including the present author, served as facilitators in the IAR4D learning initiative.

International Centre for Research in Agriculture (ICRA)

ICRA has a long-term involvement in capacity building with a focus on agricultural research for development (ARD). Its special focus of interest is in developing such capacity in the South. Aside from contributing through experience and learning resources, ICRA viewed this as an opportunity to develop partnerships in Eastern Africa for possible decentralisation of its training. Through engagement in the learning initiative, ICRA would also enhance its competence in facilitating IAR4D processes in practice. In this regard, ICRA provided one of its staff to be a facilitator in the IAR4D learning initiative.

The independent consultant

As a process consultant, Hagmann had been involved in several reform processes in Africa and elsewhere, both in the CGIAR and in national public research systems. This experience and his facilitation skills were needed to contextualise learning activities. The consultant had also facilitated the innovation competence development programme in Makerere University, as well as contributing to some stages of the NARO reform. He was therefore interested in strengthening capacity in both Makerere University and NARO to complement each other in taking forward their reforms.

African Highlands Initiative (AHI)

AHI, one of the ASARECA networks, is an established NARO partner in the region, particularly with respect to mainstreaming INRM and participatory monitoring and evaluation in the research system. Its experience in Uganda, Ethiopia, Tanzania, Kenya and Madagascar would enrich the IAR4D learning initiative. In addition to being part of the steering committee for the initiative, AHI also provided a resource person.

Overall, the integration of the diverse skills and experiences of the partners and a mix of learning resources provided a rich menu for learning. The intention was to build complementarities from a variety of approaches and experiences to make learning how to implement IAR4D relevant and applicable.

Design and implementation of the learning initiative

Design

The initiative was envisaged in three major phases: The first phase focused on enhancing capacities of teams to apply the IAR4D approach in dealing with complex problems. This would be achieved through a series of five learning workshops, alternating with periods of practice in dealing with research and development challenges (Figure 8). The second phase would focus on mainstreaming IAR4D within the partner organisations and institutionalising the capability for Makerere University to provide similar learning events for various groups of clients. In this phase, IAR4D would be integrated within the University curriculum. The third phase would then focus on scaling up the initiative within the ASARECA region, using the Ugandan experience as guidance. The discussion here, however, is limited to the first phase, implemented between March, 2004 and February, 2005.

Ideally, the initiative was intended to be an action-learning process, with workshops providing critical input to support practice in teams. The lessons generated through practice would also enrich the learning workshops. The teams were based at the ZARIs, with ZARI staff as core members. The team members from NARIs and MAK would occasionally join the ZARI team and their local partners for specific joint activities. But for the most part the ZARI core team was responsible for the day-to-day activity implementation.

With exception of the first learning workshop, which lasted 10 days, the subsequent workshops ran for 6 days each.

Implementation

As mentioned earlier, participants in this learning initiative were drawn from NARO, District Local Government and Makerere University (Table 5).

For ease of managing the learning participants were split into two groups, one group taking care of three ZARI teams and the other group taking care of four ZARI teams. Each

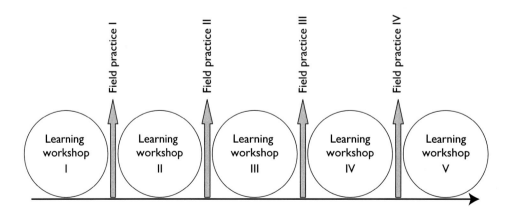

Figure 8: Design of the IAR4D learning programme.

Table 5: Composition of participants.

Institution	Number
ZARI staff	24
NARI staff	16*
Makerere University	10**
NARO partners (DLG staff)	4
Total	54

* Includes staff from NARO Secretariat some of them in administrative positions.
** Includes the three co-facilitators.

learning workshop, therefore, had two consecutive sessions, one for each group. To each team, a resource person (mentor) was attached to provide some technical back-up during the field practice, and to give feedback to help the project implementation team (PIT) plan accordingly. The mentors included the three facilitators from MAK, the resource person from AHI and three others from NARO. Three of the mentors, including the author, were also researching different aspects of this learning process as part of their PhD programmes.

Actualising the experiential or action-learning approach required reasonable time and engagement in the field, to generate adequate experiences to inform the subsequent learning events. The practice period between the workshops was, however, too short (barely one month) to provide for sufficient engagement with complex field realities. This was because the funds available for the initiative had to be used and accounted for within a fixed period (March 2004 – February 2005). The funds were drawn from an ongoing project whose accounts had to be closed within that time frame. Consequently, it turned out to be more of a knowledge acquisition process than the intended action learning type. That a pioneer activity in transforming agricultural research from a top-down to a bottom-up approach should, in the end, be driven by the rigidities of an accounting framework, brings home the point that the initiative was only a beginning. Up-scaling participation will require major transformations – eventually – in the basic ways in which donors and governments do business.

From their general experience in research, understanding of IAR4D and insights from some of field practice activities, participants expressed challenges that needed to be addressed effectively to engage in IAR4D. The following is a synthesis of challenges based on what was expressed and refined through an iterative process of workshops, field practice and mentoring, as described in the methodology section in Chapter 1.

Challenges of implementing IAR4D

These challenges are formulated in such a way that they not only present constraints or problems but also opportunities. They start with *"How to ...."* statements. Figure 9 illustrates

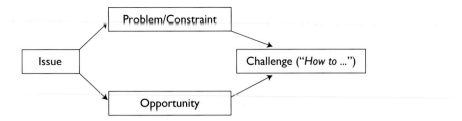

Figure 9: Formulation of challenge.

how the challenges are derived from issues. This formulation reflects the perspective of solution-oriented thinking motivating creativity and action to overcome challenges, as opposed to being overwhelmed with problems and/or critique.

The challenges of implementing IAR4D are discussed below:

How to develop and maintain effective partnerships in research and development.

Partnerships in technology development are important because of their benefits in innovation performance derived from productive relationships between organisations engaged in formal research and those engaged in use of new knowledge in economic development (Hall *et al.,* 2001). The aim of IAR4D is to enhance the impact of research on the farming community, but impact cannot be created by research alone. It can only be achieved by partnerships with other complementary service providers in a manner that can bring about the desired impact (*i.e.* as part of an innovation system). This requires a framework in which the partners can engage within their interests and mandates to contribute to impact in a coordinated way. In this case, the impact is to improve wellbeing and to reduce poverty. Such collective processes are characterised by conflicts that can only be managed with good facilitation, construction of platforms for negotiation and consensus building, joint reflection/learning, and focus on improving team performance. These skills are largely missing in research systems that have for long encouraged scientists to work independently.

How to empower farmers to demand, and effectively participate in, research

The last few decades have been characterised by attempts to establish some models of effective participatory research practice (see Friis-Hansen and Kisauzi, 2004 for a review). But some of this activity can be criticised for failing to go much beyond asking farmers questions through surveys and offering on-farm demonstrations of research products. In these cases, the research process continues to be driven largely by the researchers' agenda, and tends thus to sustain the status quo

The new approach echoes the concern of putting farmers in a position enabling them to influence the research agenda and to help the research process generate relevant outputs. While debate in this area has focused more on what needs to be done, the most important practical issue is how to empower the demand side (farmers) to influence research. Doing so requires competences for building mutual trust and respectful relationships with farmers, in addition to enhancing their organisational capacity. It also invites change in attitudes from the experts driving solutions to joint learning and discovery, and among other things requires dynamic integration of scientific and indigenous knowledge (*c.f.* Murwira *et al.,* 2001; Hagmann *et al.,* 1997).

How to design and manage integrated research with quality

An increasingly integrated world requires integrated approaches to problems (Woolcock, 2002). It is clear that many bottlenecks to adoption of agricultural technologies happen to be outside the narrow confines of the technology development process. Markets and policy, for example, are critical aspects influencing technology uptake. The argument among scientists, at this point, is often that such a mix of issues bundles together manageable research problems and unmanageable externalities. This degrades the quality of their research, as methodologies in their respective disciplines cannot take into account such a diversity of perspectives. The challenge is how to design and implement research to influence all these dimensions in a holistic way, taking into account sustainability of the natural resources and without loss of rigor. This calls for new strategies of engagement, and use of alternative research methodologies, as well as new approaches to monitoring and evaluation of research. At very least, the announcement of an effective technological intervention needs to be accompanied by a fully specified set of assumptions regarding the external environment in which a specific innovation will and will not work. This implies a multi-disciplinary approach, involving research expertise directed at innovation contexts.

How to develop and maintain multidisciplinary teams throughout the research process

Integrated agricultural research thus means integration of disciplines. Scientists are trained to excel in their disciplines as independent researchers. The complexity of reality, however, compels them to work with other disciplines interdependently – resulting in tensions between professional training ethos and practice. Earlier lessons are important here. Farming Systems Research (FSR) to a great extent only managed to understand systems from different disciplinary perspectives but did not achieve its goal of integrated interventions.

Integration of policy, social aspects, biological and ecological issues to influence social change processes remains an acute dilemma of multidisciplinary and/ or interdisciplinary research as currently encountered. The underlying issues include the need for orientation through training, to enable researchers to see beyond their disciplines and to work with other relevant disciplines so as to influence change in the system.

How to cope with the dynamism of socio-political and ecological environment

The socio-political and ecological environment is volatile. Farmers' needs and priorities are not static either. Yet "good" science is about systematisation, often characterised by following prescribed procedures towards "logical" conclusions. The gap is in the room available for quick adaptation to a changing context in which theory informs practice but yet is not a rigid prescription for practice. How can we systematize within chaos? Should agricultural science try to do that? And if it turns its back on this challenge will it remain relevant? This requires a new mindset, in which systematisation is directed towards client problems, as opposed to systematisation for conformity to theory.

How to instil a culture of honesty, ethics and transparency in the system
Sustaining multi-stakeholder engagements relies on mutual trust and therefore requires high ethical standards and transparency on the part of all partners. These are even more critical in the management of resources for joint action. Success in joint ventures very much depends on the commitment of the partners to contribute to agreed goals and satisfactory accountability in terms of responsibilities and resources. For this to work there must be a strong value base of honesty, ethics and transparency. Ethical standards in science are maintained (Ideally) by processes of "double blind" peer review. Problem oriented science will need to develop an enlarged peer review mechanism, involving all stakeholders, including farmer clients. How to make such systems work is not yet known, but the new professional training will have to alert its trainees to the issues at stake, and the renewed danger of cronyism and patronage where laboratory data sets are not the only basis for judgement. Some of the dilemmas of evolving ethical and professional standards for participatory development approaches are addressed in recent work (Mosse, 2005).

How to secure and appropriately manage resources for IAR4D
Integrated agricultural research poses a serious challenge for resource mobilization and management. Firstly, funders insist that a research proposal be focused on a specific problem, leaving little room for flexibility to address emerging issues. Secondly, how should partners commit their resources to joint engagements? Thirdly, how should resources contributed by various partners be managed? Who should be in charge and how should such resources be accounted for? Fourthly, how will credit or blame be shared, in case of success or failure respectively, among the partners? These are among important research management issues that complicate the operationalization of IAR4D. Developing research programmes that ultimately focus on impact rather than outputs is to deviate from the logical frame-based designs of research projects that researchers are now accustomed to. It therefore requires putting in place mechanisms for efficient and flexible use of resources – something that donors also have to adjust to. The effectiveness of such programmes will depend on negotiations with partners, and putting in place appropriate mechanisms for mobilisation and management of shared resources.

How appropriately to reward, motivate and retain human resources for superior organisational performance.
IAR4D requires a high level commitment from researchers, as the desired impact will come neither easily nor speedily. Only well-motivated staff can pursue the approach required with appropriate determination and persistence. The present incentive structure, including remuneration for researchers in developing countries, is far from generating the level of commitment that IAR4D requires.

Furthermore, staff performance appraisal is skewed in favour of publications rather than impact on the community. As in any academic institution the survival formula is *publish or perish*. It does not matter whether the publication translates into any visible change in the foreseeable future, so why bother so much about impact? To encourage IAR4D, the staff performance criteria need to change to appropriately reward and recognize those who strive for impact. This issue is flagged here, because it is a crucial one, but devising the right kind of incentive structure goes beyond the present scope. Clearly, however, a major methodological question is raised. Incentives need to be related to community impact criteria, but the very basis of cooperative research activity makes it hard to assign values to the contributions made by the various parties. Currently, conventional reward assessments would almost force a researcher assisting self-reliant vanilla farmers to try and claim the activity as his or her own, for example. Measuring "added value", or effective synthesis of farmer and scientist knowledge, is an area requiring specific detailed study.

The demand-driven National Agricultural Advisory Services (NAADS)

Background

The NAADS programme was created on the justification that the traditional top-down public extension had failed to influence change in productivity at the farmer level. To avert this situation, NAADS aimed at developing a decentralised, demand driven, client-oriented and farmer-led agricultural service delivery system particularly targeting the poor and women.

Vision, mission and principles
As articulated in the master document (NAADS, 2000), NAADS is envisioned to be:

> "Decentralised, farmer owned and private sector serviced extension system contributing to the realisation of agricultural sector objectives".

and driven by a mission to:

> "[Increase] farmer access to information, knowledge and technology through effective, efficient, sustainable and decentralised extension with increasing private sector involvement in line with government policy".

In pursuance of the above vision and mission, NAADS operations are guided by the following ambitions, aims and principles:
- Empowering farmers in the agricultural advisory processes and building a demand for both research and agricultural advisory services.
- Targeting agricultural services to the poor farmers, who are the majority.
- Mainstreaming gender issues.
- Deepening decentralisation to bring control of research and advisory services nearer to the farmers.
- Commercialisation, including intensification of productivity and specialisation.
- Participatory processes in planning, contracting, monitoring and evaluation.
- Managing natural resource productivity.

- Increasing institutional efficiency through contracting out services, better linkages between research, advisors and farmers.
- Harmonisation of donor supported projects with PMA principles.

NAADS components

To ensure effectiveness and efficiency, the NAADS programme was designed to have five main components, namely:

- **Advisory and information services to farmers**. This component targets orientation and capacity building of farmers to take charge of the structures and processes that drive the advisory services. It is intended to be achieved through farmer group and farmer fora formation. Farmer groups at village level progressively federate into farmer fora at sub-county level and then district and national levels. These fora provide platforms for participatory planning to identify and prioritise farmer needs. The sub-county farmer fora take the responsibility for contracting services based on aggregated and prioritised farmer needs. Whether discursive approaches alone (e.g. farmer fora) should drive the process can be debated (Richards 2006).
- **Technology development and linkages with markets**. This component is intended to enhance development and access to relevant technologies through participatory research and development, and outsourcing. Although the documents refer to this as technology development, in reality it is *"technology demonstration",* basically aimed at exposing farmers to existing technologies. The sub-county forum initiates processes for technology demonstration contracts based on their priority needs. Technology demonstration sites (TDS) are then set-up within the community, to be accessed by farmers.
- **Quality assurance services**. Quality assurance services were intended to support standards setting and regulation of service providers and technical auditing of service providers. Monitoring of standards is primarily done by technical staff at the sub-county level, complemented by the sub-county farmer forum and administration. Technical staff at the district level conduct routine auditing of service providers.
- **Private sector institutional development**. NAADS recognises that private service providers require new competences and attitudes to be effective under this arrangement. It seeks to enhance capacity for private service provision through service provider development (facilitating emerging private companies to acquire the legal status for contract eligibility), national representatives/institutional support (farmer organisations) and structural adjustment retrenchment (facilitating public extension staff to join the private sector).
- **Programme management and monitoring**. This includes supporting national and local government institutions to manage and monitor the programme, including setting up a management information system (MIS).

Challenges of the NAADS extension service delivery approach

After about five years of implementation, a lot of experiences have been generated on the NAADS approach to extension service delivery. Several studies have been conducted on its performance. Based on these studies, and some research encounters with NAADS implementation activities, the challenges described below were derived. The research encounters with NAADS activities were not specifically designed to follow-up NAADS activities, but provides some qualitative evidence to complement the documentary data.

As before, the list of challenges identified is not supposed to amount to a critique or evaluation of the NAADS programme. The intention is to point out some areas that could be improved, if the NAADS vision and mission is to be attained. Also, this list of challenges is not exhaustive with regard to the breadth of the programme; they are selectively synthesized in the context of the requirement of the present thesis to identify and analyse competences for demand driven and impact oriented service provision. The challenges are described below.

How to provide advisory and information services with a systems focus through contracted service providers

Private service providers are contracted to provide specific commodity-focused services, with no mechanism for coordination amongst the service providers. The services are therefore disconnected and not anchored in contextual constraints such as markets, natural resource management and HIV/AIDS (Eilu and Turamye, 2004; Bua *et al.*, 2004). While, for example, natural resource management and HIV/AIDS are meant to be cross-cutting issues to be integrated in the contracts, actual integration in practice has not been successful. This is not only a design issue; it is also a competence issue. From an operational view, it requires first a mindset that is appreciative of the value of integration of disciplines in services delivery. The internal drive for integration is derived from appreciation of its value. Second, it requires capabilities for networking, developing and maintaining functional partnerships. But all this has to happen in a coordinated way. The lack of specific mechanisms for coordination and creating and sustaining partnership needs to be addressed.

How to move away from training and demonstrations to learning and experimentation with farmers

The whole set-up of the NAADS system is geared towards training farmers and demonstration of technologies to farmers. The assumption behind this design is that the solution lies solely in technology and information dissemination. This is no different from other top-down approaches, like the World Bank sponsored Training and Visit (T&V) system, which NAADS replaced on the basis it has been ineffective. Application of knowledge at the farm level is compounded by other constraints concerning, for example, inputs, credit and markets (Obaa *et al.*, 2005; Oxfam and FOWODE, 2004). Addressing such complexities demands an attempt to address underlying issues via strategic interventions. Developing an appropriate strategic vision, however, requires an engagement that provides scope to learn with farmers rather than to teach them.

The training approach, and a multiplicity of contracts corresponding to specific enterprises and commodities, develops into a scenario based around creating schools for farmers. But this is problematic. Each farmer is engaged in multiple enterprises, implying that s/he is expected to attend a training session almost every day of the week, not dissimilar in fact from students attending school everyday (see Box 3).

Such responses from farmers have far-reaching implications for the perceived value of training. Indeed many service providers acknowledge progressive decline in farmer attendance at training meetings, and yet the contracts are partly evaluated on the basis of farmer attendance lists. As a way of mobilising farmers to attend training meetings, some service providers provide incentives like food and drinks. Obaa, *et al.* (*ibid.*) observed that during NAADS sensitisation activities some farmers were, indeed, attracted to the meetings by the food and drinks served.

It is well known that farmers learn more from fellow farmers. Chapter 3 illustrated the point in a rather extreme way, in describing a vanilla innovation process where extension had no input. The new situation to which NAADS is committed is a two-way flow of knowledge formation. But in practice extension workers are yet to learn much if anything from farmers, as they still carry with them into the field the mentality of being an "authority" to teach farmers. In a study by Mubangizi *et al.,* (2004), NAADS service providers listed their major sources of information as college notes, text books/manuals and NARO. Farmers as a source of information came 14th among 17 sources. The limited recognition of farmers as a source of knowledge in the agricultural system is an indication of how distant the system is from the ideal of being a learning organization. Given the present orientation just described service

---

Box 3: Are we taking farmers to school?

In one of the training sessions on farmer institutions development observed in Mukono district, the trainer came with a box of exercise books and pens distributed to farmers to enable them take notes. Then the trainer started teaching about farmer groups – why there is need for a group, the leadership structure of the group and responsibilities for each leadership position. Though occasionally punctuated by questions to the farmers, it was not different from a typical "lecture".

When I asked him what else he was going to do in that village with regard to farmer institution development, he said his organisation had only a three month contract to do the job. He did not envisage himself doing much more in that village as he had several other villages to cover.

After this training, I had a conversation with one of the farmers who complained *"we should also get holidays!"* He was referring to trainings that take place every day, turning them into full-time students. Students do in fact get holidays, and he argued that farmers also deserve holidays. But the approach seems basically misconceived, since the training is still formulated around the notion of a contract to supply. It would be better to start by asking what farmers think they lack, and then build a demand driven training curriculum.

---

providers are hardly likely to engage with farmers to learn and jointly experiment promising options to key problems. The point to be stressed here is that change needs to be twofold: in addition to attitude change, it requires a different set of competences to effectively engage in learning processes with farmers. Listening to farmers is a skill like any other. Extension professionals need to be trained to listen.

How to develop strong farmer institutions capable of articulating quality service demands and fostering accountability for services and resources

A pillar for farmer driven services is strong farmer organisations capable of processing and articulating farmer needs in an operationally precise and yet inclusive manner, *i.e.* there is a need to move beyond wish-lists put together by vocal community leaders in "instant" meetings. Real demand can only emerge out of a situation where farmers have a clear and shared developmental goal. Based on this goal, they then develop with professional assistance workable strategies for which the necessary services are identified. Inclusiveness here means taking care of different levels of needs among different classes of farmers. Even small-scale farmers are not homogeneous. For example, Magnall *et al.* (2004) expressed the difficulty of delivering information to the poor who are food insecure and rarely interact with the market. Richards (1993) argues that agriculture as a performance is part of a wider performance of social life in which technological needs and innovation possibilities cannot be separated at all readily from a range of often unequal relationships tying small-scale resource-poor farmers into various kinds of dependency relationships. Such people do not farm for commercial purposes. Their farming is part of a way of life, and this way of life has complex interconnections not always fully comprehended by various systems approaches (such as farming systems research and the household livelihoods approach). This makes it very difficult to "represent" farmers, unless farmers themselves have organised the mode of representation and worked through some of the political issues dividing them.

The lack of true democratic representativeness of even participatory rural development activity has been a subject of recent comment (Mosse, 2005; Richards, 2006). In Uganda, it has been noted that the only people who benefit from NAADS are those with convertible assets such as a cow, or have access to external financing such as remittances (Oxfam and FOWODE, 2004). For inclusiveness, service demand has to be differentiated so that services can be targeted and tailored to each relevant farmer group and class; otherwise commercial demand automatically excludes many - and probably the ones most in need of what poverty targeting programmes are intended to provide.

Within genuinely democratic and accountable farmer organisations, farmer representatives would be able to follow up a range of interests and demand accountability in terms of service delivery and resource utilisation. This entails having competences for mobilisation, leadership, lobbying and advocacy, networking and business analysis among others, at farmer organization level. It is only then that we can talk of farmer empowerment. Developing viable organisations and sufficient skilled organisers at this level will require long term engagement and skills. This is a major challenge for the new agricultural professionals, working with farmers. It also leaves aside whether or not there is sufficient political commitment to democracy to allow farmers to organise in ways that genuinely empower. Where local confidence is sufficient to demand better services it may also demand far-reaching political change as well.

It is noted that formation of many farmer groups in NAADS was induced, often with unrealistic material promises (Obaa *et al.*, 2005; CEED, 2004) and, therefore, groups lack internally driven common interests. By the nature of their contracts, service providers invited to develop farmer institutions invariably induce farmer group formation. They do not go all the way to strengthen local capacity for self-organisation, which might then lead to real service demands around development interests. Self-organisation for farmers requires a prior reasonable level of emancipation, to challenge the system to be accountable. The risk is that otherwise platforms created in order to articulate demand will be hijacked by a few elite farmers who connive with service providers around their own interests.

How to build the capacity of the private service providers to deliver effective demand driven advisory services
Moving from a supply-driven to demand-driven service delivery approach calls for much more than structural changes. Inherent is, as argued, a critical need to develop competences that fit the new thinking. One of the major reasons for failure of reform processes is too narrow a focus concerning what it takes to do things differently. Most often, the temptation is to do new things in old ways, which tends to change little.

While one of the components of NAADS is private sector institutional development, this has been limited to supporting attainment of legal status for service providers. No investment has been made in the functional competences of service providers to make them effective in delivering demand-driven services. It is rather unrealistic to expect that by merely changing the "rules of the game" - as in the present case - service providers would respond by offering quality services. Service providers can only do what they know how, and are able, to do. They must be enabled to do things differently. Once again, we see clearly the need for new competences.

Implications for competence

Based on the challenges explained above for both research and extension, it is clear that the shift from a supply driven to demand driven service delivery has serious implication for competence development, on both supply and demand sides. The supply side in this case is the service provider, while demand for services is the province of the farmers. The key competences on both sides, as derived from the challenges just discussed, are now outlined.

Key competences for the supply side

In addition to proficiency in their speciality technical skills, service providers should have the abilities (attitudes and skills) to:
- **Facilitate action learning processes with farmers, to enhance experimentation and joint discovery**. Developing mutual trust and integration of indigenous and technical knowledge are key elements here. Service providers could, for example, develop a scientific

dimension to farmer experimentation to arrive at logical findings acceptable to both parties and capable of being scaled up or out to other farmers. Joint critical reflections are also essential for exchanging views and opinions, in order to enhance learning and adaptation.

- **Serve as information and knowledge brokers.** Information and knowledge brokerage is not just dissemination of information. It is about linking those who have information and knowledge to those who need it (*i.e.* knowing who has it and who needs it, and how to bring them together). This might be a matter of linking farmers themselves, or it might involve linking farmers and service providers. In this case the broker has interests on both sides, and hence enhances a mutual interaction and networking. The broker can also help to negotiate fair deals for all the parties. Brokers also develop a knowledge management function to allow effective accumulation and exchange of knowledge and experiences (they know where to find information). It also implies that the brokers should be able to document and manage information for future reference.
- **Develop local organisations and facilitate farmer empowerment processes.** This goes beyond formation of organisations to enabling emergent organisations to come up with their own development agenda. On the basis of this agenda, genuine demand for services can be articulated. Empowerment also means developing potentials that enable organised groups to identify and take advantage of existing opportunities. Ability to mobilise for social action, to ensure accountability for services and resources at all levels, are also key elements of local organisational development and empowerment. In turn this requires leadership, awareness of rights and how effectively to use the powers that people have.
- **Apply system-wide perspectives in programme design, implementation and impact assessment.** This is thinking beyond outputs to focus on ultimate impact, which in this case is poverty alleviation. In a systems perspective, one is able to see what it takes to influence impact and consequently design appropriate processes and mechanisms to link the different actors to contribute to impact. Clarity about what it is that the different partners are contributing to impact, and how all the various contributions complement each other, is critical. In such mechanisms, strategic planning, participatory monitoring and evaluation of impact are embedded aspects.
- **Develop and promote teamwork, and be good team players themselves.** Firstly, they should be aware of how effective teams function and have the techniques to enhance teamwork. Managing group dynamics, self-awareness, and self-control are key skills here. Also critical are functional communication skills for influencing change – *i.e.* negotiation, lobbying, advocacy and conflict resolution skills.
- **Facilitate development and manage partnerships for collective action.** Impact on livelihoods is an outcome of activity by multiple actors. For the actors to work in a complementary manner towards developmental impacts requires several process management skills. The key ones include facilitating stakeholder platforms to develop a shared agenda, negotiating roles and responsibilities, and setting-up management arrangements for coordinated action. Conflict management is part-and-parcel of these processes.
- **Support enterprise development.** This requires skills for strategic and business planning as well as entrepreneurial skills. Understanding enterprises in a broader market system helps in assessing their viability.

Key competences for the demand side

The demand side too needs to be able to:

- **Self organise and mobilise people and resources for a shared development goal.** Firstly this requires having a shared development agenda and then mobilising social energy to pursue that agenda with perseverance. Secondly, it requires awareness of farmer rights and/ or entitlements, as well as skills for mobilising to enforce accountability at all levels. There is beginning to be a literature on how, practically, to develop a rights-based approach among farmer client groups in Africa (*cf.* Archibald and Richards, 2002).

- **Lobby, advocate and negotiate for services.** Farmers should be able to identify the type of services they need and use their leaders to lobby, advocate and negotiate for those services with service providers and politicians. This requires confidence, determination and persistence. Leaders, it is said, are born not made, but in fact much can be done to prepare leaders, once popularly chosen, to carry out their functions more effectively. Internal motivation emanates from commitment to development desires (and poverty in Africa is sometimes clearly the effect of poor local leadership) but new professionals need to know how to help improve the capacity of farmer leaders.

- **Elect and support visionary local leadership that is accountable.** This is based on awareness of good leadership qualities and exercising freedom to elect their leaders without manipulation. In effect, further extension of the basic agenda of democracy and good governance, to which most African countries have now committed themselves, is a basic requirement for the implementation of the technical reforms here envisaged. Farmers need to accept the responsibility to use their legitimate power to enforce accountability by their leaders.

- **Demonstrate entrepreneurial skills in their business.** Farmers need to be able to analyse situations to see opportunities among challenges and to engage with challenges in a positive way. Poverty alleviation requires, on the demand side, a more proactive approach (rejection of the "victim" culture) in which local groups take responsibility for their own development. This is possible through appropriate investment in skills of self-awareness, and challenging oneself to develop unutilised potentials.

- **Engage in learning processes with intention to experiment options for potential solutions.** Learning requires positive thinking and action towards a solution – hence experimentation. This should be supported by consciousness to reflect on processes and outcomes to draw lessons for success. It also requires, at times, local adaptation of the scientific (evidence-based) approach as a means of sifting viable and non-viable approaches and treatments. People's science is not an impossible dream, as shown by the success of integrated pest management approaches based on farmer learning (Richards, 1995).

It is perhaps worth pointing out, finally, that competences on the demand and supply sides appear to be mutually dependent. One way of looking at this is to recognise that the supply side has a responsibility to facilitate the emergence of requisite competences on the demand side, while the demand side provides all-important feedback controls. Figure 10 illustrates this

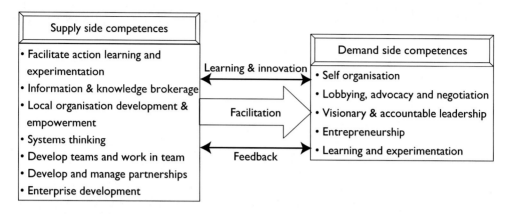

Figure 10: Interaction of competences.

interaction and interdependence of supply and demand side competences. The interaction is effective only if both parties engage, with a motive to learn for mutual benefit. The relationship is dynamised and sustained by honest feedback.

Conclusion

This chapter has discussed generic competences for the effectiveness of the entire value chain in an innovation systems perspective. They are generic in a sense that they cut across disciplinary boundaries. The implication is that such skills have to be integrated in the professional training for all those likely to work in the value chain. The subsequent chapters will focus on how universities can prepare themselves to integrate those skills in their training programme, with an example of a specific initiative at Makerere University. First, the university must ensure that these skills exist among the academic staff, otherwise they cannot be provided. Specifically, the next chapter (Chapter 5) will present a design process for learning about innovation competences by university lecturers. Internal learning within the university as an organisation then prepares it to be in position to provide services (training, research and outreach) in a different way to meet emerging demands on the university and graduates.

CHAPTER FIVE

Getting it right from the start: designing innovation competence development programmes in universities

Introduction

The literature is very rich on why universities all over the world need fundamental reforms to be relevant to the development challenges of the 21st century (Sutz, 2005; Sterling, 2001; Altbach, 1998; Harvey and Knight, 1996; Corcoran and Wals, 2004). However, it is deficient in cases of how such reforms can be designed and implemented. The contemporary university suffers from a lack of self-confidence and has lost some of the support from society it enjoyed in the past half-century or so (Altbach, 1998). Universities claim to be champions of change and yet they are themselves criticized for being resistant to change (Forster and Hewson, 1998; Swinnerton-Dyer, 1984; Allen, 1988). For this reason, there is an emerging rather radical proposal that the only way to reform universities is to create new ones (Goldschmid, 1998, 1999; Juma, 2005) founded on thinking that matches the needs of the day, such as the Earth University in Costa Rica.

While it is imperative that universities reform to become and remain relevant to the changing development context, the question is how such reforms should be designed and facilitated. The assumption that universities should be able to steer their own reforms is like telling a patient to heal him/herself. The paradigm shifts towards transformative learning (Mezirow, 1991, 2000, 2003), lifelong learning (Knapper and Cropley, 1985) and the learning organization (Levin and Greenwood, 2001; Senge, 1990) all demand fundamental changes in a wide range of aspects, including mindsets, competence, management and curricula. Sterling (2004), for example, argues that the possibility of reorientation of higher education in the context of sustainability depends on widespread and deep learning within the higher education community. Such learning should precede and accompany matching change in learning provision and practice. This chapter describes processes of designing staff competence programmes that lead to change in learning provision and practice. The first chapter already explained the meaning of competence in context of this thesis.

Developing competence is a transformative process that takes into account the mind, the body and spirit of the individual. Mezirow (2003: 59) expounds on the wholeness of transformative learning with reference to a problematic based on frames of reference - sets of fixed assumptions and expectations (habits of mind, meaning perspectives, mindsets). He further elaborates:

> "Taken–for-granted frames of reference include fixed interpersonal relationships, political orientations, cultural bias, ideologies, schemata, stereotyped attitudes and practices, occupational habits of mind, moral-ethical norms, psychological references

and schema, paradigms on science and mathematics, frames in linguistics and social sciences and aesthetical values and standards".

As Hervey and Knight (1996: 158) put it: "if students are to be transformed during their undergraduate careers, then universities need to transform themselves, moving from the rituals of teaching to the mysteries of learning." Questions that remain unanswered include:

- Are universities themselves capable of designing and facilitating such comprehensive reforms of a system they are a product and part of?
- Are universities capable of providing new forms of education, research and service to community that they themselves have no experience of?

This chapter addresses these questions by presenting and discussing experiences with the design of a pilot competence development programme for transforming university teaching, research and consultancy in an agricultural context. But before going into the design, some background to the programme is provided.

Background to the programme

Since 1991, the Forum on Agricultural Resource Husbandry (FORUM), a Rockefeller Foundation (RF) funded programme, had been funding Masters training in agriculture in five Eastern and Southern African countries, namely Kenya, Uganda, Malawi, Mozambique and Zimbabwe. The overall objective of the programme was to develop the human resources that would influence food security and poverty alleviation in the region. After about ten years there were few indications that the programme would achieve the anticipated impact on food security and poverty alleviation. RF then convened a workshop at Bellagio, Italy on *'Curriculum Development and Transformation in Rural Development and Natural Resource Management'*. The workshop, attended by 27 agricultural scientists from 17 African universities, including seven Deans of Faculties of Agriculture, discussed issues around curriculum development and strategies for preparing university graduates to meet the challenges of rural transformation in Africa. The shared insight from the discussion was that the profile of graduates of the agricultural faculties did not correspond with the actual competence demand of the labour market (Patel *et al.*, 2001).

In addition to proficiency in their technical subject matter, the desired graduates would need to have much more capacity to integrate across disciplines and possess both "hard" and "soft" skills. They would be critical thinkers, creative and responsible to develop themselves, and team players able to facilitate learning in groups and communities, as well as having substantial management capacities and excellent communication skills (Hagmann, 2002). The Bellagio meeting confirmed or revealed that current curricula largely address the agricultural science skills (hard skills) albeit with challenges, they are grossly deficient in social skills (soft skills) for enhancing performance on the job. Building on Checkland's (1981) notion of soft systems, Röling (2004) argued that a soft system implies a process of joint learning by which people come to accept shared goals, agreed boundaries, and scenarios for moving ahead. The soft skills therefore are an integral component of innovation competence to influence change through complementary engagement with multiple stakeholders.

The dilemma then was who would provide the soft skills since the academic staff are largely a product and part of a system devoid of such skills? Integration of the systems approach into university training required new ways of thinking and learning. The starting point then was designing a competence development programme for the academic staff to:

- target a shift towards systemic thinking that allows for broader integration of disciplines and knowledge systems;
- impart skills for facilitating interactive learning;
- change mindsets and build values that support the new ways of thinking and learning.

In the context of systems thinking, transformative learning and learning organizations, a plausible option for Makerere University was to focus on innovation competence founded on Personal Mastery and Soft Skills (PM/SS) as core elements for building change skills. The idea of applying PM/SS as an entry point for change was developed by Hagmann using his 15 years of experience in facilitating change particularly in research and extension organisations. The programme was then commonly referred to as the 'PM/SS learning programme'. Personal mastery as described by Senge (1990) in his well-known book, *The Fifth Discipline*, aims continually to clarify and deepen personal vision, which as already explained in Chapter 1 is a basic element of innovation competence.

In response to the challenge, Makerere University developed a concept paper to pilot an innovation competence development programme for lecturers in three related faculties of Agriculture, Veterinary Medicine and Forestry and Nature Conservation. With the initiative coming from the university, Hagmann, a process consultant was contracted by RF to design and facilitate the programme.

Designing the competence development process

Framework for process design

To contextualize the competence program to particular organization and individuals involved a generic framework, as described in Figure 11. This framework is based on lessons from the PM/SS learning programme. It is a generic framework for designing competence development for organizational change. Basically, it highlights the key areas of consideration in designing such programmes.

The framework distinguishes three areas of pragmatic action, each of them bound by a broader context as illustrated by two nested triangles (Figure 11). The outer triangle represents the contextual dimensions while the inner triangle represents the pragmatic actions in the design process. Central to all these are regular consultations and feedback between the organization management, programme participants and other stakeholders. The pragmatic actions are explained with respect to the context.

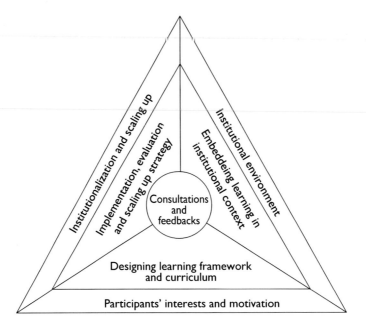

Figure 11: Framework for designing competence development programme.

Embedding the programme in institutional environment

The first pragmatic action is embedding the learning in institutional context for relevance and ownership by the target organization. Staff development needs a context; otherwise, it will fail to respond to the changing needs of the university and teaching staff (Orsmond and Stiles, 2002). This involves scanning the institutional environment to gain understanding of the institutional cultures, norms, and exploring potential opportunities and constraints of the programme. Scanning the environment increases awareness of the institutional context so as to design a process that stands a relatively high chance of success.

Designing the learning framework and curriculum

Based on the understanding of the context, a suitable learning framework is designed outlining the learning approaches, sequence and content. A good framework and a responsive curriculum jointly determine the success of competence development initiatives. Successful planning and change efforts in institutions of higher education are likely to occur when there is a close alignment between the needs and expectations of the external stakeholders and the competences, interests, and aspirations of the staff (Cowen, 1995). This stage requires good analysis of the potential participants' interests and motivation to engage in learning, with a reasonable degree of commitment. Other things to consider here include mechanisms for sustaining ownership of the programme by management, involving them in its evaluation and developing a commitment to scale up the positive outcomes of the programme.

Implementation and scaling up strategy

Making the programme flexible enough to be able to adapt to emerging interests and issues is very critical. This is the bait in the learning process that creates incentives for learning and change. Continuous evaluation of outcomes/impacts vis-à-vis the vision helps to bring back the programme on course. This process also involves serious thought and initiatives for institutionalization and scaling up of the programme.

All these actions are anchored by consultations and feedback with management at various levels to seek their input, update them on progress, enable them to internalise the process and outcomes, and help them see the value of the programme in their institutional change process. A stepwise process describes how the framework was applied in the design of the PM/SS programme.

Stepwise process of the PM/SS programme design

Step 1: Identifying the challenge and developing a vision

The objective of the Bellagio meeting was to discuss curriculum review, but starting with curriculum review would only deal with the symptoms of the problem. To get to the roots of the matter the meeting looked beyond curriculum by first imagining what the graduates would be able to do if they were to have impact on food security, poverty alleviation and natural resource management. The exercise resulted in a profile of the desired graduate. From the profile it was then easy to identify the gaps in the curriculum. Moving beyond curriculum to competence created a vision, which then led to the questioning of the capacity within the universities to help develop the necessary competences.

This is how the consensus on the intervention at the lecturer level was reached. It was apparent that unless the lecturers shared the vision and gained the capacity to develop the required competences in the students, change in curriculum would not automatically translate into more competent graduates. In view of the new competences outlined as the basis of the programme, the goal of the PM/SS programme was later defined as:

> "Enhancing the adaptive capacity of people to use and enlarge their space and freedom to operate and to foster personal growth and productivity as a member of their social system".

This goal gives room for integration of various aspects to develop the whole person to be effective in a system. Nevertheless, those who are to be part of the programme must first appreciate its value in relation to their organisational challenges.

Step 2: Creating curiosity and ownership of the process by management

Aware that success of such a programme largely depends on the support from management, the initial consultations by the process consultant aimed at creating curiosity and local ownership of the programme. Even though the Dean and some professors of the Faculty of Agriculture were in the Bellagio meeting, interest in the programme needed to extend beyond those few.

The consultant together with an influential professor (also coordinator of the programme) made wider consultations in the university. The overall objective of the consultations was to enhance ownership of the programme by management so that they pursue it as their experiment, and not just another donor driven programme. Specifically, the consultations aimed at: (1) explaining the background, purpose and rationale of the proposed programme to a wider group of managers and potential participants, (2) establishing the relevance of the programme, (3) discussing how such a programme would be set up to fit into the broader institutional context, (4) developing criteria for selection of participants, and (5) agreeing on how the programme would be monitored, evaluated and institutionalized. Among those consulted were: Deans, Heads of departments, and selected academic staff members in the targeted faculties, the academic registrar, managers of other innovative projects in the university, e.g. the 'I@mak.com' project, university planners, and other stakeholders outside the university system.

The consultations expanded the shared vision beyond the few people who attended the Bellagio meeting. Relevance of university training to the national development needs was a challenge that the university was already grappling with. A study commissioned by the university (Asiimwe et al., 2001) had already pointed out glaring gaps between university training and the job competences required by employers, especially the District Local Governments (DLGs). On this basis, the 'I@mak.com' project was initiated in the effort to realign university training and ensure that research would be more relevant to national development needs, particularly the DLGs. The PM/SS programme was therefore perceived as complementary to on-going efforts, but with an emphasis on staff development. The university managers (i.e. Deans and Heads of Departments) committed themselves to support the programme. They took responsibility to select the participants for the programme, monitor its implementation and participate in its evaluation. Since the aim was to improve learning in the university, the School of Education, though not planned for originally, was invited to nominate two participants to the programme.

With the understanding that the learning programme would extend over a period of 1½ years, it was agreed that the major criterion for selection of participants would be their commitment to go through the entire learning cycle. The target was 25 participants in total, with representation of all the departments in the three core participating faculties, including the two participants from the School of Education. The Deans, in consultation with their Heads of Departments, nominated the participants to the programme. Table 6 shows the composition of participants by faculty.

It turned out that the majority of the participants were relatively young lecturers. Only four (including the programme coordinator) were at the level of senior lecturer or above. The fact that all the Faculties mainly nominated young lecturers suggests four propositions. First is that in view of the managers, it is the young lecturers who needed such competence training more. The assumption might be that the senior lecturers are more competent than younger lecturers. Second is that the senior lecturers might be less willing to commit themselves to a long-term learning process, since the major criterion was full commitment to the entire learning cycle. Third is that it was a strategic choice by the managers on the basis that young lecturers would

Table 6: Composition of participants.

Faculty	No. of participants
Agriculture*	12
Veterinary Medicine	8
Forestry and Nature Conservation	4
Education**	2
Total	26

* The number includes the coordinator and author of this thesis. The author had a special interest in researching the process.

** Second participant dropped off early on realizing that the programme was not to do with computer software, which was his interest.

have higher motivation to champion reform since they have a much longer career life in the university than their senior colleagues. Fourth is that the young lecturers would have less power to make a difference, which might have been a sop to conservative forces in charge. Whatever the case, the younger lecturers were potentially more beneficial to the university since they would be able to influence the system much longer. The danger is that they may get better opportunities and leave the university early.

On realising the fundamental change that the programme had initiated in their personal lives and professional careers, the participants coined the identity "Win26". Win – standing for Windsor hotel where the learning workshops took place and 26 signifying the pioneer members of the programme. Thereafter, they were commonly referred to as Win26, or simply "Winners".

Step 3: Designing the learning programme

The learning model

Designing a learning programme that aims at holistic change in terms of mindsets, values and practice is comparable to the reconstruction of the whole person. With this picture of reconstruction, the PM/SS learning was modelled as the frame involved in constructing a house – the personal mastery house (Figure 12). This model was developed by Hagmann based on his experience in developing facilitation and change competence among extension officers in Zimbabwe and South Africa (Moyo and Hagmann, 2000). Basically the house had three major parts: foundation, pillars and roof. These are explained in relation to the learning programme.

Foundation: The foundation of the house rests on shared vision, values and commitment of the stakeholders, *i.e.* learners, managers and facilitators. The vision of enabling universities

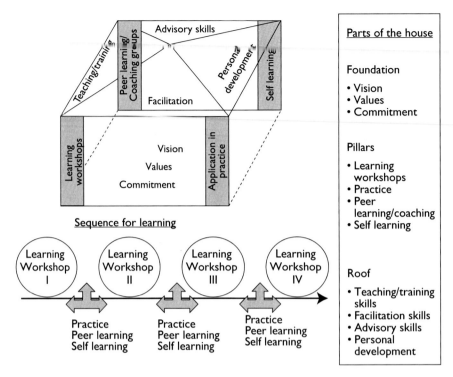

Figure 12: The PM/SS Learning model.

actively to influence development through training, research and service to community was the core of the foundation. Through consultations and joint planning with managers this vision was concretized with commitments. The Rockefeller Foundation committed funds to the programme. But ultimately results can only be achieved with the willing engagement of participants, which in turn depended on their values and interests.

The participants, too, articulated their expectations of the programme to fit into the broader vision. At this level, the goal was to enhance effectiveness and productivity for personal and organisational benefits. To achieve this, some guiding principles were agreed upon by the participants at the beginning of the learning programme as follows:

- That it would be *"learning"* and not a *"training"* programme per se. This meant sharing and exchanging knowledge, skills, experiences and recognizing that everyone had something worthwhile to contribute to the learning.

- Ownership of the process and outcomes by the participants. The participants contributed to design of daily learning process through a steering committee comprising of participants representatives and facilitators. The committee discussed at the end of each day what went well and what did not go well, in order to co-design the process for the next day.

- Appreciation of every contribution to encourage participation and learning from each other. Open dialogue and transparency were encouraged to ensure inclusiveness and to create space for everyone to contribute freely.

- Iterative and adaptive learning. The learning was meant to fit the interests of the participants and their organisation. In this view, it would be iterative and adaptive to emerging issues of interest.

These principles created an informal and relaxed atmosphere, which enhanced interaction and mutual trust as well as generating collective inspiration to engage in the learning.

The pillars: The pillars of the programme were four complementary learning approaches - namely, learning workshops, practice, peer-learning/coaching groups and self-learning. These are explained as follows:

- *Facilitated learning workshops.* These were for introducing conceptual issues, skills building, joint reflection on process learning experiences, and developing a common frame for application of knowledge and skills gained. Four learning workshops were conducted - one in each semester break and facilitated by two external facilitators (Jürgen Hagmann and Ulrike Breitschuh) over a period of 1½ years. The first learning workshop was ten days, the second lasted five days and the third and fourth lasted seven days each.
- *Application by practicing.* During the semester the lecturers practiced new ways of facilitating learning and other skills learnt. The classroom provided a 'safe' environment for practicing new skills of facilitation - safe in that the risk of losing face in case it did not work out well was much less than if it happened outside the class (*cf.* Hagmann and Almekinders *et al.*, 2003). This period also provided opportunities to test and apply some of the concepts, such as personal feedback, to generate experiences that would be processed to enrich subsequent learning workshops. Lessons drawn were documented and used as a learning resource.
- *Peer learning/coaching groups.* Stevenson *et al.* (2005) in their study of "Fostering Faculty Collaboration in Learning Communities" found that peer learning among staff enhanced learning to engage in collaborative behaviours, thinking outside the disciplinary borders, and the employment of a specific template as a heuristic for course development. At the end of the first learning workshop four peer-learning groups were formed around interest areas for the participants to continue learning and supporting each other through sharing experiences. The four areas of interest for peer learning were: enhancing undergraduate training, enhancing graduate training and research, facilitating community learning initiatives, and facilitating institutional change processes. Groups were formed based on individual interests. Members of each peer-learning group would engage individually or collectively in activities associated with their interest and schedule meetings to share their experiences as a continuation of the learning. A general meeting was organised before the next learning workshop to share experiences across peer-learning groups.
- *Self-learning.* These were mainly for individuals to enhance their learning by reading more about the concepts discussed in the learning workshops and utilising related materials from elsewhere. The facilitators enabling individual exploration provided several resource books and handouts and sought to deepen understanding of the conceptual elements of the learning, but also the participants took the initiative to search for information from other sources.

The roof: The roof represents anticipated outcomes of the learning process. The roof is the visible desired outcomes that create motivation for others to engage in the programme. In this case the roof should display better teaching/training approaches, facilitation skills, advisory skills and personal development.

The learning sequence

As illustrated in Figure 10, the programme was designed as action learning anchored in learning from experience. The four learning workshops were intermitted by practice, peer learning and self-learning as the action part of the learning. Dreyfus and Wals (2000) encourage taking action to implement potential solutions as a means to understand the problem better and to contribute to a democratic society. The action and reflection continuously improved the relevance of the learning. Through reflective processes, lessons learnt from action were synthesized in the next workshop to deepen the learning.

Step 4: Composing the curriculum

Given low morale due to inadequate remuneration, a major challenge was how to motivate the participants to engage in the learning programme with high level of commitment. What would be the incentive for the lecturers to want to improve their teaching abilities? After all, teaching by itself does not significantly count in career advancement, as university promotions are largely based on publication in peer-refereed journals. The prospect of just being a *"good lecturer"* would not be an adequate incentive to engage in a competence development programme.

The strategy to this was to focus on systemic skills that open up opportunities for personal benefits while at the same time enhancing professional abilities. Staff development is concerned with people, therefore understanding people is fundamental to what they do and what they can achieve (Webb, 996). In this view, the consultations and situation analysis revealed that the lecturers earn a larger part of their income from research and private consultancy. The programme then targeted competences for process consultancy and action research as the "carrot" to sustain motivation for engagement. Around these competences, other fields were constructed in an integrated way. For example, facilitation skills, which are essential in process consultancy, offer many opportunities outside teaching and at the same time improve teaching. Similarly, action research would increase the impact of university research on development, increase chances of winning research funds and enhance publication for professional advancement. To be able to do these effectively, one would have to strengthen personal qualities for interaction and be able to perform in multi-disciplinary teams. With facilitation skills and feedback as crosscutting elements, the content of the learning programme was composed into six major themes (Figure 13):

- **Personal development** sought to focus on individual social aspects such as emotional intelligence as an internal driver for enhanced performance and productivity. Jaeger (2003) found a strong relationship between emotional intelligence and academic performance. And as Bernett (1994) argues, the university has become less a place of broad educational and personal development, via an interactive process deemed valuable in itself, and more a place in which knowledge is viewed as a commodity, picked up by those who pass through

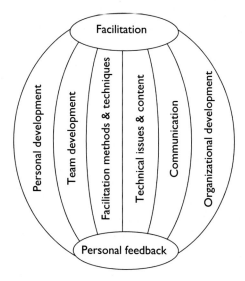

Figure 13: Integrated curriculum content.

seeking the latest technical competences and analytical capacities. Personal development therefore provides a wide range of soft skills to increase one's performance in personal and professional engagement.

- **Team development** aimed to develop individual characteristics to enable effective teamwork, understand team dynamics and help manage teams for improved organisational performance.

- **Facilitation methods and techniques** focused on building skills for facilitating learning and other collective action processes. The prime role of the staff developer is to encourage staff to be at ease with the notion of mixing approaches from across the continuum (Orsmond and Stiles, 2002). Facilitation methods and techniques were intended to provide alternative approaches to the conventional lecture method of teaching.

- **Communication** was viewed as part of a set of personal attributes. Knowledge about teaching is primarily communicative rather than instrumental, *i.e.* it is about understanding ourselves, others, and the norms of the organisation, community, and society in which we live (Cranton and King, 2003). Emphasis was placed on application of communication tools for problem solving. Negotiation skills and conflict resolution are examples of such communicative capacities.

- **Organisational development** focused on understanding organisations as social systems. Inducing and managing change and developing adaptive capacity for organisations to cope with dynamic environments were key components. The peculiarity of continuing professional development (CPD) in universities is that while universities are major providers of CPD for other professions, this activity has had little influence on the rhythms of its own institutional life (Clegg, 2003). Blandy *et al.*, (1985 quoted by Clegg) assert that innovation, flexibility and adaptability to change require attention not only to the people in the organisation but also to the social system within which they work. Organisational development therefore gives a broader view of change management.

- **Technical issues and content** targeted the building of technical skills in facilitating and managing interactive learning processes, designing and conducting impact oriented research (action research), and improved consultancy skills.

Step 5: Implementing the curriculum

To create a holistic picture of the relationships between the thematic components, lateral integration as opposed to the common sequential modular approach was preferred. Again, this approach was based on Hagmann's ideas and experience in developing systemic competence. The intention was to seek depth of content, but in an integrated way. Each learning workshop covered therefore related aspects from all the six themes in the form of a *"sandwich"*. Figure 14 illustrates the lateral integration with subsequent workshops going deeper and deeper into the content.

This lateral integration allowed interlocking of the content to create appreciation of the inter-relatedness of elements – building a holistic picture. As mentioned earlier, personal feedback and facilitation skills were crosscutting issues applied as tools in all exercises, including small group activities. For example, giving personal feedback and practicing facilitation were part of every group assignment. Table 7 presents the content outline as applied in the learning workshops.

Content of the themes was flexible and responsive to emerging issues and interest of the participants, *i.e.* flowing with the energy of the group. Comparing this to music, flowing with

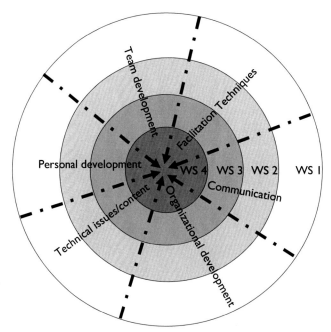

Key

The centric circles labelled **WS1-WS4** represent the four learning workshops

Broken lines separate the six thematic areas of content. The broken lines are also intended to signify diffusion across themes, hence integration.

Arrows pointing to the centre mean going deeper into the thematic content from WS1 to WS4. Also note that the shading intensifies towards the centre to further illustrate depth of content

Figure 14: Lateral integration and depth.

Table 7: Content outline for the learning workshops.

Workshop	Content outline
Workshop 1 (10 days)	Introductions and setting the scene
	Personal development (emotional intelligence, Johari window, personal feedback, myself as a development project)
	Systems thinking and the perspective of change (types of systems, inducing change in systems, action learning/research, the art of questioning)
	Understanding the dynamics of change in social/organisational systems (the concept of adaptive capacity, phases of change in social system/organisational change, creating a learning environment, examples of change processes in university)
	Learning about facilitation in practice (preparing teaching units, practicing facilitation, reflecting on own learning history, selecting appropriate teaching techniques)
	Personal growth (the dimensional world of personal growth)
	Building peer-learning groups
	Workshop evaluation
Workshop 2 (5 days)	Introduction and setting the scene
	Looking back and looking forward – major challenges (Processing experiences of PLGs, major challenges derived from experience)
	Exploring solutions to the challenges
	Conceptualizing consultancy (Assessing the demand side, characteristics of process and expert consultancy, the concept of clouds, stages and focus of the consultancy process, conceptual framework for managing successful consultancy, the learning wheel methodology, designing a consultancy marketing strategy)
	Strengthening PLGs (roles, tasks and resources for PLGs, PLG plans for the next phase of practice)
	Workshop evaluation
Workshop 3 (7 days)	Introduction and setting the scene
	Emerging issues about facilitation
	Sharing experiences and exploring issues
	Understanding more about facilitation (key elements, visualization, practicing facilitation, synthesis of challenges and lessons learnt, process documentation, process observation and analysis)
	Developing a vision of the impact of the PM/SS
	Some concepts and tools of communication (negotiation, the adrenaline concept, active listening, reframing)
	Understanding action research (what is action research, criteria for design of action research, contextualizing action research, sample cases of action research)
	Conceptualizing action research (critical success/failure factors)
	Personal development (drivers in us, reflection on drivers in PLGs, the Riemann/Thoman model of personality)
	Team building (Distinguishing features of teams, stages of team building, applying criteria of high performance teams to PLGs, types of conflicts, stages of conflict resolution process)
	Next steps (scaling up, training of trainers)
	Workshop evaluation

Table 7: Continued.

Workshop	Content outline
Workshop 4 (7 days)	Warming up and setting the scene
	Review of peer learning concept (experiences from peer-learning groups, how to apply peer-learning in an academic environment, developing principles and guidelines for effective PLGs)
	Deepening understanding of process observation
	Facilitating interactive learning (critical success/failure factors)
	Application of the learning wheel methodology
	Aspects of personal development (My inner-team; working in a culture of suspicion, jealousy, envy; the staircase construction of reality, self-positioning)
	Impact oriented monitoring systems for projects
	Knowledge management
	The future of Win 26
	Evaluation of the learning process and workshop

the energy would be equivalent to the rhythm of a song. Music is interesting if the words fit into the rhythm. Similarly, the learning becomes interesting and relevant if it can be adapted to the emerging interest of the learners. Iteration and continuous evaluation of the environment (in plenary sessions and through the steering committee) helped to identify the emerging issues of interest to which the content was adapted. This is a departure from the modular approach, with rather inflexible content. Flexibility requires expertise to adjust quickly and manage the learning without deviating from the major goal. Iteration also helps to refine and internalize issues, as more insights are gained along the way, thus making the learning truly experiential.

Step 6: Sustaining ownership and involvement of management
Involvement and ownership of the programme by management was sustained in three ways: gallery exposures to managers; feedback by participants to the faculties; and making the managers evaluate their experiment.

Gallery exposures
At the end of every learning workshop, the managers in the participating faculties and top executives, including the Vice-Chancellor, were invited to a half-day "gallery exposure". Gallery exposures were sessions at the end of each learning workshop where the programme participants demonstrated and explained the relevance of what had been learnt to invited guests. This was usually organised in form of a gallery using visual materials generated in learning workshops. The reputation and influence of the programme coordinator helped to convince even the top-level managers to participate. In these sessions, participants organised gallery presentation of key messages from the learning to share with their managers. This was a platform for interaction, which enhanced appreciation of the value of the programme as

the participants explained its relevance in the university context. The exposure consequently generated more support from the managers. In addition, the sessions provided a mechanism through which the managers could monitor and update themselves with the processes and outcomes of the programme throughout its implementation.

Feedback to the faculties

With support of their managers, participants from each faculty organized feedback to their faculty colleagues to share some aspects of the PM/SS programme they found to be critical to improvement of the system. In essence, this was a mechanism for ongoing sharing with other staff and at the same time provided accountability to the organisation. They also practiced feedback with their managers and colleagues to influence the way things are done in their faculties. The inspiration from these activities challenged the managers to support the programme more. For example, the Faculties of Agriculture and Forestry and Nature Conservation sponsored 2-3 day workshops for in-depth exposure of other staff to PM/SS.

Making the managers evaluate their experiment

Since it was agreed in the beginning that this was *their* experiment, the responsibility to evaluate the programme was brought back to them at the end of the learning programme. The managers were consulted on how "objectively" to evaluate the programme. Through these consultations, they agreed to create an "independent" assessment team (comprising of staff who were not part of the programme) to give the perspective of an "outsider". The detailed composition of the assessment team and the entire assessment processes are elaborated in the next chapter (Chapter 6).

Step 7: Deciding on scaling up and institutionalisation

The independent assessment team reported its findings to the managers (Deans and Heads of Departments) together with the programme participants. Using the outcomes as key input, areas of human resource development where innovation competence was considered important were discussed. Options for repackaging the PM/SS programme to involve specific categories of staff *i.e.* lecturers, managers and support staff were also suggested. To solicit top level support, a two-day exposure workshop on the application of some elements of innovation competences in management was organized for the top executive managers (*i.e.* Vice-Chancellor, Deputy Vice-Chancellors, University Planner, University Secretary, Academic Registrar and some Deans of Faculties). By engaging them in practicing some tools such as giving and receiving feedback to enhance staff performance, team building, and use of emotional intelligence, they appreciated more how the PM/SS type of programme could enhance their management capabilities. With this and previous exposures, a verbal commitment was made to anchor the innovation competence part of the human resource development programmes in the newly created Human Resource Department (HRD).

Step 8: Scaling up

Scaling-up the PM/SS programme university-wide and beyond depended on the availability of a pool of facilitators to undertake the task at affordable cost. It would not be right to assume that all those who went through the programme would be willing to facilitate its scaling up. Those who were interested in facilitating the scaling up programme were requested to apply for a Training of Trainers (ToT) orientation to prepare them for the task. Fifteen expressed interest and attended a one-week ToT workshop. From this pool, a team of five started facilitating the first phase of scaling up, involving 35 participants from eight units of the university. These include Faculties of Agriculture, Veterinary Medicine, Forestry & Nature Conservation, Education, Social Science, the School of Graduate Studies, the Continuing Agricultural Education Centre (CAEC), and the Department of Human Resources Development (HRD). Involvement of the HRD department at this stage was critical as it had to prepare to manage the programme in the near future.

Design challenges

Engagement in competence development programmes with a high level of commitment depends to a large degree on the intrinsic motivation of the participants. Creating incentives that stimulate that motivation in all the four pillars of learning (see Figure 12) and fitting that into the work environment was a challenge. The peer-learning groups (PLGs), for example, did not function in the way they were planned to. In the design it was thought that PLGs would meet periodically on agreed schedules to share and learn from each other's experiences. It did not work that way because:

- Some players, particularly the institutional development and community development PLGs, did not have opportunities for practical engagement in their choice of interest to acquire learning experiences. The first meetings of such groups focused on identifying possible opportunities for engagement rather than sharing experiences from their engagements. Since such opportunities were not forthcoming, the relevance of, and morale for, PLG meetings faded.
- The work overload and unforeseen commitments, some of them related to *"survival"* strategies, made many unavailable for the formally planned PLG meetings. The teaching load was so enormous that it did not allow much time for PLG activities. Generally, all departments operate much below their planned staff capacities, creating an overload on the existing staff in terms of teaching load. Yet the staff have to engage in many other private activities in order to make a living, since their university remuneration is inadequate. Combining the workload and other commitments made it difficult for the PLGs to function as planned.

Instead, the PLGs worked more informally and on an ad-hoc basis. Consultations and sharing of experiences tended to be around activities with economic gains and not necessarily between members of the same PLGs. Such activities were around short-term consultancies (studies and facilitation of workshops and meetings).

Lessons learnt

From the design and implementation stage of a competence development programme, the following lessons were drawn:

- **Time of engagement**. Competence development is itself a change process that takes time. It requires exploration and internalization of issues, appreciation and perfection of skills through practice. Using experiences from practice as a learning resource is the strength of competence development. In this context 1½ years is about the minimum period required for meaningful engagement, otherwise it can easily turn out to be simply a knowledge acquisition exercise that does not fundamentally change the way people think about or do things.

- **Finding the triggers for change**. People will not engage in competence development for the sake of it – participation must translate into benefits. It is therefore important at the design stage to identify what it is that will motivate and keep the learners committed. In this case, focusing on research, consultancy and systemic skills that bring immediate benefits to the participants was the trigger. To sustain application of competences acquired, organisations must ensure appropriate rewards for new performance criteria. Therefore, alongside competence development, appropriate reward systems have to be put in place.

- **The factor of a champion**. However good the design may be, it may not succeed without key people within the system to deal with the internal *"politics"* of the organisation. Such persons must be respectable and credible among managers and participants. In this case, a highly regarded professor played the role of champion. His willingness and humility in fully engaging in the learning process inspired the participants and his credibility and influence helped convince the management.

- **Creating ownership among the management**. Taking up an intervention as a normal way of doing business in an organisation depends on the extent to which the managers take responsibility for it. It is extremely important that the managers own the intervention right from the beginning and remain part of it throughout. They should be made responsible for critical decisions to create ownership. This way, they cannot easily evade or distance themselves from their own decisions. Mechanisms for continuous update, exposure to outcomes of the programme, and accountability to the organisation make ownership and institutionalization easier.

- **Pressure to change**. If there is no pressure to change, then there would be no motivation for undertaking a competence development programme. Existing institutions resist change and prefer the status quo, especially in the absence of social and economic pressure (Goldschmid, 1999). Competence development is more appreciated if it is part of a change process in an organisation. The discomfort with the status quo especially at the level of management is the motivation for positive response to competence development. In this case, Makerere University was under immense pressure from the local governments, NGOs and donors to make its training more relevant to current development needs. The decentralization and privatization policies created new competence demands, as local governments and private sector became the main employers of university graduates. At the same time, the private sponsorship scheme had increased the stakes of students, parents and other sponsors in the university training as they sought to get value for money. Faced with inadequate funding from the central government, the university was under pressure to respond to criticism of the relevance of its education and training. Innovation competence development fitted very well in the university's response to such criticisms, which undoubtedly contributed to the support and commitment to the programme by the management.

- **Facilitation capacity**. Influencing change in any system requires high quality facilitation skills. The ability to contextualize change and focus on important emerging issues increases the motivation for learning and change. One of the critical aspects of facilitation is being able quickly to analyse the environment and adapt the learning to emerging issues and interests without losing focus. Successes in this programme are largely attributable to the quality facilitation and flexible process design. Now that scaling up is facilitated by the first trainees, sustaining the quality of facilitation is achieved by the mentoring and coaching of the facilitators.

Conclusion

Competence development is not just a matter of influencing skills and attitudes; it is also about exploring underlying causes for the status quo, and creating awareness of the environment that necessitates new competences. While the ultimate aim is change in the organisation, finding the motivators for individual staff engagements increases the chances of success. It is around these that organisational interests are constructed to ensure that as people change in order to meet their personal development goals, they also enhance performance of the organisations they work for. Such change is embedded in learning processes, which require a combination of complementary learning approaches and integrated content that in meaningful interaction lead to change in knowledge, skills and mindsets. Only a well-facilitated, iterative and flexible process that builds on experience and emerging interests of the participants enables internalisation and application of the learning.

Competence development is a means for organisational change. Its success therefore depends on the level of commitment and ownership of the process by management. A strategy for creating ownership by management and sustaining it throughout the process is part of the design process. Making the leadership take responsibility to make critical decisions enhances institutionalisation and up-scaling of the change through competence development. Champions play a valuable role to in getting the management involved and in making them co-owners of the initiative. Champions must command a reasonable level of respect from the management and also become role models who inspire the pioneers of change. Therefore, identification and involvement of champion(s) right at the start is as important as the process design itself.

Having discussed the design and implementation of the competence development programme as a change process, the next chapter looks at how the learning programme was evaluated. A visionary approach that emphasizes improvements gained through flexible learning processes was applied as a departure from the conventional judgemental approaches based on pre-determined criteria.

CHAPTER SIX

Vision-based assessment of learning for change: the case of an innovation competence development programme

Introduction

We are beginning to see signs of professional education narrowing to sets of practical skills – indeed, to competences – and behavioural operations, with clients reduced to being recipients of those skills rather than joint authors of the professional service that they require (Barnett, 1994). Barnett argues that skills cannot be a sufficient way of describing genuinely open-ended transactions of the kind that should characterize professional-client relationship. Education is not a service for a customer (much less a product to be consumed) but an ongoing process of transformation of the participants (Harvey and Knight, 1996). For this transformation to take place, education must genuinely embrace the ethos and champion the praxis of participation. The new sciences of complexity, concerned with emergence and chaos in non-linear systems, indicate that we live in fundamentally participative world that is both unpredictable and inherently creative (Sterling, 2001). Participation is an underlying core value for educational concepts such as action learning, reflective learning, life-long learning and transformative learning, which aim to prepare learners for adaptation in the unpredictable world. Actualizing participation in all learning activities is easier stated than done. Its practice requires high level competence, but as Raven (2001: 21) puts it:

> "It has become clear that there is very little formal understanding of the nature of high-level competence, how its components are to be nurtured, or how these components are to be assessed".

While education is a participative process (Harvey and Knight, *ibid.*), universities remain the home for "experts" who teach and examine learners based on what they think the learners should have learnt and not necessarily what they actually learnt. Knapper and Cropley (1985) describe a situation where university teachers claim the aim of their courses is to offer higher order learning skills such as creativity and critical thinking but the examinations and tests they give only reveal low-level learning characterised by the memorization of facts. Such situations bring in three levels of contention. The first level is the intention of the learning. The second level refers to what is actually learnt, while the third level refers to what is assessed or evaluated. These levels can be reconciled through participatory engagement of the learners and the facilitators of the learning to create a common frame of reference. The value of innovative learning approaches can be easily downgraded if their assessment falls back to the prescriptive expert type. Assessment of learning should be seen as a continuation of learning rather than as the end of learning.

One of the hindrances to participatory learning is the adherence to prescriptive procedures and standards for evaluation of the learning. Many teachers will ask how objectively to assess the participatory learning processes in accordance with academic standards. Objectivity in this sense means each learner being judged on the basis of whether s/he knows a particular answer. This is often based on the view that assessment is an exclusively judgmental process clearly distinct from the learning process. The alternative option is to test whether the learners can make a logical argument in a particular context, in which case the assessment enhances learning. Therefore, participatory learning also calls for creativity in assessment of such learning.

The fundamental question is to what extent should the learners participate in determining standards and ensuring quality in education? Harvey and Knight (*ibid.*) argue that the transformative view of quality is rooted in the notion of qualitative change that enhances (value addition in knowledge, abilities and skills) and empowers participants through student evaluation, guaranteeing students minimum standards of provision, more control over their own learning and developing students' critical ability. Student evaluation in this sense is used more as a feedback mechanism about their learning. Good assessment is a form of learning and should provide guidance and support to address learning needs (Epstein and Hundert, 2002). With this line of argument, learners have to participate in determining criteria for assessment of their own learning in order to reconcile what is intended, what is actually learnt and what is assessed.

Competence is context-dependent (Epstein and Hundert, *ibid.*), meaning that it emerges in a context. This calls for creativity in the design and assessment of competence development programmes. The previous chapter discussed a creative design process for innovation competence development (the PM/SS) in a university context. This chapter discusses the vision-based assessment of the programme – an approach developed by Hagmann and applied in several other cases (Hagmann, 2000). As explained in the previous chapter, the vision is to make university training, research and consultancy more relevant to national development. Vision-based assessment is a departure from the judgement-driven expert assessment. It focuses on improvement in performance within the framework of the vision and seeks for convergence of observations and opinions, making it a learning process in and by itself. The methodology focuses on processes and perspectives within triangulation, with the aim of assessing improvements towards a shared vision. These processes and perspectives are explained further and illustrated in Figure 15.

Triangulation: processes within a process

Many scholars of the case study method (Yin, 1994; Verschuren, 1997; Creswell, 1998, 1994) recommend triangulation for attainment of adequacy. Triangulation in most cases refers to situations where a researcher applies more than one tool/method to gather evidence and/or gather evidence from different sources. Truly, the tools/methods and sources of information are chosen based on what the researcher thinks is important in the investigation. The researcher determines what evidence to gather and applies the tools to the source(s) of data. The tools/methods of data collection used include interviews, participant observation and self-assessment. Sources of data include programme participants, students and managers. In addition, the criteria applied in gathering some of the data were established by the programme participants and the independent assessment team.

In the present case, another dimension was added, namely, the triangulation of perceptions, whereby participants', in their perceptions, also determine what is important in the investigation and what evidence should be gathered. These collective choices of variables/evidence by people other than the researcher were also considered data. Allowing for this takes the research process beyond triangulation as it is commonly understood to what may be termed "poly-angulation". This means that within the process of triangulation there were several distinct processes at work, as illustrated by Figure 15.

Using the analogy of spectacles, the meta-level has three pairs of spectacles (perspectives) for assessing the outcomes of the learning process, namely from the action research perspective, from the perspective of an independent assessment team, and self-assessment (intersecting circles in Figure 15). But each pair of spectacles had a combination of lenses (tools, methods and processes) for observing the evidence and gathering data. The different lenses enable scrutiny of the same things, perhaps with different precisions, but they also enable different

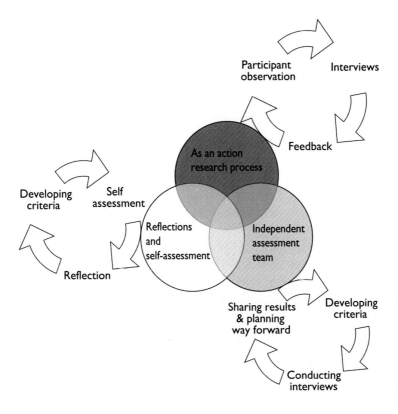

Figure 15: Processes within the triangulation process.

perspectives of the same thing. Different pairs of spectacles fitted with different lenses increase the reliability of the assessment, especially in learning processes that are subject to different perceptions. In assessing critically reflective learning, Bronckbank and McGill (1998: 100) emphasize the value of multiple approaches:

> "If critically reflective learning has occurred then the first person to know about this is the learner. When this learning is communicated to others in writing or verbally, then this is known as 'self-report'. When others, possibly fellow students or tutors, report on their observations or experience of the learners to a third party, this is known as 'other-report'. Clearly the presence of other-report supports self report, and if added to by a presumed independent other, e.g. the tutor, then the well-known reliability of triangulation is achieved".

Repetitiveness of observations serves as a reliability check while the complementarities from different perspectives further enhance this reliability. This reliability, in combination with frequent validity checks obtained through frequent mirroring of the findings with the participants (feedback loops), ensures the adequacy of the research. However, complementarities are achieved when all perspectives focus the assessment of a shared vision. The shared vision becomes the ultimate guide (guiding star) of the different perspectives to be integrated in the assessment. From a systems context, the different perspectives enable us to see how the intervention influences the whole system.

Putting processes into practice

As illustrated in Figure 15 above, each of the perspectives had its own process and tools. These processes and tools are described in the context they were applied.

As an action research process

A fundamental position in action research is that it seeks to create a research situation where active manipulation of the material and social world defines the inquiry process (Levin and Greenwood, 2001). The PM/SS programme was set-up as an experiment in an action research mode. In addition to being a participant in the programme, I was also researching the programme. However, the research interest was clarified to the group at the beginning of the programme. As a researcher I took the responsibility of documenting all activities of the learning programme. This increased my credibility in the group and also provided me the mandate and privilege to observe and take record of all activities. The detailed documentation of the learning workshops provided a full account of the processes and outcomes of every activity, including small-group and plenary discussions, role-plays and exercises as captured in their original form. The participants relied on these reports for their reference, but it was also an opportunity for them to verify that the documentation represented a true account of what transpired. In an action research process, participant and process observation, interviews and feedback are the main tools for data collection. How these were applied in this study is now explained in more detail.

Participant/process observation

By putting forward the research interest in a transparent manner and offering to document the learning process, I was always invited by the participants to take part in activities outside the learning workshops. Such activities included PLG meetings and in some occasions to situations for practicing some skills such as facilitation of strategic planning for departments and joint development of research projects. Observations made on those occasions were fed back to groups or individuals verbally and in writing as part of the reflective process. In reality, the participants did not perceive me as someone collecting data about them but rather as someone learning with them. These collegial interactions created rapport between myself and other participants to the extent that I engaged intensively with some of them in consultancy assignments, like facilitating workshops. This helped tremendously when probing specific experiences during interviews.

Individual interviews

Individual interviews were used for two purposes: (1) to monitor the learning and (2) to assess the impact of the programme at the individual level. For monitoring purposes, the intention was to find out what participants found useful or not so useful from the previous workshop, and what they wished to learn more about in the next workshops. Two such interviews were conducted, one before the second and one before the third workshop. The second interview, however, did not yield large differences from the first, given that subsequent workshops largely deepened the understanding of the same concepts (see Figure 14). It was therefore not necessary to conduct a similar interview before the fourth workshop. Interviews were conducted after the fourth learning workshop to establish what individuals considered to be the overall impact of the learning programme with respect to their personal and professional activities but also to find out what elements of the programme contributed to those impacts the most. Box 4 presents the checklists used in these interviews.

Within the open-ended type of questions there was room to probe and deepen the discussions with clarification in a reflective mode. This went beyond just eliciting responses. It also helped the interviewees to distil and internalize key learning points. In essence, the interviews triggered a deep reflection on experiences, and by so doing went beyond a mere question–answer type of interaction. At the end, both the interviewer and the interviewee gained more insights into what learning actually took place.

Feedback

All workshop documentations and reports of observations of specific activities were given to the participants only a few days after the event to get their comments. Workshop reports were sent to all participants, while specific activity reports were sent to only those involved in the activity. Other than for their record, this was intended to get approval of accuracy of the information and to allow for corrections where necessary. Similarly, all interview transcripts

---

Box 4: Interview checklists.

Checklist for monitoring learning
- What have you found useful so far in the PM/SS learning programme?
- Why have those things been so useful to you?
- How have you applied them in your private and professional activities?
- What are your experiences in application of those things (opportunities and challenges)?
- What are your experiences in the PLGs (positive, negative and challenges)?
- Based on your experience, how can peer learning be improved?
- What would you like to learn more about in the next workshop?
- What have you not found so useful so far in the PM/SS learning programme?

Checklist for assessment of impact
- What can you say has changed in the way you think and do things that you can associate with the PM/SS learning programme?
- Reflecting on those changes, what do you think have been the major triggers?
- What challenges have you encountered with respect to those changes?

---

were sent to the respective interviewees for their approval and correction. Feedback was thus a mechanism for validation of data.

Assessment by the independent team

After the fourth learning workshop, managers were consulted on how the programme should be evaluated objectively. The consultations extended beyond the participating faculties to include the Faculty of Social Science, the School of Graduate Studies and the Academic Registrar. Through this process, the managers agreed to nominate an independent team (non-participants in the learning programme) to assess the outcomes/impacts of the programme. A team of twelve people was nominated from seven units to carry out the assessment (see Table 8).

In a facilitated process, the team developed assessment criteria based on the vision of the programme, did the assessment through field interviews and reported their findings to the managers. This was done using the following steps:

Step 1: Workshop to develop the assessment criteria
The first task for the team was to develop criteria for assessing the programme. In a two-day workshop facilitated by Hagmann, criteria were developed within the context of the vision of the programme. Reference points were:
- the profile of the preferred graduates – with the Bellagio outline (Box 5) as starting point;
- purpose and content of the programme; and
- current and future university competence challenges.

Table 8: Composition of assessment team.

Unit	No. of people
Faculty of Agriculture	2
Faculty of Veterinary Medicine	2
Faculty of Forestry & Nature Conservation	2
School of Education	2
Faculty of Social Sciences	1
Academic Registrar's office	2
School of Graduate Studies	1
Total	12

Box 5: Additional qualities required of agricultural graduates.

Beyond the technical knowledge and skills in agriculture, the preferred graduate should:
- Display ethical conduct based on fairness, honesty and responsibility as core values.
- Display entrepreneurial skills and innovativeness in pursuance of personal and professional goals.
- Communicate effectively with different categories of people including superiors, peers, subordinates and clients.
- Possess sound management and leadership competence to promote efficient resource utilization.
- Think critically and in a systemic perspective.
- Build and facilitate high performing teams to promote collective action and achievement of common goals.

With this guide, the team explored the required staff capabilities to contribute to the desired qualities of graduates. In addition to assessing those aspects, the team also explored opinions and issues for scaling up the programme within the university. Box 6 presents a checklist that guided the assessment.

Step 2: Conducting the assessment

The team split into three small groups of about four members, each group conducting the assessment in one faculty. The groups were allocated to the faculties in a way that would prevent them from assessing their own faculty. This encouraged exposure of the teams to other faculties. In each faculty the group interviewed programme participants, some of their peers who did not participate in the learning programme, and managers (Deans and some Heads of Departments), and held group discussion with some students taught by the programme

---

Box 6: Checklist for assessment of outcomes/impact of the programme.

Areas to explore for impact/change
- Development of personal skills and confidence.
- Establishment of a feedback culture with students and among colleagues.
- Innovations in teaching, research and consultancy.
- Interdisciplinary engagement in research, training and consultancy.
- Teamwork and networking.
- Enhancement in management qualities.
- Being exemplary or role models in professional conduct.
- Pro-activeness in responding to opportunities and expectations of stakeholders.

Issues and challenges for scaling-up and institutionalization of the PM/SS
- How to scale-up and mainstream the PM/SS in the University programmes.
- Options and approaches for scaling-up given resource constraints.
- How to create awareness of the PM/SS across all categories of staff including non-academic staff.
- Which are the priority levels of staff to scale-up.
- How to link and harmonize the PM/SS with other ongoing competence related programmes such as the pedagogical training by the School of Education.
- How to institutionalize the PM/SS in the University set-up. Who will house it? Who is the champion?
- How to schedule scaling up activities to fit the university calendar and programmes.
- How to maintain and effectively utilize competence of the pioneer trainees (the Win26 group).

---

participants. The intention was to establish whether other people noticed any difference in those who participated in the programme.

The assessment exercise covered a period of two weeks (not full time), though the total time of engagement was estimated to be about three working days. Through this exercise the assessment team became better informed about what the PM/SS programme entailed. In a way it was a learning exercise for the assessors too. The focus of the assessment was to look for improvement rather than to make judgements.

Step 3: Synthesis of results and planning the way forward
After the assessment the team convened in a three-day workshop. The first two days of the workshop focused on the synthesis and harmonisation of findings before reporting to the managers and programme participants. The major recommendation of the assessment team was that the PM/SS programme provided cross-cutting skills essential for all categories of university staff, *i.e.* managers, academic staff and support staff. Chapter 7 integrates the specific findings in the presentation of the overall outcomes.

The findings were then used as input for planning scaling-up strategies as a way forward. Planning scaling-up strategies was a joint engagement of the assessment team, programme participants and the managers. This further strengthened the ownership of the programme and opened new windows of opportunity for application of innovation competences in an organisation-wide set-up. Bearing in mind the need for institutionalisation, it was suggested that the most appropriate host unit for the programme was the newly created Human Resource Development (HRD) Department.

Reflections and self-assessment

People learn in cycles, moving naturally between action and reflection, between activity and repose (Cambron-McCabe and Dutton, 2000). Becoming critically reflective of one's own assumptions is the key to transforming taken-for-granted frames of reference, and is therefore an indispensable dimension of learning for adapting to change (Mezorow, 1997). Reflection and self-evaluation were integral parts of the programme. In a programme shaped and guided by participants' interests, it is not easy to pre-determine what the assessment criteria should be. Appropriate assessment criteria emerged through reflective processes with the learners themselves. In this type of learning there is some danger that a reductionist approach based on pre- and post-tests will devalue the action learning processes. For this reason, visionary reflections were applied to construct a composite profile and criteria for assessment of the PM/SS programme. It was 'visionary' in that it involved stepping out of "*what is*" to questions based on "*what would be*", in which the imagination of what might be possible depends upon a vision. The following explains how this was done.

Developing the composite profile of the PM/SS
Throughout the PM/SS programme participants engaged in several self-assessment exercises, either individually or in groups. However, for overall impact of the PM/SS programme there was a need for a profile against which the individuals would assess themselves. This profile was created at the end of the third learning workshop after which participants had a clearer view of what the programme could influence and what not.

The profile was developed based on experiences in the light of an overall vision. A guiding question was "*If a person was successful in PM/SS, what would this person do/do differently?*" This question allowed the learners to articulate what "*it would be*", based on their experience and the overall purpose of the programme. In buzz groups of 3-4 people, participants generated their views on cards. The cards were clustered and titles were generated to label the clusters. The cluster titles represented a composite profile with twelve elements (see Box 7) each element having underlying or constituent sub-elements. This then allowed the elements of the composite profile to be assessed using their constituent sub-elements (See Appendix 2).

Self-assessment against the profile
To assess oneself against elements of the composite PM/SS profile, the constituent sub-elements were assigned a Likert scale of 1-10. The participants then rated themselves on

Box 7: Composite profile of PM/SS.

A successful person in PM/SS ...
- uses professional networks and alliances for exchange of information and experiences and to pursue common interests;
- promotes team development and consensus building in teams;
- initiates and facilitates group processes of joint reflection, strategy and vision development and decision making;
- manages and minimizes conflicts;
- actively seeks to develop him/herself professionally and personally;
- tries out new things with courage and without fear of failure;
- deals with unforeseen situations in a positive and solution-oriented way;
- shares information in a free and transparent and accountable manner;
- gives and receives feedback as a tool to develop him/herself and others personally;
- develops and pursues clear vision and values in his/her professional environment;
- assumes leadership roles (formal and informal) to enhance individual, team and organisational performance;
- pursues a balanced life style.

this scale based on self-estimated scores before and after the learning programme. Twenty one (81%) of the original 26 members participated in the self-assessment. At the time of the assessment, two had left the university, another two were out of the country on study leave and as earlier mentioned in Chapter 5, one dropped out early. In addition to self-scores, they also identified what elements of the PM/SS programme contributed to a change in each element and how the change manifested itself in reality. This process yielded a comprehensive self-assessment instrument (Appendix 2). In this instrument the present situation is the realistic reference point for estimating where participants start from with regard to each criterion. The instrument could only be developed utilising the experiences generated by the programme itself. Without such experience, there would be no realistic reference point and self-scores would be arbitrary. Figures 16 and 17 provide a summary of the self-assessment results.

Impact of the PM/SS programme on individual profiles

Profile enhancement

The self-assessment scores for each element of the composite profile as listed in Box 7 were calculated as the mean of the scores of its constituent sub-elements. Figure 16 maps out the mean scores of all participants before and after, to illustrate the overall impact of the programme.

Figure 16 demonstrates profile enhancement at varying degrees. Putting it in another way, the variation illustrates a learning curve if the mean enhancement scores are plotted against the profiles. This is better visualized in Figure 17.

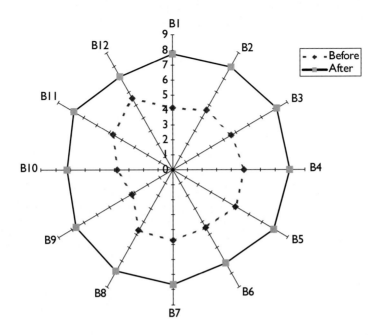

Figure 16: Profile ratings before and after the PM/SS programme.

Key

B1 = Uses professional networks and alliances for exchange of information and experiences and to pursue common interest.

B2 = Promotes team development and consensus building in teams.

B3 = Initiates and facilitates group processes of joint reflection, strategy and vision development and decision making.

B4 = Manages and minimizes conflicts.

B5 = Actively seeks to develop him/herself professionally and personally.

B6 = Tries out new things with courage and without fear of failure.

B7 = Deals with unforeseen situations in a positive and solution oriented way.

B8 = Shares information in a free, transparent and accountable manner.

B9 = Gives and receives feedback as a tool to develop him/herself and others personally

B10 = Develops and pursues clear vision and values in his/her professional environment.

B11 = Assumes leadership roles (formal and informal) to enhance individual, team and organizational performance.

B12 = Pursues a balanced lifestyle.

It is clear from the two figures that elements of the profile were not the result of participation in the PM/SS programme; they existed in the individuals even before the programme. Figure 16 shows that none of the profile elements had a mean score of zero before the programme. It is also true that development of these profiles is a continuous process and could not be fully achieved in the duration of this programme. Figures 16 and 17 simply illustrate enhancement of

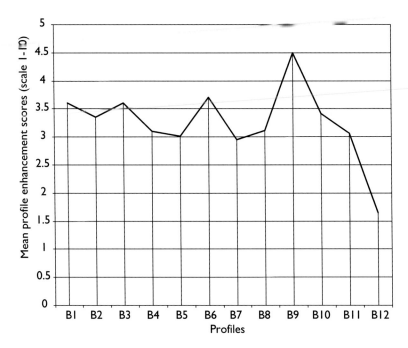

Figure 17: Learning curve for PM/SS programme.

the profile elements of the PM/SS. Most profile elements were considerably enhanced by more than three points on a ten point scale, with B9 shooting up to about 4.5. The enhancement was attributed to specific content elements (triggers) in the PM/SS programme.

Triggers for profile enhancement

Key content elements of the programme that triggered this enhancement, and the indicators of the enhancement as identified by participants, are summarized in Table 9. The Effects of the profile enhancement are part of the overall outcomes of the programme, as discussed in Chapter 7.

By their inter-relatedness, one trigger may enhance several profile elements. The cross-cutting triggers however, tended to be those that targeted mindsets and personal development. It therefore appears that mindsets and personal development are the key nodes for change in the process through which individuals move towards being innovative. They are thus identified as key entry points for influencing the way people do things, as the alternative ways of doing things must fit the mind frame and reward structure of individuals, both socially and economically.

Lessons learnt

Based on processes of vision-based assessment described in this chapter, the following lessons emerged:

- Facilitated evaluation creates more coherence in action learning processes than the expert judgemental type of evaluation. It is a shift from judgement to focusing on improvements, in line with the overall vision of the organisation. In the broader performance context, the shift implies focusing on "*doing the right thing*" rather than "*doing things right*". Doing the right thing involves challenging the participant's own values, practices and institutional cultures to enhance performance, while doing things right reinforces conformity to established rules and procedures that often do not give room for innovations.
- Engaging the learners in developing appropriate criteria for assessment of their learning brings them to new horizons of understanding. The reflective process helps to internalise the learning, but in addition it challenges the participant with reference to the core purpose of the learning. It is getting "*out of the box*" to see the world in a different way.
- Self-assessment requires realistic points of reference, otherwise it becomes arbitrary. The reference points are created after the learners appreciate outcomes of the learning. Without this they cannot imagine how "*it could be*" in reference to "*what is*". Self-assessment therefore is about questioning the self with reference to new frames.
- Involving stakeholders in assessing a learning programme within a vision of the organisation creates clarity about the behavioural changes required of the programme. For example, the development of a composite profile for PM/SS clarified the behavioural characteristics (profile elements) that the programme can influence. This is a way of creating congruence between intended and actual outcomes of the learning programmes, and therefore a solid basis for realistic assessment (in the sense of Pawson and Tilley, 1997).
- This type of evaluation is a continuation of the learning process allowing people to explore and discover new dimensions and increase awareness of their own change. In this case the programme assessors readily subscribed to the learning process. Emphasis is on monitoring the outcomes rather than judgement based on pre-determined indicators. It is in fact a reversal of the logframe-based type of evaluation.

This chapter presented comprehensive poly-angulated processes for evaluating the learning programme. Only results of the profile enhancements have been discussed in this chapter. The next chapter (Chapter 7) presents a detailed synthesis of outcomes of all evaluation processes discussed.

Table 9: Triggers and profile indicators.

Profile elements	Triggers	Indicators
B1 = Uses professional networks and alliances for exchange of information and to pursue common interest	Team development and teamwork Peer learning groups Emotional intelligence Personal feedback Negotiation as an aspect of communication	Improved interpersonal relationships and motivation to work in teams Sharing information via e-mails and other channels Joint reflection meetings Openness to and supporting one another to improve
B2 = Promotes team development and consensus building in teams	Principles of working together and team development processes Personal feedback Johari window Facilitation – tools and tips Active listening and negotiation skills Peer learning groups Understanding social systems and social change	Engage with others to exchange experiences and feedback Facilitating joint activities and creating shared ownership Respect of divergent opinions and self control to give others chance to participate/contribute
B3 = Initiates and facilitates group processes of joint reflection, strategy vision development and decision making	Facilitation – tools and tips Principles of working together Active listening Visioning and developing shared goals	Volunteers to facilitate interactive processes, synthesise and visualize synergies Confidence and fluency in articulating issues Providing leadership in teams towards shared goals Document processes and outcomes of group activities
B4 = Manages and minimizes conflicts	Negotiation and conflict resolution Active listening, reframing and adrenaline model in communication Emotional intelligence Facilitation – tools and tips The staircase construction of reality	Accommodative and patient with others Express opinions in non-judgmental way and seek for synergies and common ground Focus discussion on issues and not personalities
B5 = Actively seeks to develop him/herself professionally and personally	Johari window Facilitation – tools and tips Visioning - myself as a development project Emotional intelligence Personal SWOT analysis Personal feedback Our inner drivers The clouds concept to enhance our potentials and solution oriented thinking Principles of working together Peer learning groups Relating the research and development continuum and social change	Explores to discover more through self learning and sharing with others Overcomes the "victim" feeling and looks for opportunities in every situation Open to new ideas and use them to improve performance Pursue opportunities with a vision and clear targets Self confidence Empathetic and guided by ethical values

Table 9: Continued.

Profile elements	Triggers	Indicators
B6= Tries out new things with courage and without fear of failure	Facilitation – tools and tips Personal feedback Our inner drivers The Clouds concept to enhance our hidden potentials Personal SWOT and self positioning	Courage to try out or experiment new things – learn by doing Ask for feedback and support from peers and other people
B7= Deals with unforeseen situations in a positive and solution-oriented way	Understanding systems dynamics of social change processes Facilitation – tools and tips Emotional intelligence Reframing Our inner drivers	Looks for learning from failure and documents lessons Applies a variety of tools and strategies to adapt to different situations Committed to accomplishing tasks
B8= Shares information in a free and transparent manner	Application of principles of working together in peer learning groups Personal feedback Emotional intelligence Reframing as an aspect of communication	Exchange information and ideas freely without fear of criticism Not selfish – share information on both opportunities and challenges
B9= Gives and receives feedback as a tool to develop him/herself and others personally	Personal feedback (role plays on feedback) Emotional intelligence Active listening Johari window Practicing feedback in peer learning groups The art of questioning	Gives constructive feedback to develop others and improve relationships Interacts freely with colleagues and subordinates Controls his/her emotions and takes responsibility for own mistakes Helps others to develop their potentials
B10= Develops and pursues clear vision and values in his/her professional environment	Visioning Peer learning groups Emotional intelligence	for a common goal Seeks and encourages dialogue Focussed committed and trustworthy Proactive in pursuing opportunities
B11= Assumes leadership roles (formal and informal) to enhance their individual, team and organisational performance	Teamwork and characteristics of high performing teams Active listening Emotional intelligence Understanding organisations as social systems Performance oriented management Reflects to learns from experience Leadership concepts Feedback Riemann-Thoman model of personalities Facilitation – tools and tips	Good team player and engages in peer learning activities Respect others and recognises their contributions to team efforts Realistically accepts responsibility and not frightened by challenges Receives and gives feedback in a constructive way
B12= pursues a balanced life style	Emotional intelligence Johari window Personal SWOT analysis The inner team Personal vision Feedback	Pursues healthy behaviours e.g. exercising the body Manages stress and conscious about balancing time for work, family and other activities Reflects on implications of their behaviours to themselves and others Adheres to prescribed moral values e.g. spiritual values

CHAPTER SEVEN

Outcomes of the competence development programme

Introduction

The previous chapter described an assessment process for the PM/SS learning programme. Triangulation of the assessment brought out repeated but also complementary findings on the influence of the PM/SS programme on individual participants, and to some extent, on their units (faculties and departments). The overall intention of the PM/SS programme was to have competences reflected in the quality of graduates, but at this stage assessment focuses on the impact on lecturers. Being a pilot programme with only a very small number of staff, running over 1½ years, it is not possible yet to assess impact on students, although the independent assessment team did try and obtain some impressions from students.

The outcomes presented in this chapter are a synthesis of the results of several assessment methods and procedures as described in Chapter 6. They are inter-related and sometimes difficult to untangle, which is not atypical for systemic elements. However, this chapter attempts to distinguish and at the same time explain the linkages, in order to bring out their inter-connectedness more clearly. The chapter will also discuss challenges in sustaining these outcomes.

Outcomes

Self-awareness and discovery of hidden potentials

One of the most exciting elements of the PM/SS programme was a better self-understanding of personality and behaviour and how these influence interaction with others, including students. Several elements of personal development (see Table 7), such as emotional intelligence, Johari window, feedback and related exercises that the participants engaged in, were very powerful tools for revealing individual personalities with their associated weaknesses and strengths. Self-awareness is always taken for granted, but in the interviews all participants stressed it as one of the most valuable things that they got from the programme. It challenged them to critically analyze how their personalities influenced the way they do things and helped them appreciate why other people tend to do things differently. The urge for self-understanding induced conscious reflection but also made participants more open to constructive feedback from peers for purposes of improvement in their personal and professional performance. For example, with regard to social relationship, one participant explained:

> "In my family there are more females than males. I am a person who always wants quick
> results but I have come to appreciate that this is not the way ladies deal with things. I

have learnt that ladies need a lot more care and a bit more time to get them to perform well. By appreciating these differences, I am able to cope with less stress. I have also learnt to consult my children, which has helped me understand them more".

From a professional perspective, another participant explained:

"I now appreciate differences among people. These days when I pose a question in class, I allow students to explain different perspectives based on how they understand the question. I do not immediately dismiss any answers as wrong but I allow a bit of discussion around the issue and eventually we agree on possibilities in that context".

Self-awareness and appreciation of others' personalities and abilities is the basis for seeking complementarity through teamwork. It is also, arguably, the "glue" for social relationships based on trust and empathy. The independent assessment team stressed the importance of self-regulation, openness and transparency as some of the factors that enhance relationships between the "winners", their peers and the partners they work with. It can therefore be argued that self-awareness is the basis for respecting different bodies of knowledge and paves the way for integrating them effectively to deal with complex situations. Box 8 presents some of these personal experiences of self-discovery in relation to social relationships.

The trigger for this rise in self-awareness was largely the exposure to personal development concepts and tools related to emotional intelligence, the use of the Johari window technique, and feedback. Elements of emotional intelligence, *i.e.* self-awareness, self-regulation, motivation,

---

Box 8: Some personal experiences on self-discovery.

"I have explained to my wife how to analyze myself as a development project and she was very excited about it. I have also shared with her about the Johari window and we have used it to discover ourselves more".

"The Johari window helped me to understand myself better. In the past few months I have been working very hard to enlarge my public person. As a result, I have improved my relationships with colleagues and friends. I interact more with them".

"I have found empathy more important in my private life. With empathy you are able to put yourself in the position of another and imagine what you would feel if you were in the other person's shoes. You get a feeling for others and this has improved the way I relate with my family".

"Understanding myself has made me appreciate my weaknesses, which I strive to improve, but it has also made me appreciate why I need to work with other people to do the things that I cannot do well".

"I have come to understand that sometimes I appear rude to others but when I reflect, I put myself in the other's shoes and I imagine what it feels. This has given me another view of how to relate with other people better".

---

empathy and social skills focus on understanding personal characteristics for enhancing individual and team performance in an organisational set-up. Social life (as argued by Emile Durkheim and many others following his lead, *cf.* Bellah [2005]) is intrinsically performative; every human being aspires to be recognised as a performer in whatever they do. Emotional intelligence then induces self-reflection on the extent to which personal characteristics are oriented towards effective performance. The Johari window and feedback are tools that one can use to increase emotional intelligence.

Contextualisation of these concepts and tools and their immediate application enhanced internalisation and appreciation through critical self-examination. Self-awareness however, does not just come automatically. It is a quality that has to be developed and nurtured in a particular context. As one of the participants said:

> "This was not my first time to hear about Johari window but the way it was introduced and applied here made me understand why I do things in certain ways and why other people also do things differently. It challenged me to understand myself more".

The underlying message behind self-awareness is that *"if you want to change others, you must first change yourself."* Training, research and development are all about influencing social and technical change – implying that those engaged in such processes need to reflect on their values and their thinking to change themselves in order to influence others to change. Self-awareness is the precursor for critical reflection. We cannot critically reflect on an assumption until we are aware of it, we cannot engage in discourse on something we have not identified, and we cannot change a habit of mind without thinking about it in some way (Cranton, 2002). Reflection is a key competence for influencing learning and development, but often taken for granted. It is always assumed that everybody can reflect, but doing so for purposes of life-long learning requires some guiding principles.

Social relationships are part of living, especially given the "dense" collective tendencies of most African societies. This density partly explains why aspects that enhance relationships generated high motivation for immediate application among lecturers in an African institution. In this context, therefore, social cohesion and empathy are among the most important values influencing learning and change. Unfortunately, however, formal Western education systems, first superimposed on many of these societies by colonialism, do not pay much attention to social density. In one of the learning workshops, a participant put this very clearly:

> "What we are learning in these workshops are very important things in our everyday living which are never taught in our education system".

Putting it another way, our education system misses out some critical virtues that ought to be integrated within it. Specifying in what respects, or to what extent, African social life differs from social life in other continents is a topic that has vexed social anthropologists and African politicians. Concepts such as "African socialism" are now held in low regard, and have been replaced by the emphasis (especially by donors) on more congenial (but perhaps no less incoherent) concepts such as "social capital". There is no opportunity to discuss these debates here, except to state that it is a finding of this study (and many others) that when standard Western institutions are imposed in African setting many participants feel something vital is missing. That African intellectuals need to engage further on this topic is clear, and it is a theme picked up again in the concluding chapter, under the heading of authenticity.

Influencing change from within through feedback

Feedback is another concept that was picked up and applied immediately. Giving personal feedback that is intended to enhance personal growth and improvement of systems was very exciting to all the participants. It is a tool to understand oneself better through other people; the idea is well captured in the South African proverb *"you are what you are because of what others say you are"*. The guidelines for giving personal feedback challenge one to analyze the characteristics of the other person from both ends – the positive and negative. Usually, people tend to focus on only negative things in others, which is often demoralizing and provocative of defensive tendencies. Like one of the participants commented:

> "All along, I have known feedback as negative, but now I know it is something positive and rewarding to the person receiving it". Another one too said: "Before, I did not know how to give feedback without hurting the person receiving it. But now I can give feedback that is motivating and encouraging to the person receiving it".

Personal feedback brought in a new pathway for enhancing mutual capacities, so that the group could build on the strengths of each person to achieve a common goal. This was found relevant in all spheres of life; opening up to improve trust and relationships in families and among colleagues, building a non-threatening relationship with students for interactive learning in teaching, and building a more effective and transparent system where the subordinates and superiors interact in an interdependent manner in management. For feedback to be constructive, however, it is essential to ensure that the person receiving it is prepared psychologically. From experience, one participant cautioned:

> "Feedback is important but you have to make sure that the person receiving is ready for it. It is very useful if both the person giving and the one receiving appreciate its value".

Nearly everyone applied feedback in their private social life, e.g. in their families, churches and other social relations. Many examples can be cited such as:

> "Feedback has improved my relationship with my family. They now tell me a lot of things that they used not to. My daughter even writes to me letters appreciating what I discuss with her. They tell me what they like and what they do not like. This was not happening before".

While discussing the application of feedback in learning and change, it was generally concluded that feedback is also a tool for a non-confrontational way of challenging the hierarchical and power dominated cultures that suppress the freedom to explore and question conventional thinking. Learning is about exercising freedom and gaining space to explore and to challenge common knowledge. But most African cultures are so power dominated that this freedom is suppressed right from the family level and extended to the education system. One participant emphatically put it like this:

> "Feedback is not part of our culture. The families we grew in and the schools we went to are so hierarchical and do not encourage free interaction, especially with superiors, to be able to provide feedback. We do not even do it with our wives and children. We have to start building this culture now".

In African societies, children are not expected to challenge their elders as this is interpreted as mischief or being disrespectful. Similarly, subordinates are not expected to challenge their leaders. This results in a culture based on chieftaincy leadership, which stands in the way of honest and realistic feedback to the leadership. The same scenario exists in the education system, where normally students have no freedom to challenge their teachers. The teacher is supposed to know and the student is expected to listen and absorb. This is power-dominated culture is challenged by feedback to create a favorable environment for discovery learning. The case in Box 9 illustrates how feedback worked with superiors.

Box 9: Inducing change through feedback.

A group of participants analyzed the challenges of their Faculty and made an appointment to meet and discuss with their Dean. They started by giving feedback to their Dean recognizing the positive things that he had done and also highlighting the challenges that the Faculty faced. They suggested what they could do to support him to deal with those challenges. In this experience, the Dean felt overwhelmed that since he became Dean several years ago nobody had ever come to his office to appreciate his efforts and offer themselves to help in dealing with the problems that there were. "He said, everybody who comes to my office comes with a problem for me to solve and nobody comes with solutions to any problem". He committed some funds for this group to organize and facilitate a meeting with other members of staff including all heads of departments to brainstorm on the challenges and possible ways of dealing with them. A one-day meeting was organized and facilitated by the group. The key outcome of the meeting was shared responsibility for the challenges, and commitment collectively to deal with the challenges. This impressed the Dean so much that he was challenged to commit funds for a 3-day workshop to expose more staff in the Faculty to the important aspects of the PM/SS programme.

Application of feedback in teaching yielded positive results too. It dissolves the communication barrier between students and lecturers, allowing for the two to interact more freely and for mutual exchange of knowledge and information. Feedback provides space for students to share their problems, suggests improvement in delivery approaches, and in general co-creates an environment for better learning. Box 10 provides some impressions from the lecturers on how feedback worked in their interaction with students.

The independent assessment team also reported that lecturers proactively sought the opinions of students and colleagues for the purpose of improving their teaching methods. At the beginning of a course the lecturers explored students' expectations and attempted to adjust the course structure to accommodate students' learning interests. For the purpose of improving effectiveness in teaching, the lectures proactively sought honest feedback from students about their teaching styles in a non-intimidating manner. For the same reason, some lecturers invited peers to sit in on their classes to give them constructive feedback to help enhance their teaching skills.

Feedback creates the space and freedom for dialogue between students and lecturers to improve a system for effective learning. After interviewing the lecturers and some students, the independent assessment team recognized emergence of a feedback culture that encouraged students to give critical and constructive feedback about their learning without fear of being reprimanded. This was seen as a desirable move to address a general concern from students that the system does not provide opportunities for critical feedback. There are no functional mechanisms for students to give feedback to influence how they are taught. Feedback improved student-lecturer interactions, which benefited students through more consultations with their lecturers, especially with respect to research projects supervision.

Taking initiative to work in teams and promote peer learning

Greater appreciation of teamwork arose from continuous engagement in group activities throughout the learning programme. Peer learning as a pillar of the programme (see Figure 12) deepened the team spirit by providing a platform for continued mutual learning outside the learning workshops. As one participant put it:

Box 10: Experiences of feedback with students.

"When I introduced feedback with students, they opened up and started telling me all their problems, including their fears with lecturers".

"I have developed a good relationship with students and the number of students coming to consult me has increased tremendously. I suppose this is because of the way I now treat them".

"In teaching I use feedback at two levels: first is between me and students and the other level I encourage students to give each other feedback. It has narrowed the gap between me and the students that on one occasion a student challenged me to explain why other lecturers cannot give constructive feedback".

Learning to make change

> "The training introduced the aspect of peer learning, which I found very useful. I learnt to consult more with colleagues to learn from their experiences. In addition to learning from peers, you also develop brotherly relationships. I feel very close to the colleagues in my peer learning group".

Appreciation of the value of teamwork is the trigger for seeking complementarity through multidisciplinary approaches. It promotes co-operative inquiry – a way of working with other people with similar interests to increase self-awareness, to develop creativity to look at things differently, and to learn to change the world around oneself, and increase one's performance (Heron and Reason, 2001). The independent assessment team found that the lecturers were working more in teams across disciplines/faculties as a result of the relationships established during the PM/SS programme. They also encouraged teamwork and peer learning among students through group assignments where students explore their own learning. The lecturers then facilitated the exchange of knowledge and experiences across groups. This mode of learning widened student interaction with other disciplines as they searched for learning materials from other faculties. As such it represents the beginning of a more holistic type of learning that builds linkages across disciplines.

Although in most cases the peer learning did not function in a formal way, based on scheduled meetings for reflection and sharing experiences, as was planned. Instead it took a different form – informal consultations and exchange, even across peer learning groups. For peer support and sharing expertise, participants preferred to work with colleagues in small consultancy activities, such as facilitating workshops. Reflecting on this trend, one participant affirmed that:

> "Before we came to this learning programme, we worked as individuals but now we work together, even in writing proposals and supervision of students".

This signifies a shift from purely individual activity to teamwork as an internalised value for effectiveness and efficiency. This is likely to influence a tendency towards partnerships, and ensure beneficial impact on training, research and consultancy activity.

Facilitation skills for interactive learning and collective action processes

The PM/SS was built around an assumption that facilitation skills are the key that opens the door for new forms of interaction with people. Skills in facilitation were widely applied in teaching, workshops/meetings and other social interactions such as in church life. Practicing facilitation was an integral component of all activities of the learning programme. This served not only to build confidence in its application in teaching but facilitation capacity was also seen as a marketable skill, especially in process-oriented consultancy, where donors place great stress on impact and participation of citizens. The classroom therefore provided a safe environment for practicing facilitation to gain experience and confidence. It should perhaps be added that what the development practitioners tend to call facilitation is quite widely practised in universities where teaching is by seminars as well as lectures, but that seminar skills tend not to have flourished in the African university due both to the power relationship implicit in lecturing (as mentioned above) but also due to weight of numbers. Facilitation is labour intensive, and requires a better staff-student ratio than commonly met with in the African university setting. This is a point which is reverted to below and in the conclusion of this thesis. Box 11 presents some experiences of facilitative teaching.

Through a more facilitative approach to teaching, lecturers came to realize that students were also a source of knowledge to be utilized in teaching and learning. At the same time they came to see themselves more as co-learners and not as the sole authority of knowledge. Mezirow (1997) emphasizes the educator functions as a facilitator and provocateur rather than as an absolute authority. Ideally, the facilitator tries to escape the authority role by becoming a co-learner progressively transferring her/his leadership to the group, allowing for the group to become more self-directive. The force of the word "ideally" should be noted. Critiques have drawn attention to some of the complexity of the role (*cf.* Richards, 1995; Mosse, 2005), and attention needs to be paid in developing the PM/SS approach to the need for best practice rules to be adopted. Support factors for such "best practice" interaction include personal feedback generating dialogue and free exchange of ideas.

Box 11: Experiences of facilitating interactive learning.

"I now have a wide range of tools for teaching. You see all these (while pointing to a pile of charts and cards), I use them in my classes. I have introduced group discussions in my class and when I shared my experiences with my colleagues in the department, some of them adopted the approach in their classes too. One professor for example invited me to his class to witness how the group discussion innovation made the teaching more interesting. I engage students to think beyond the course to imagine how they would apply knowledge acquired from the course in their future careers. This enables me to develop learning goals together with students...."

"Since I introduced group discussion and presentations in class, students have gained confidence to express themselves and argue issues. They now feel free to ask questions. Indeed one student confessed: *I have always dodged asking or answering questions in class, it is only in this class that I have felt confident to talk.* This is basically because I put it clearly right at the beginning that learning is two way and that we can only learn from each other if we interact freely".

"…. It is even more interesting with students who have some field experience. I have made students generate knowledge from which I also learn a lot. This is a shift from when I was the sole deliverer of knowledge and students were on the receiving end. I use a lot of questioning to stimulate thinking and sharing experiences, in the process, students also ask a lot of questions, which never used to happen before".

"I am very different in teaching. I used to go to class and dictate notes to students, but now I facilitate a lot of discussions. The students bring in a lot of new information and this forces me to read more about the subject".

"My teaching is still instructive but I have introduced some group work and the students contribute more in class than before".

Facilitation skills had profound influence on teaching styles. The engagement in facilitation led to the conceptualisation of an operational framework for interactive learning in this context. The emergent framework is presented as a learning wheel (Figure 18). The learning wheel methodology was developed earlier by Hagmann (2005) to generate experience-based conceptual frameworks from practice. It builds on the lessons and success factors of practical case examples in an appreciative manner. The cornerstones of the learning wheel are fundamental to successful systemic interventions. In this sense, it serves as a checklist which can also be used for self-reflection and evaluation. The cornerstones are those things that have to be in place to make interactive learning possible in this particular context. The learning wheel is both a conceptual and operational framework for putting interactive learning in practice.

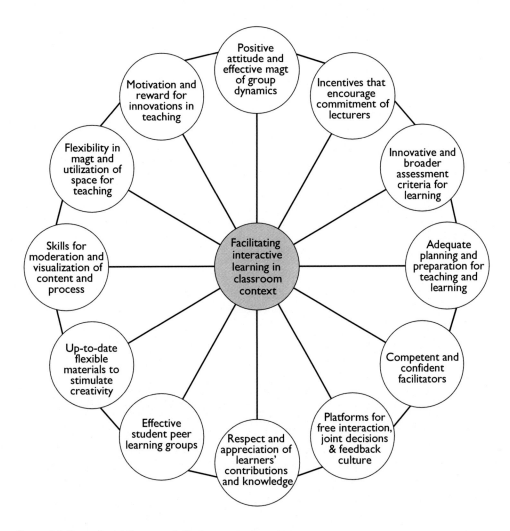

Figure 18: Operational framework for interactive learning.

Based on practice experience in facilitating interactive learning, twelve success factors were distilled (by the programme participants) for interactive learning in this particular context of Makerere University:

- A positive attitude towards interactive learning and an ability to effectively manage group dynamics. A positive attitude is needed both from lecturers and the students.
- Incentives that encourage commitment of lecturers. Interactive learning takes more time in preparation and to continue doing so requires a relatively high level of job satisfaction. This takes into account staff remuneration and welfare.
- Innovative and broader assessment of the learning. For the learners to be appropriately rewarded from interactive learning, the assessment has to go beyond memorisation of knowledge to the analytical and application levels. Also a variety of tools and methods of assessment is required including peer assessment. Without these, it becomes irrelevant in terms of its contribution to academic achievement.
- Adequate planning and preparation for teaching and learning. Effective interactive learning within the limited time allocation for a course, demands good planning and preparation for both the lecturers and students.
- Competent and confident facilitators. Competence here refers to both a sufficient grasp of the subject matter and adequate process management. The facilitator must also be confident enough to deal with unanticipated issues without getting disoriented.
- Platforms for free interaction, joint decision making and conducive to a feedback culture. Dialogue and feedback between students and lecturers set the benchmarks for interactive learning.
- Respect and appreciation of learners' contributions and knowledge. Recognition that learners are a resource of their own learning creates the space and confidence to share experiences and knowledge.
- Effective student peer learning groups. These have to be initiated and nurtured as platforms for peer exchanges. Group work is necessary as it advances communication skills, reinforces the importance of citizen participation, creates meaningful learning situations for students, utilises the interests, creativity and curiosity of students. In diverse groups, it also triggers intra-group dissonance which can become a source of conceptual change (Wals *et al.,* 2004).
- Up-to-date and flexible learning materials that stimulate creativity. Availability and access to materials in different forms that can be shared for self-learning, peer-learning as well as instructional learning.
- Skills for moderation, synthesis and visualisation of process and content. Ability to bring things together with clear linkages and relationships is extremely important. This is aided by good visualisation to create a mental picture of how things are connected.
- Flexibility in management and utilisation of space for learning. Flexible sitting arrangements that allow interaction amongst students create an ideal environment for interactive learning. Similarly, the class size has to be manageable for effective learning.
- Motivation and reward for innovation in teaching. If the lecturers are to invest their time and creativity in interactive learning, it has to contribute significantly to their career advancement. At the moment, publications are the single most important factor for

promotion. Objective indicators of the impact of publications – e.g. citations on Google scholar – seem easier to devise than objective indicators of teaching impact and excellence. This creates a disincentive for improving teaching.

Beyond teaching, many of the lecturers who participated in the PM/SS programme, including the present writer (see Appendix 1), have taken on facilitation and process documentation as a new direction of professional to supplement their meagre income from the university. In affirming this, one participant testified:

> "I can surely say that since I completed the PM/SS programme, I do not entirely depend on my salary like before. In fact I can survive without it. With the facilitation skills I have acquired, I can supplement my salary to have a decent life".

Demand for quality facilitation is high within and outside the university. Opportunities for the lecturers to be hired to facilitate meetings, workshops and other platforms for multi-stakeholder engagement motivated them to practice facilitation skills in class as a training ground. It could be argued that this is only sustainable while donors and development agencies maintain their enthusiasm for workshops and other discursive modes of popular participation, but meanwhile it has the definite advantage that the quality of university teachers to teach is improved, while at the same time others benefit from this enhanced level of skill when lecturers work outside the university.

Overcoming fear to try out new things as reflective practitioners

The concept of life-long learning is based on the ability to reflect and learn from our actions. Fear of failure is a major hindrance to progress in pursuing our personal and organizational goals. This fear is sometimes overwhelming among academics because of their "expert" mental models. This limits their space for exploration in complex and unpredictable situations. Overcoming fear is a precondition for developing the adaptive capacity that drives innovations and entrepreneurship.

A reflective practitioner is one who consciously engages in dialogue between the thinking that attaches to actions and the thinking that deals in more abstracted propositional knowledge (Harvey and Knight, 1996). The iterative and reflective nature of the PM/SS programme allowed participants to re-examine whatever they did and draw lessons from various experiences, and stimulated the consciousness for reflective practice. Reflection is also a mechanism for self-control as it permits re-examination of one's own actions, values and thoughts with a view to identifying alternative options. One of the participants summarized its value in this way:

> "Personal reflection allows you to take a step back to examine and critique why and how you do things for purposes of improving your performance. It also brings in a sense of

responsibility for your own behaviours and practices to see where you go wrong rather than blame others for your own weaknesses".

The positive attitude towards learning from experience and social support for reflective practice increased the confidence and courage to dare to try out new things. Social support here means a group of people willing to help each other to learn from their experiences, including their failures, without feeling embarrassed. With a reasonable level of self-positioning, they developed a sense of security to take on challenging tasks, such as providing leadership in strategic planning and managing contentious meetings in and outside their units.

Enhancing communication for problem solving

Through analysis of the various exercises on conflict management, negotiation and consensus building it was discovered that active listening is the core of effective communication for problem solving. Unfortunately listening is an aspect of communication that is often taken for granted. Lecturers are taught to speak in public and practice to perfect articulation of ideas, but there is less emphasis on being taught to listen (except, of course, "listening" to lectures and the careful critical dissection of written statements). On realizing the value of active listening in one of the workshops, a participant lamented:

> "Usually it is those who speak eloquently that are recognized and considered talented but those who actively listen to understand their opinions are never recognized!"

There is no public incentive for active listening and yet it is critical in learning and problem solving. In nearly all interviews, learning to listen actively was specifically mentioned as a benefit from the PM/SS programme. It is active listening that makes two-way communication effective. Therefore operationalising interactive learning, providing feedback and conducting action research requires that lecturers learn to listen actively. Only through active listening do we understand and appreciate different opinions even if we do not agree with them. This is very critical in conflict resolution, negotiation and consensus building processes.

Listening is also a way of controlling our power to provide space for others to participate. When we listen, we are also giving a chance to others to contribute. As discussed earlier, learning is a participative process that is very much influenced by power relations. By virtue of their position, lecturers (or teachers) have more power in the lecturer-student relationship. If the lecturers have to learn from this relationship, they have to learn to listen. Theoretically it sounds unimportant, but in reality it has a big impact on the learning transaction.

Thinking "out of the box" to influence development impact through action research and process consultancy

In specialized technical training we tend to limit our view of the world within the confines of our disciplines. The imaginary boundaries of our disciplines are even more emphasized in a university context. In the university, even departments within the same faculty tend to exist as "silos" with little to share functionally. Coming from this background of disciplinary independence, exposure to systems thinking and social change phenomena opened a window to programme participants to look at the world in a new light. Reflecting on the impact of their research, for example, the participants began to see the inadequacies of their disciplinary approach in influencing visible change in society. The dynamics of change in social systems challenged their perceptions of the role of "change agents". Examples of change processes within the university, such as the attempted merger of five units (*i.e.* Faculties of Agriculture; Veterinary Medicine; Forestry and Nature Conservation; Institute of Environment and Natural Resources and Department of Fisheries and Aquaculture) into a college under the initiative code-named "Plan-4-five," were used to demonstrate complexity in social systems[2]. Such real-life examples enhanced interest in alternative approaches to influence change in social systems. It also challenged the participants to contextualize their disciplines in a systems perspective. In this respect, one of them reported:

> "Beyond the subject matter, I take some time to discuss with students other issues that would make them more effective in the field. Through such discussions, I am compiling a list of challenges that the students anticipate in their career so that I can integrate them in the learning in the future".

This is a starting point in developing a vision for curriculum review. The lecturers gain clarity on what else is important beyond specialist subject matter. With this realization, an integrated curriculum can then be pursued.

One way of integrating disciplines in a systems perspective is through action research and process consultancy. These two were the "carrot" in the learning programme, around which participants worked intensively.

Action research

The systems perspective made it clear that influencing change in society either through research or service delivery required a new form of engagement. As one of the participants put it:

> "Understanding the dynamics of systems and social system change helped me to see how we can influence change in communities through research. To me this is particularly important in the research that I am engaged in currently".

Linking real-life challenges and systems thinking laid the foundation for an appreciation of action research as an approach to increase the impact of research in communities. Amidst the challenge from donors and government for the university to demonstrate the relevance of its research in development, action research provided a plausible option. It also presented

---

[2] The process to merge the five units into one college has apparently stalled due to insufficient consultations, transparency and consensus leading to suspicions of hidden agendas among the partners. To some of the partners, the change was seen as an unnecessary imposition.

opportunities for the lecturers to access research funds, as many funding agencies were getting more concerned about impact and sustainability. Based on experiences in research an operational framework for action research was developed (Figure 19).

The framework is composed of the following cornerstones (*i.e.* what needs to be in place, developed or considered):

- Competent, committed and interdisciplinary research teams taking into account the technical and social dimensions of the research.
- Farmer experimentation and innovation capacity for active farmer participation in the research. This involves recognition of farmer innovations as well as creating the curiosity and confidence for farmers to experiment and innovate.

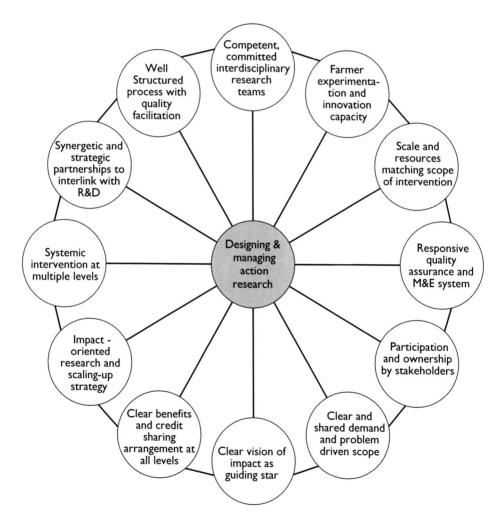

Figure 19: Framework for putting action research into practice.

- Operational scale and resources matching scope of intervention. Realistically plan and allocate resources bearing in mind the scope of systemic intervention. Starting with pilots offers lessons and realistic estimates for scaling up.
- Responsive quality assurance and monitoring and evaluation system. Joint reflections to assess progress in view of anticipated impact and participatory impact assessment are integral components of the quality assurance system.
- Participation and ownership by stakeholders. Inclusiveness of all stakeholders, clarity of roles and responsibility and credible accountability systems enhance ownership, efficiency and sustainability.
- Clear and shared demand and problem driven scope. Informed problem definition with stakeholders in the context of strategic development goals.
- Clear vision of impact as guiding star. Vision and clearly defined impacts determine the strategy. Flexibility of strategy is a critical success factor.
- Fair benefit and credit sharing arrangement at all levels. Sustained multi-stakeholder engagement to a great extent depends on level of consensus on sharing of both the tangible and intangible benefits of the research.
- Consistent impact-oriented research strategy with clear research questions and scaling up perspective.
- Systemic intervention at multiple levels. Appropriately dealing with complexities in the system including the social and political dynamics.
- Synergetic and strategic partnerships to interlink research and development – utilizing existing networks and building new ones.
- Well structured action learning/research process with quality facilitation and feedback mechanisms.

This operational framework provides guidelines for designing and implementing action research. Since this emerged out of participants' own experience and conceptual thinking, the guidelines offer a pathway for doing research differently. The important thing is to be aware of all the aspects (cornerstones) as a check for design and implementation. They do not all have to be in place at the same time but the most critical ones are identified and worked on first as others are tackled along the way.

Process-oriented consultancy

Like action research, process consultancy was of high interest, as it offers direct benefits to individuals. In comparison to the most common short-term expert type of consultancy, process consultancy presented better opportunities. The skills gained in the PM/SS programme were needed to get into a new form of consulting. The curiosity and interest in this area culminated in a conceptual framework for managing an effective process consultancy in form of a learning wheel (Figure 20). The cornerstones are self-explanatory, and simply present a checklist of what is required to manage an effective process consultancy.

Conceptualizing this from experience and new exposure depicts new thinking and a new approach towards consultancy directed towards impact in a systemic perspective. This horizon

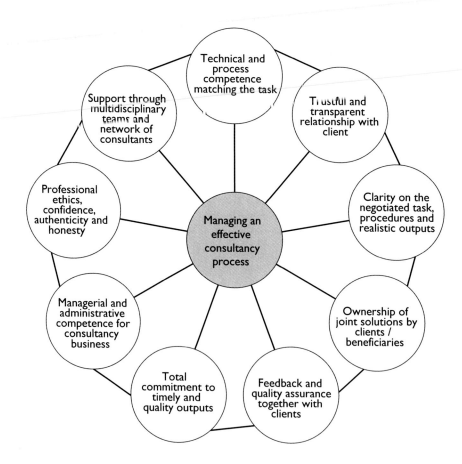

Figure 20: Framework for managing effective consultancy.

of thinking supported by acquired skills in facilitation, action research, and work on inter-personal relations and communication make the lecturers a new breed of consultants highly in demand in development type consulting. For example, the African Highland Initiative, a member of the CGIAR, preferentially sought consulting services from the "Win26" group to support setting up a communication and information centre for a community in Kabale District (see Box 12).

Such experiences spot-light the value of skills for systemic interventions through research and consultancy. It is these types of engagements that increase the visibility of the university on the development scene. They illustrate the need to develop and mainstream such competences in the university system, starting with the lecturers.

Box 12: The AHI Acacia project.

The African Highlands Initiative (AHI), a regional research program of ASARECA, works where the people and landscapes in the densely populated highlands of Eastern Africa are under pressure. In doing so AHI articulated their challenges as:

- Under-utilized potential of local people to manage their resources sustainably and to articulate their demands.
- Conventional research approaches that are not addressing complexity of NRM and the real demands arising from local levels.
- Limited capacity of researchers and their organizations and policy makers to respond to challenges of working in an integrated, participatory manner.

The objective of the Acacia project was to develop a system and strategies for improving flows of information in rural communities to support enterprise development, natural resource management, and well-being. Specifically, the project intended to: (i) design and test improved communication and information support to key initiatives, programs and schools that are providing support to community development, (ii) catalyze the formulation of a local development communication *"community of practice"* partnership, (iii) expand the community and service provider capacity to manage information related to enterprise development and NRM, and (iv) monitor, document and widely share lessons learned.

The management of AHI contacted "Win 26" to provide consultancy support to this project. Within the guidelines for a process consultancy framework, the group then responded with a proposal that made the AHI management defend their preferential choice of consultants before their donors as opposed to open bidding. Basing on their experience and knowledge of consultancy firms, management argued that the process skills required in this type of work were rare to find in local firms. Two lecturers were entrusted by their colleagues to lead this consultancy.

Developing a culture of commitment and integrity

Based on participants' observations there were indications of higher commitment, elevated passion for work and an increased desire to build a legacy of integrity. This seems to be an outcome of the interaction of many factors, but responses suggested two main ones:

First there is the development of empathetic feelings. By challenging their own values and practices, participants developed more dedication to work, including volunteering to take on assignments on behalf of their units. A participant who has now moved into an administrative position explained how she sacrifices her time for the sake of giving the best of her services because she is empathetic to those she serves. Similarly, others said they now attend to their students more because they can imagine how it would feel if they were the students. Some of the managers acknowledged this commitment and dedication. A Dean of Faculty for example assented to assigning more tasks to staff from this programme because he was confident they would deliver. Though he seemed to doubt whether others would do the same if they went through the programme (implicitly, he wonders whether the early participants are somehow already more motivated than the general cohort) he acknowledged a difference in those who attended the programme.

A second explanation can be found in the challenge to be exemplary, and to live by example. Many said that on one hand, some of their colleagues perceived them as role models for transformation, while on the other hand they recognized envy, jealousy and suspicion from others. Peer pressure to uphold the impression of being exemplary inspired commitment, passion for work and a desire to build a legacy of integrity. Unconsciously, this also demonstrated leadership qualities which, indeed, some have very well used to propel themselves into leadership positions. Within the period of 1½ years, four participants acquired administrative positions – successes that they strongly associate with personalities and skills gained from the PM/SS programme, though it might also have been due to the attention they attracted to themselves as programme pioneers. These are a 'new breed' of leaders with a different view (from the conventional) of how to improve teaching and research in the university. Their leadership positions therefore present opportunities to more widely influence innovations in the university teaching and research. However, it is a problem to be overcome in subsequent up-scaling to ensure that these pioneers are not seen as in any way an elite treading a special path inaccessible to the rank-and-file. In this respect the *esprit de corps* of 'Win26' might prove a two-edged sword.

Challenges for enhancing and sustaining impact of the PM/SS programme

The outcomes described above did not happen without challenges. The challenges of designing such a competence development programme were already discussed in chapter five. Here the focus is on challenges for enhancing and sustaining the impact of the PM/SS programme. These challenges are particularly related to institutional factors and perceptions.

Challenges in the institutional environment

Challenges related to the context in which the learning was applied include:

Inadequate infrastructure and resources to support interactive learning
Interactive learning necessitates access to a variety of materials and tools for visualization and contextualization. As teaching in the university is largely lecture-based, simple materials, such as flip-charts, manila cards, and marker pens that aid visualization, were not easily available when needed by the lecturers. Requests for such materials by lecturers were sometimes perceived by administrators as deviation from the "normal". The normal is the lecture, and in some cases lecturers needed to justify why they needed "unique" materials by comparison with their colleagues.

Effective lecturer-student and student-student interaction requires a flexible classroom set-up where it is possible to rearrange the seating according to need. The set-up of "lecture theatres" is inflexible, with fixed seats – making it difficult to organize group exercises within the class. This is exacerbated by the ever increasing student numbers. Some classes, for example in Faculty of Agriculture, are attended by well over 250 students, and in the humanities these numbers can more than double. Such increases have not been matched by corresponding increases in facilities and staffing levels. Even with good intentions, efforts at interactive learning are frustrated by these adverse conditions. Indeed interactive teaching was practiced more in relatively small classes. As noted above, facilitative (i.e. seminar) styles of teaching (and advocates of their virtues!) are generally more likely to be encountered in richer institutions.

Inappropriate reward system for competence

The motivation for enhancing individual performance is related to the incentives that the system attaches to performance. Just being a good lecturer is not a strong incentive, since career growth is, as pointed out earlier, principally based on publications and not on how well one teaches (Harvey and Knight, *ibid.*). The attitude easily becomes one of "who cares if I can't teach well, as long as I can publish and be promoted!" Capabilities for teaching are not even among the key criteria for staff recruitment. The lecturers come in through what Cranton and King (2003) call a circuitous route, one that does not include training on how to teach. The most critical measure of academic abilities for staff recruitment is the class of first degree, possession of higher degrees, e.g. Masters and PhD, and publications. The value of teaching competence is less significant compared to these other criteria, though North American and British universities frequently request a seminar or teaching performance as part of an extended job assessment process. Much low wages and higher staff shortages mean that few African universities can afford to be so picky. Moreover, teaching competence as a component of staff development lags behind emphasis on other skills, e.g. facilitation skills for participatory learning. To encourage acquisition and application of new competences in teaching, teaching abilities must be more appropriately rewarded than by the occasional award of a teaching prize in some universities. African universities need now to take on board the practice of some British and other universities in awarding salary increments for teaching competence.

Lack of mechanisms for students to influence the learning

In a system that promotes interactive learning, the students, lecturers and management have to recognize each other as partners with a stake in a shared system, and collectively seek to improve its efficiency and effectiveness. The learning is not only for the students but also for the system to adjust accordingly. However, the African university system as it is today treats students largely as repositories of knowledge. Consequently there are no functional mechanisms for students to make an input into their learning. While students are enthusiastic to provide feedback on the way they are taught and the relevance of their academic programs, there is no mechanism for doing so, and even if there was there is no requirement in sight to ensure that students' opinions have any bearing on the staff performance appraisal. A feedback culture has to be supported by mechanisms that have consequence for the way the system functions. It is only then that students can be regarded as active partners in the learning process.

Fragmentation of curricula based on disciplines

Disciplinary disconnects in the curriculum do not enable learning to be embedded within its context, to enable students to see how different bodies of knowledge relate and complement each other in reality. These kinds of curricula lack rhythmic engagement with complex external problems requiring synergies and complementarities between disciplines. Therefore integrating systemic thinking in such curricula is difficult, as emphasis is normally on the depth of content rather than its breadth. Competence-based learning is not only about approaches and methods but also has a lot to do with a curriculum design that offers space and encouragement to lateral thinking as well.

Changing institutional cultures and practices to promote innovation

Entrenched institutional cultures and power structures of control limit the space and freedom for innovation, especially if the innovation comes from those who hold less power. One such culture is that of lecturing – a reason it is more common to refer to university academic staff as "lecturers" and "professors" and not as teachers. The main professional union for British lecturers is in fact the Association of University Teachers, but in the African setting the notion of lecturing as something different from teaching has become reified. I had a discussion on this with senior professors in my Faculty over coffee, and they asserted that they are meant to lecture and not to teach. They argued specifically that they do not require competence in teaching because they are lecturers not teachers. By reminding them that "a lecture is just a method of teaching" and challenging them to think about what it is that they want to influence through lecturing one of them came to me a week later saying *"I now seem to agree with you. We need to re-examine some of these labels we have carried for long"*.

This partly explains why the ability to teach is not emphasized in recruitment and staff development in Makerere University. Lecturing is regarded as an end in itself rather than as a means. Those who attempt innovative teaching may be considered a misfit in the academic society. Clearly the attitude is premised on notions of power and control in which challenge from below is interpreted as a challenge to due authority. The fear/insecurity of challenging authority creates tension leading to defensive responses that suffocate innovation. Promoting innovations in the African university, therefore, requires supportive and visionary leadership capable of and willing to challenge institutional cultures reinforcing rigidity and conservatism.

Challenges of perceptions

The challenges related to orientation of the mind include:

Changing student attitudes and stereotypes in learning styles

Change in attitudes to support discovery learning or life-long learning is required for both lecturers and students. As the lecturers strive to change their teaching methods, students too have to change their attitudes on what their role is in a learning process. The entire Ugandan education system is characterized by stereotypes of dependence - a "spoon-feeding syndrome".

The teacher is regarded as the sole source of knowledge and determines what the students should learn and how they should learn it. All that the students have to do is to get ready with their pens and paper to write down as much as the teacher can give – a stereotype carried over into the university as well.

From this background, introducing learning approaches for exploring issues and developing critical thinking appear strange to some students, and are sometimes interpreted as evidence of a teacher's lack of command of the subject matter. The mindset is that of "receive and give back" rather than "give and take" or, better yet, "give, take and co-create". The latter two fit interactive learning processes of joint exploration to develop critical thinking, whereas the former encourages students to absorb from the teacher as much as possible and give it back to the teacher during examination. As some lecturers reported, some students perceived interactive learning as lack of command in the subject matter on part of the lecturers. It takes time, persistency and large scale application of interactive learning approaches to change this mindset.

Suspicion of the change itself

During the PM/SS programme a team spirit across faculties emerged among the participants. As this was not a common phenomenon, it aroused suspicion from colleagues about what PM/SS was all about. Initiatives to create awareness about the programme in some instances evoked old rivalries between faculties, further deepening suspicions that "hidden" agendas were at work. The skeptical ones likened it to a "club" or sodality whose agenda was not well understood to non-initiates. On a few occasions it raised the question of how the participants in the programme were selected. Such reactions are normal to change in social systems but they create tensions and fear among the pioneers of change. The benefits to the individuals, however, helped to diffuse these tensions and fears, as exemplified by the high interest to participate in the scaling up of the PM/SS programme.

Tension of being role models versus jealousy

On one hand, those who appreciated the impact of the PM/SS programme so far held high expectations from the participants of the programme as role models. Such expectations especially from their managers usually translated into more responsibilities assigned to them. On the other hand, some people felt jealousy. A discussion on how to manage the tension between being a role model and jealousy at being one of the privileged few led to conceptualizing a framework for countering the culture of jealousy, envy suspicion and gossip (see Figure 21).

The cornerstones in this framework illustrate the practical aspects of creating a performance culture.

- Need to be aware of jealousy, suspicion, envy and gossip, and need for mechanisms to counter it.
- Importance of appreciative and solution-oriented attitudes promoting fairness, trust, and recognition of people's contributions.
- Culture of transparency and feedback promoting free interaction, sharing of ideas and accountability at all levels.

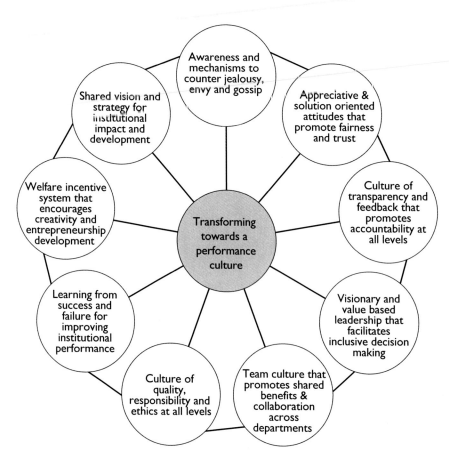

Figure 21: Conceptual framework for transforming the culture of jealousy, envy, suspicion and gossip into a confidence-based performance culture.

- Visionary, service-oriented, value based leadership facilitating inclusive decision-making and nurturing personal and professional growth of staff.
- Shared vision and strategy for institutional impact and development.
- Team culture promoting shared benefits, peer learning and collaboration across departments, faculties and Universities.
- Ensuring quality, responsibility and ethics at all levels of the institution.
- Performance and welfare incentive system that encourages creativity, innovation and development of entrepreneurship potentials.
- Continuous learning from success and failures for improving institutional performance and culture.

But one other point needs to be addressed. Change often does require the club-like bonding of a change-oriented elite. In other words, the suspicion of outsiders is perhaps well-justified. In such circumstances it is essential to take steps to ensure that the changes are translated as soon as possible into general benefits, rather than becoming the basis for the continued privilege of a few. The entire development "industry" needs reform in this regard, since highly-paid international change agents are generally tasked with ensuring a few emblematic successes before handing over "up-scaling" to nationals, on much less favourable terms. Other studies parallel to this thesis will draw detailed attention to this intrinsic challenge to up-scaling, but here it is appropriate to state that jealousy rapidly spreads unless steps are taken not only to counteract misinformation but also to extend the benefits to the larger target group as quickly as possible.

The outcomes presented in this chapter imply a diversity of competences cutting across personal, group and organizational boundaries. The intention is to relate these competences with the competence gaps discussed in chapter four in view of the functions for agricultural professionals highlighted in chapter three. The concluding chapter builds on this relationship and expounds on generic innovation competences in the university that can be associated with the PM/SS learning programme. These competences are discussed in relation to the challenges of universities to enhance their direct contributions in the development arena, and simultaneously to bridge between university and society.

CHAPTER EIGHT

Discussion and conclusions: towards a new African university for the 21st century

Towards innovation competence for development

In addition to providing education and training, universities are also expected to influence change in society through research and outreach, consultancy included. Correspondingly, if universities in Africa are to reproduce, maintain and enhance their position as centres of excellence, then their staff must actively become involved in re-inventing their institutions as places contributing to the current demands of a contemporary client group. Without radical moves, universities in Africa risk becoming – rightly – obsolete in the face of the huge challenges posed by poverty and international commitments such as the Millennium Development Goals. An assumption underlying this research is that universities will remain prominent centres for human resource development to which society looks for solutions to complex problems. This complexity arises out of the fused multi-dimensional characteristics of social and development problems, yet universities, as has been argued in Chapter 1, tend to address these problems as if they were well configured to be addressed by existing academic disciplines. Prior experience in sub-Saharan Africa but elsewhere as well, suggests that a narrow technological focus, as the driver of development, is unlikely to eliminate pervasive poverty and food insecurity. The challenge is not only technological, but also involves important social and political dimensions. Time and time again technology has been parachuted into farming communities without real, sustainable impact, and repeatedly it has been shown that "community" is far from being the neutral social playing field technology developers often assumed. Professionals who are likely to influence change in such situations, therefore, need to have not only technical competence in the field of agriculture but, most importantly – so this thesis has argued - the social skills for change management.

Training institutions, including universities, often respond to demand for new forms of education via curriculum reviews and/ or new academic programmes. Rarely do they think about their own competence to provide the quality of education being demanded. Education and research competence in universities is assumed, since it is a place where the most highly educated are found. The complexity of development problems facing a country like Uganda now requires universities to develop a different form of learning. Universities themselves need to learn to influence change in a complex environment. Most critical is the issue of their competence to provide training, research and outreach services that appropriately address real-life problems. The struggle to find integrated solutions through participatory, multi-disciplinary, innovation systems seems important, but universities have not yet been very effective in developing the corresponding competences neither within their own staff nor within their students. Yet, African universities are increasingly expected to take on societal and developmental functions, in addition to their academic functions. Hence there is a need to re-examine their capacity to do so.

This study has been inspired by the critical need to develop the necessary innovation competence African universities and their graduates need to become more capable in responding to development challenges in an agricultural context. The focus has been on how to transform the African university – specifically Makerere University in Uganda – to ensure greater relevance and responsiveness to the development challenges of a new century. Clearly, as the study shows, transformation involves many facets, and by no means is one able to exhaust all dimensions of transformation in a single study. The present thesis has examined transformation specifically from the perspective of learning, innovation and change in agriculture.

Competence has been treated as the capability to learn and influence learning. Innovation has been viewed as an adaptation and translation of learning into options for solving real-life problems in a complex and dynamic environment, while change has been seen as the desirable outcome of learning and innovation leading to improvement of life (or better development). Learning, as the research reiterates, is to a large degree a social phenomenon, meaning that all institutions of learning require social skills as part of package of innovation competence to be effective in influencing learning, while 'development' becomes social change based on learning. Hence, this research shows that various levels of development require the social competences for learning. This thesis points at the relevance of enhancing the capacity of agricultural professionals to activate and strengthen social learning in communities, and at the same time identifies competence gaps affecting both agricultural professionals and farmers when they engage in collaborative learning for change. It is such engagement that results into innovations that are likely to liberate farmers from poverty trap – an alternative to the failed technology transfer model. Innovation competences required at university are those that support learning and innovation for development. University lecturers must come down from the 'pulpit' for lecturing and begin to influence learning for development. This means building a relationship between competences at various levels: university, development service providers and the grass-roots community (specifically small-scale farmers, as has been shown in the Ugandan case (Chapter 3). Figure 22 provides a summary of the key elements, functions and relationships that, when holistically considered, make up innovation competence.

Competences of the agricultural professionals, as they emerged in the research, are based on their expected functions in a social learning context. In a sense, they are cross-cutting competences for influencing change in society, especially where, as in Uganda, smallholder farmers dominate the development landscape. By no means is it implied that these are the *only* competences required, nor are disciplinary specialties being devalued. The research shows primarily that additional competences are needed if technical knowledge and disciplinary know-how is to have any impact. Chapter 4 makes clear that agricultural professionals have a responsibility in facilitating the acquisition of required competences among the farmers. Not only do they need to have equivalent or complementary competences as aspects of their own performance, but they are also expected to be effective competence developers. This suggests that competences at the university level have to be at the meta-level, to ensure agricultural professionals and farmers can be linked. There is no way university lecturers can train their graduates to influence and facilitate change processes in the community when they have no idea how it can be done practically. Chapter 3 has shown that farmers innovate and change

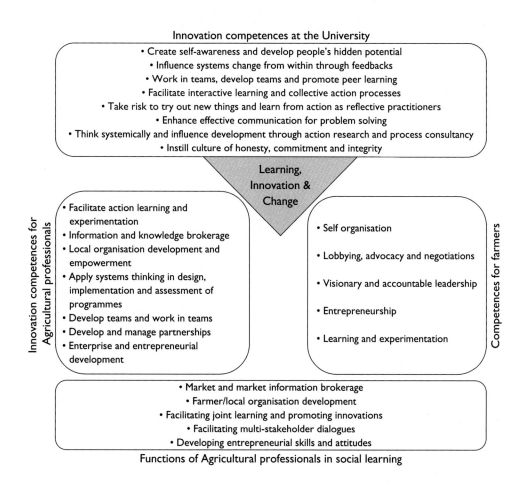

Innovation competences at the University
- Create self-awareness and develop people's hidden potential
- Influence systems change from within through feedbacks
- Work in teams, develop teams and promote peer learning
- Facilitate interactive learning and collective action processes
- Take risk to try out new things and learn from action as reflective practitioners
- Enhance effective communication for problem solving
- Think systemically and influence development through action research and process consultancy
- Instill culture of honesty, commitment and integrity

Learning, Innovation & Change

Innovation competences for Agricultural professionals
- Facilitate action learning and experimentation
- Information and knowledge brokerage
- Local organisation development and empowerment
- Apply systems thinking in design, implementation and assessment of programmes
- Develop teams and work in teams
- Develop and manage partnerships
- Enterprise and entrepreneurial development

Competences for farmers
- Self organisation
- Lobbying, advocacy and negotiations
- Visionary and accountable leadership
- Entrepreneurship
- Learning and experimentation

- Market and market information brokerage
- Farmer/local organisation development
- Facilitating joint learning and promoting innovations
- Facilitating multi-stakeholder dialogues
- Developing entrepreneurial skills and attitudes

Functions of Agricultural professionals in social learning

Figure 22: Constructing innovation competence in agriculture.

by learning from each other how things are done in real-life and that there is a wealth of knowledge within the community for the agricultural professionals to learn from to influence change. The thesis points at the importance of (a) building relationships across the different levels with regard to learning and change as individual and collective action processes, (b) inducing and managing change in social systems, (c) development of and access to tools for making change, (d) achieving solution-oriented thinking and practice, and (e) attaining to a culture of authenticity. I will briefly touch upon all five of these challenges.

Learning for change: going beyond individualism to enhancing collective action

A review of history suggests that the African university has maintained a colonial mind-frame that aimed at turning out individuals who excel at executing instructions from their colonial masters rather than creative thinkers to deal with unique problems. This is sustained by insisting on lecturing and rewarding those capable of reproducing the lectures during examination. It is evident that political independence did not fully liberate the Africans in thinking and creativity to be able to solve problems in society. Another phase is needed to 'decolonise' their mind – possibly by a reorientation of educationists to focus on learning that enables people to solve problems that exist in society as this thesis argues. The three empirical case studies featured in the research illustrate that all involved (university lecturers, researchers, extension workers and farmers) have an inherent capacity to learn, particularly with respect to what they already know or have experienced. Their learning history shapes their reference frames. How much the participants in the case studies learn depends to a large degree on how much they know about themselves and their environment. To develop people's personal learning potential, and hence their capacity to learn, has shown to be quite a challenge, but when it happens, a quantum leap in learning competence seems to take place much along the way Harri-Augstein and Webb (1995) describe in their work on self-organized learning. The competence to learn therefore cannot be taken for granted. A Chinese proverb makes the point very well, in asserting that there are three types of people:
- those who know
- those who don't know, and
- those who don't know that they don't know.

Knowing that we don't know is probably the main element of our competence to learn. This is enabled by awareness of our own behaviour and deficiencies, and in giving room to others to let us know what we are not aware of ourselves. This appeared to be a crucial step in the learning of the participants in the case studies. Once we increase our awareness of what we don't know, then we can undertake action to learn and change as individuals. Similarly we can assist others to learn by making them understand themselves better. The same applies to institutions. Chapter 5 explained how the innovation competence development initiative emerged out universities engaging with external agencies in this case, the Rockefeller Foundation to be able to see the critical gaps in training agricultural professionals who can influence reduction in poverty and food insecurity among smallholder farmers. Fundamental change for the African University to be relevant to community needs therefore requires continuous engagement with other stakeholders who can provide critical but constructive feedback to the university.

As the vanilla farmers showed, taking action to change is both an individual and a collective process. We rely on other people to let us know what we do not know about ourselves. This means we have to have a mutually reinforcing social relationship with others; we must be able to listen and understand the context and content of what others tell us, and above all, we must respect their way of knowing, and thus their opinions. These are the foundations for social learning and collective action that underpin individual and social system change, and hence lead to development. Chapter 3 has shown that social learning and collective action are critical among smallholder farmers who as individuals cannot influence or even access the external competitive markets. Competitive and individualistic learning where folks steal from each other and hide the best bits for themselves only leads to their being exploited by opportunistic businessmen. In this kind of situation, it is important to get the social relations right as it constitutes a key resource for the resource poor farmers to manage crises and shocks and to sustain steady growth (Woolcock, 2002). Elsewhere, Fafchamps and Minten (2002) show how social networks enhance the vital trustworthy and efficiency in smallholder agriculture business. Strengthening capabilities for social learning among smallholder farmers is the way to enable them adapt to 'turbulent' market dynamics.

Enhancing social learning among the vanilla farmers involved creating relationships and having time for learning and reflection. To be able to support such learning extension workers need to understand and sense the dynamics of teamwork, but also need to be able to work in teams themselves. The cases do confirm one of the initial presumptions put forward in Chapter 1 suggesting that in order for graduates to influence change in society the university must develop innovation competence within its own staff in order to be able to develop such competence among the students. As Chapter 5 shows, developing innovation competence in an African university where staff motivation is very low is more complicated than just designing a training programme. A more holistic programme is necessary targeting change in mindsets and integrating competences that reward staff through teaching, research and consultancy. An important first step is to enhance self-awareness as a primary competence for enhancing learning for personal growth and social change which by nature is participative – based on interactive exchanges of knowledge and experiences. It is such participative engagements that may lead to more democratic and accountable societies that trigger and support grassroots development and systemic innovations. Based on this research it can be concluded that without capabilities for self-awareness, academics and their graduates will always find it difficult to influence development and consequently their anticipated contribution to building democratic societies will remain largely rhetorical.

Inducing and managing change in social systems

Unpredictability of people's responses is often what makes change in social systems especially complicated. As discussed in Chapter 2, people resist to be changed, but it is often a pleasure when they are motivated to change themselves. In fact "we" cannot change people; educators can only influence change through learning. The challenge of development practitioners is to create motivation for individuals and organisations to learn and change themselves according to the changing environment. It has been argued, based on management literature that organisations learn through people who learn – hence organisational learning is an outcome of individuals learning together. The thesis has documented an exercise in individuals learning together based on the assumption that the way to sustain individual and organisational learning is to create a shift in the mind-sets of people, so that they begin to see the world differently, so opening up new frontiers for learning.

The personal mastery and systemic 'soft' skills approach used in the competence development programme sets a platform for change in mindsets where people begin to explore their own processes of change. Personal feedback, for example, opens new grounds for learning in an inspirational way. As people become more aware of what else they could do beyond their present capabilities, they begin to desire to take action and change. The interactive processes of inspiring one another collectively lead to organisational learning and change. With new mind-frames to accommodate alternative views, a shared organisational vision takes shape, providing a basis for re-examination of organisational cultures, rules and structures. The basic theory of the process examined is that the value realised by individuals from their own change processes creates the social energy and motivation for organisational change. Outcomes of the innovation competence development case, as described in this thesis, then provided evidence that the aggregate effect of individual change increased the potential for organisational change. People are motivated to change by their dissatisfaction with the status quo, and by having options for achieving a shared vision. However, it has been shown that pursuing change is not easy; it requires social support through collective action and shared responsibility.

Theory suggested that through continuous reflection, people can better understand their organisation and take initiative to explore other dimensions of change that ultimately lead to improved organisational performance, and that such systemic interventions may trigger change in the entire system, resulting in effects far exceeding expectations. From the innovation competence development case study, this thesis has provided evidence that change in mindsets of individuals was capable of effectively and beneficially influencing the way professionals conduct training, research and consultancy. We also saw that those individuals then begin to influence the management of the social system. The most important intervention for social change, it has been suggested, is the shift in mindsets which creates fertile ground for new learning. This type of learning opens doors for system-wide change that is less threatening and therefore more likely to be sustainable.

The core of organisational development and system change processes, as suggested by the outcomes of the innovation competence development case (Chapter 7), lies in the ability to create alternative worldviews in people while at the same time supporting them to gain confidence to manage their own change. In the context of rural development, expert knowledge and skills only come in to support a change process in motion, but they themselves cannot induce change in a social system. Expert knowledge is an essential but scarce public good – hence the need to find the most effective way to utilise the scarce resource. Effective utilisation of the scarce resource requires an organised demand side – the smallholder farmers to articulate exactly what they want from the 'experts'. Chapter 3 showed the inability of vanilla farmers to demand services, even for problems related to soil-borne diseases and nutrient management, where they thought research and extension might have a solution. A demand-driven agricultural service delivery that the Ugandan Government has embarked on (Chapter 4) will be severely hampered unless smallholder farmers are assisted to organise themselves to generate demand for expert knowledge. Farmers also need to have opportunities to engage in the mind-set changing activities through which lecturers in research and extension have engaged. This remains a major challenge for scaling up of results reported in this thesis beyond the university.

Development of and access to tools for making change

To induce and manage change in social systems, two critical tools are required: facilitation and communication skills (*cf.* Woolcock, 2006). They are essential in all professional activities as discussed below.

Facilitation

Acting in an innovation system is a new paradigm for African universities (Makerere is just an example). This new paradigm is emerging out of dilemmas of dealing with complex development challenges such as poverty. Chapter 1 portrayed recent policy reforms in many African countries as aiming at increasing efficiency to deal with development challenges where poverty is at the core. Universities as flag-bearers of education cannot escape the pressure to justify their relevance to those challenges. In order to cope with pressures that often arise, we have to learn new ways of mentally tackling situations, which frequently involve changes in procedures, the way we relate to others and how we physically perform tasks (Harri-Augstein and Webb, 1995). In this view, university lecturers have to absorb new ways of training, and learn new ways of doing research and consultancy resulting in development impact, a demand that was never made explicit before. Chapter 7 presented facilitation competence as a key tool for steering mental, social and physical change in the way people do things; a mental shift is the primary change required at all levels (farmers, agricultural professionals, lecturers and students). The mental shift, however, has to be guided by a new vision for personal and organizational performance. Chapter 5 described how such a compelling vision could be developed to commit the university leadership and lecturers to ensure continuous change and adaptation. Similarly Chapter 4 illustrated the centrality of facilitation competence to influence change in the community, and especially in innovation systems characterized by multiple stakeholder engagement and conflicts typical for such an arrangement. It is therefore concluded that facilitation competence is an important tool for fostering learning for change in a development context.

Facilitation competence should not be separated from professional training. Our own personal experiences with education and basic teaching and learning preferences shape our habits of mind about how we influence others to learn (Cranton and King, 2003). If students have never experienced facilitative learning it is unlikely that they will apply it in their future professional career. In training people to work with community, universities must apply facilitative approaches that instill the values of shared learning among future professionals because whatever they are expected to do to influence change in society will require facilitation.

Communication

Like facilitation, communication is a basic tool for professional practice in the field of agriculture – influencing change among farmers is a communicative process. Emphasis on communication here is different from simply taking or offering a course on communication as part of the curriculum. A review of literature has shown that universities cannot fundamentally change the quality of their graduates via curriculum reviews. The underlying challenge is how the curriculum is implemented – *i.e.* how the curriculum content is taught. Chapter 7 provides evidence that what changes a person is not necessarily 'what' but 'how' a subject is taught to her/him. Passing an exam (as usually happens in a university) in a communication course, for example, does not guarantee that one can actually communicate anything at all outside the exam room. The outcomes of the innovation competence development case study (Chapter 7) suggested that communication for practitioners who are pre-occupied with problem solving requires practical engagement processes through which people learn among other things to:

- talk to one another in a respectful manner regardless of their social and technical diversity;
- respect different opinions, appreciate how the diversity of opinions enriches the learning process and become comfortable with living with diversity;
- listen actively to others, as much as lecturers or researchers are listened to – give others a chance to put forward their views as much as they would like to be allowed to put forward their own views;
- encourage and support others to develop their full potential through constructive feedback;
- challenge conventional thinking, culture, and values without appearing arrogant, and build consensus to redirect focus towards personal and shared benefits;
- resolve conflicts of understanding, perception and interpersonal relationships to build teams that strive to achieve a common goal.

Development and access to facilitating and communication tools demands practical engagement and can be enhanced by peer-coaching. Unlike academics, who communicate primarily with peers, practitioners find themselves at the interface of many different worlds – researchers, donors, governments, multi-lateral agencies, activists, NGOs, and poor communities, and thus need to be able to operate in multiple communicative modalities (Woolcock, 2006). For this Woolcock says development professionals need the core competences of 'detectives', 'translators', and 'diplomats', all of which from his explanation have strong elements of communication.

In short, communication is the tool that integrates professionals in society and allows them effectively to influence change from within as members of that social system. But universities train students as if all were destined to become academics who largely communicate with peers. They focus on teaching scientific writing and presentation, forgetting that most graduates will end up working with communities where scientific communication skills are not required. The essential communication skills for interacting with communities of farmers and poor people are acquired through practice and not by just studying them. In Chapter 7 it was shown that interactive learning approaches open up both the lecturers and students to exchange knowledge, or to co-create knowledge through communicative processes. Interaction between the university and the rural community, as proposed in Chapter 1 (*cf.* FAO and World Bank,

2000), enhances the development of communication and facilitation competences for both the students and lecturers in actual situations with smallholder farmers.

Therefore if universities are to produce the professionals that society expects to bring about social change they must ensure that their graduates are well equipped with facilitation and communication competences, but it also follows that those competences must exist among university lecturers in the first place. To acquire such competences class sizes must be reasonable enough to allow practical engagement. This thesis (Chapter 7) has provided evidence that lecturers who worked with relatively small class sizes practiced interactive teaching more than those who had large classes. Therefore, a 'bloated' student intake as a source of revenue without corresponding increase in facilities and staff at the university will undoubtedly curtail access to such critical competences.

Solution-oriented thinking and practice in an African university

We talk of innovations because we are looking for solutions that fit problems as they appear in a specific context and change is only possible if we are committed to going through the challenges it presents with determination and hope. However, solution oriented thinking and commitment to undertake change in the community is not in the mainstream of academia, particularly in the African context. For example, the primary objective of developing a research project by university lecturers is publication in peer-refereed journals, because that is what counts most in their career development. Development, to which universities are now challenged to contribute, is all about finding solutions to existing problems, and poverty is the biggest problem of all in the case of Uganda. This requires re-orientation of thinking and new skills in adapting the traditional functions of universities: viz., training, research and consultancy. The competence development case study presented in this thesis illustrates how developing competences for action research and process consultancy is one way to fulfil academic functions while at the same time contributing to development and poverty alleviation. If this approach seems convincing then it means that African universities have to forego, or better still challenge the relevance of, some of their traditional ways of doing science. Ingenuity is needed to adapt ways of doing science to the poverty agenda. To encourage this type of creativity, the African university must develop new criteria for staff performance appraisal and reward. In the new performance criteria for the African university of the 21st century, contribution to development and quality of teaching will need to feature more prominently.

This thesis (Chapter 4) has also shown that for agricultural professionals to enhance innovations in the community they must forego their traditional roles of 'problem solvers' and become co-learners finding joint solutions with farmers and other stakeholders through participatory experimentation. African scientists need to be able to break out of routines that reinforce the status quo and explore creative and unorthodox ways of solving complex problems. Through such engagement creativity will be unleashed, as scientists begin to rise to and relish the challenge of solving neglected and complex problems drawn to their attention through community engagement This will imply much risk taking. But taking a risk and trying out new things will depend on building up the ability of researchers to reflect on their actions, draw lessons and adapt accordingly – in short, they must become reflective practitioners. This is the type of transformation that the innovation competence development programme at Makerere seeks to pioneer. In addition to technical "experts" the African university will also have to produce "change makers", if it is at all to adapt itself to current development challenges.

When people find solutions that work for them they take charge of their own development and become entrepreneurial thinkers. I borrow Gibb's (2000) notion of entrepreneurship as it relates to ways in which people, in all kinds of organisations, behave in coping with and taking advantage of uncertainty and complexity, and how in turn this can become embodied in ways of feeling, communicating and learning things. It has already been argued in this thesis (Chapter 1) that the African university needs to produce more entrepreneurs than bureaucrats. But entrepreneurship is not acquired by proclaiming it, or by teaching its theory, as happens in so many universities. It is rather an emergent property of practical engagement in solution finding. To produce entrepreneurs university lecturers must also become entrepreneurs, in the sense that they must also find workable solutions to problems in diverse contexts. Action research and process consultancy have been highlighted in this thesis as mechanisms for enabling lecturers to become educational or research entrepreneurs, and thus in effect the true educators characterised by Cranton and King (2003) as thriving on the application of their learning. In this type of engagement, the focus shifts from getting tasks done to getting a problem solved, which involves a lot of creativity and adaptation. In justifying their existence, African universities must not only claim to be contributing to solving national problems through their actions, they must be seen to be doing so. This in itself will be a value change resulting from self-awareness, respecting other forms of expertise and engaging with other to find solutions and a commitment to make change. This thesis has discussed an example of the design and implementation of a learning programme to attain just such a value change. It is one way the African university could break out of its colonial inheritance to offer innovative and promising solutions to 21st century problems. Otherwise the university will remain on the periphery of development, with the rest of African society regarding it as an expensive irrelevance.

Developing a culture of authenticity

Authenticity is the expression of the genuine self in a community (Cranton, 2001). It is distinguishing oneself from the others with respect to norms and values. One of the outcomes of the innovation competence development case study was an emerging culture of commitment, accountability and desire to build a legacy of authenticity. Education should be seen as a way of promoting good citizenship, socialising people to fit into a profession or organisation, providing building blocks of democracy, improving productivity, cultivating future leaders and freeing people from oppression (Cranton and King, *ibid.*). University lecturers, who are at the apex of the education 'pyramid', are expected to be role models and leaders in promoting those values by example. But it is a critical challenge to incorporate ethical and aesthetical dimensions of learning in the curriculum (Wals *et al.,* 2004). Morals and ethical conduct are not seen as a responsibility of the university, yet the university expects its_graduates to behave ethically and in a morally acceptable way. Development without a strong moral base remains fragile. African universities need to re-discover and champion the moral values of African societies which largely have been eroded by corruption and bad governance. It needs to promote a strategy for building authentic professional leaders. These values include being accountable to society, a commitment to professional service, honesty and transparency in professional transactions, and a_passion to serve for reasons that go beyond money.

In other words the African university should be a place for building a generation whose activities and values will lay the foundation for the prosperity of future generations. Though the task is far from easy, and opinions vary even about the basic standards, this thesis has described a process which opens up gains in empathetic feelings, care for others and social responsibility, on which a culture of authenticity might be founded. Without the university embracing this task, the would-be 'liberators' (university graduates) of society may turn out to be those who undermine collectivity. As we strive to *"build for the future"*, as the Makerere University motto says, we need to be aware of the possible unintended consequences of an education that undermines Africa in the 21st century by failing to spread respect for social solidarity and human rights.

Conclusions

This thesis has described an attempt to transform education and research in a specific African university. The cycle of change is as yet in its early stages, so it is not possible to offer an analysis based on widespread impact. What has been attempted here is to describe the change process, and to analyse as clearly as possible its underlying logic, pointing out on the way any obvious problems posed and overcome. Time will tell whether the initiative has indeed laid the foundations for a new kind of poverty-alleviating professionalism among Ugandan agricultural professionals. It would be inappropriate to speculate on these longer terms outcomes. But the three case studies do allow some conclusions to be drawn, in terms of possible lessons for the African university more generally:

1. **The African university and the community**. The dynamics of the market for agricultural products in smallholder agriculture has surpassed the response capacity of research and extension organisations, and by implication the scope of university education. It is argued that focus on traditional export cash crops (such as coffee and cotton for Uganda) by research, extension and in agricultural training, will only increase poverty among the smallholder farmers, as prices for such products rapidly and consistently decline. New opportunities for smallholder farmers emerge with non-traditional niche market crops such as vanilla (in the case of Uganda) in which research and extension are unable to respond fast enough while the demand lasts. This thesis has shown how farmers adapt to new opportunities through social learning. By their training, agricultural professionals are 'shy' and incapable of engaging with farmers in social learning processes, because their functions in such situations are quite different from the "expert" advisors they were trained to be. In

such circumstances agricultural professionals become irrelevant in helping smallholder farmers gain the adaptive capacity to cope in a rapidly changing environment. It is therefore imperative that the African universities re-orient their programmes to produce graduates capable of enhancing innovation and social change in the community of smallholder farmers. But university lecturers must acquire the necessary competences first. What is desired is a transformation where the 'expert' of yesterday becomes the 'change maker' of today who is actively welcomed into rural social networks as a trusted knowledge broker.

2. **Policy.** From a policy perspective, the participative and democratic paradigms of development have implicitly imposed new roles for development professionals but in practice the professionals have not changed. Inclusiveness, people determining their own development agenda, and their involvement throughout the development process, have rendered top-down approaches irrelevant. In Uganda, for example, agricultural research and extension organisations have inevitably had to adopt a demand-led approach to service delivery. They are required to account for their activities by way of their impact on livelihoods (or development) and not necessarily in terms of scientific production and productivity as before. These new forms of accountability have exposed competence deficiencies for agricultural professionals. Woolcock (2006) puts it clearly that development is not a single (if highly complex) technical problem awaiting a solution from a lone genius or a single discipline; development is necessarily inherently a multi-dimensional problem, and thus will require multi-dimensional responses and integrated skills sets (cf. Hobart, 1993: 1). But mere change in policy and institutional structures will not result alone in effective demand-led service delivery. Deliberate efforts are needed to address the competence challenges of such a system, since the current training regimes are not in fact fit-for-purpose_ in a collaborative demand-led world. For the professionals, specialised technical expertise is not enough. They need social skills to foster innovation and change among smallholder farmers. The farmers, too, need basic skills to be able to demand relevant services. Consequently, education institutions are challenged to produce a new "breed" of professionals for the contemporary development paradigms. The present thesis has shown one route towards such new competences.

3. **The meta-challenge for the African university of the 21st century.** Competence deficiencies of agricultural professionals reflect the short-comings of their training. Universities as the main source of agricultural professionals are responsible for providing education that does not fit current development needs. Undoubtedly universities need to redesign their curricula, but before that they have to re-examine their own capacity to provide the type of education that ensures the competences demanded by contemporary African society. To shift from producing merely disciplinary 'experts' to producing 'change makers', the African university will have to build its own competence first. This thesis has made clear that the effort requires not only a change in knowledge and skills; the larger task is to transform a 'technical' university into a 'developmental' university, and this (it has been argued) demands a shift in attitudes, mindsets, values and responsibilities. The thesis does not purport to prove that the Makerere experiment is the only way to tackle the task, or that success is guaranteed. What it has done, however, is to show through description

and analysis that the problem is being logically and effectively addressed, and that the signs are so far encouraging.

4. **Transforming the African university.** African universities on their own are incapable of initiating and pursuing fundamental reforms in their way of doing things. They need external help to stimulate systemic thinking that is not in the mainstream of conventional academic practice in richer countries. The African university finds itself on the cutting edge of interventions intended to bring about fundamental organisational change, 'depoliticise' change processes to allow disciplinary integration and collective action, and provide quality facilitation for holistic change within a well-articulated vision. Support is needed to help universities such as Makerere manage their own change processes. There is no panacea for such an intervention. It is a comprehensive change process whose design has to grow from within, taking into account the national and institutional context, motivation and commitment of the staff to engage in a process of learning to change, and potential strategies for mainstreaming and up-scaling change to transcend entrenched institutional cultures.

5. **Triggers for change in the African university.** Targeting change in mindsets with a comprehensive and integrated learning programme is desirable for stimulating fundamental change in the African university. The starting point is to challenge some entrenched beliefs and values, in order to awaken consciousness and desire for personal change towards a preferred future. The incentives for personal change in the African context are benefits that enhance social relations, potential to supplement meagre salaries through worthwhile consultancy activity and professional or career growth. As individuals change, they become more capable to influence change in others and sometimes thereby trigger change in the larger system through new patterns of behaviour and ways of doing things. The point about inspirational champions has been made above, but it is one worth repeating in conclusion. It is sometimes claimed that Africa has plunged into extreme poverty through failures of leadership. The African university of the 21st century is challenged – perhaps above all – to change itself as an act of inspired leadership. The university itself should become the champion of poverty alleviation.

Appendices

Appendix 1: Reflection on my own learning through doing a PhD

Introduction

The thesis, *Learning to make change* is all about learning. As described in the first chapter, the methods used to generate data namely; interviewing, workshops, documentary reviews, participant observation and self-assessment do not adequately represent my own learning in the process of doing this work. I cannot hesitate to say that probably I have learnt more than anybody else referred to in this thesis yet I feel this is not well articulated. It is a general weakness in research and research methods that the investigators appear neutral to the research when actually they are not. Even in situations where researchers are fully engaged like in action research, the methods used to generate data tend to exclude the researcher. As researchers, we observe, listen, ask questions, count, measure and interpret the outcomes as though we ourselves come out of these processes 'unaffected'. We deny ourselves the opportunity to explain our own learning and what changes in us as a result of our engagement in the research.

Even Alvesson and Sköldberg's (2000) description of reflection or reflexivity as "interpreting one's own interpretations, looking at one's own perspective from other perspectives, and turning a self-critical eye onto one's own authority as interpreter and author", focuses on how we present our findings but misses out our own learning journeys. In this case one would say that if the thesis is examined and successfully defended, then what obviously changes about the researcher is a title against his name. The fact is that more important changes have taken place than a mere title. I therefore use this opportunity to reflect on my own learning journey through the process of doing a PhD. For purposes of structure, I reflect on my experiences with respect to phases of the PhD process.

Why a PhD?

If you asked people why they chose to or wish to do a PhD, there can be as many different reasons as the people asked. Our motivations to go through the not so pleasant processes are diverse. Some people describe it as "Permanent head Damage" and yet many more are striving to have it. From my interactions with people who go or wish to go through that level of academic achievement, the main reasons could be one or more of the three:
- It is a requirement for job security and/or increases opportunities for better jobs.
- It is a prestigious achievement for self actualisation. Only a minute percentage of the world population have it and it is worth the struggle.
- If there is an opportunity, why not? Once an opportunity presents itself, one just takes it on.

For my case, I happened to be in the first category. A PhD is a requirement for my employment in the university. If I don't get it, I have to think of alternative employment. What is apparent in all these grounds is the self-centredness of higher education. It appears, the higher you go in academic ranks, the more you think about and for yourself. In contrast, when I ask children what they would like to be, they often give answers like these:

- "I want to be a doctor because I want to treat people".
- "I want to be a police man/woman because I want to arrest wrong people". In other words, they want to contribute to law and order in society.
- "I want to be an engineer because I want to have nice buildings in the city".

At this level, children are clear what they want to do for society if they succeeded. In their wishes, they express a strong feeling for others and a sense of responsibility to society. At the highest levels of education, people tend to emphasise what they want to do for themselves. It appears that advancement in education is accompanied by a transition from thinking and feeling for society to thinking and feeling for self.

I had never reflected on this transition until I started a PhD. More interestingly, this happened outside the 'normal' PhD activities. It was in a workshop on enhancing professional skills where the facilitators posed the question: *looking back at your personal background, organisation and the critical problems you face in your country, what would your PhD change?* As Cranton (2002) says, sometimes to ask the right challenging question at the right moment is the most important thing we can do to bring about transformation in a student. This question turned my worldview of a PhD. I started to think about its value beyond satisfying my personal desires. The power of that question was in the opportunity to reflect on my background and the relevance of my academic achievement to others. Having come from a poor rural background, my educational achievement is attributed more to many coincidences rather than my ambitions and abilities per se. By coincidences I mean the instances like at various levels of education, you are lucky to have a relative who can pay your school fees, another one who can provide accommodation, and probably another one who can support with scholastic materials. A majority of intelligent students in Africa cannot go far in pursuing their educational ambitions just because they lack those basic necessities. With that background, I was challenged to think beyond my self.

This reflection made me not only change my research topic but also how to conduct the research. Initially, I intended to study farmer organisations – why they fail or succeed. This would obviously be achieved by interviewing people, analysing the responses and writing a thesis. Likely it would not change anything in reality like many other good studies haven't. Challenged by what my PhD would change, I developed the motivation to engage in research that would contribute to changing something in reality. Indeed I was inspired to learn to make change. That is how I came to do my research on a change process within my institution (Makerere University), which again I would describe as another coincidence of opportunity.

Falling into the academic trap: the divide between academics and development

With the motivation and vision described above, I started developing the research proposal in which the research questions were phrased starting with, "*How to...*". For this, I was challenged whether what I wanted to do was academic or development. Ideally academic research questions are phrased starting with, "*What ....*" Presumably the 'what' allow critique from an 'independent' view, which is the essence of academic research. The 'how' puts you in a position of doing things or for that matter finding solutions and that is understood to be development. It was tough and at some point frustrating to defend the "how to ..." in academic research. I had strong conviction and a compelling vision of what I wanted to do but then it was being challenged in the mainstream academics. To my consolation, there were some academics who were more encouraging and supportive of my thinking. I maintained my intentions though with adjustments in the phrasing of research questions but well aware of the challenge to make the research satisfactory from an academic view.

From these challenges, I came to understand that in academics, what matters most is the argument put forward rather than how things really are. Rigor of analysis is what lends credence to the argument or debate. Through this, I learnt that 'thesis' basically means an 'argument'. One can draw a parallel of this type of academic with the practice of law. Winning or losing a case in court depends on how well a lawyer argues the case but that does not necessarily mean that an offence or crime was/was not committed. The aim of the defendant is to discredit the evidence presented by prosecution to prove innocence. Relating this to the critical problems we face in Africa such as poverty and hunger, I was not convinced that we needed to invest so much into merely putting up critical arguments or debates. Not that I am against critical debates, but such debates would be more beneficial if situated in practical solutions to the problems we face. May be we need a new type of "academics" for Africa.

The lesson I learnt from these experiences is that we cannot run away from critical thinking, systemitisation and rigorous analysis, otherwise we get lost in doing things and end up making mistakes that would otherwise be avoided. What is critical is to be able to design rigorous processes that explore issues at depth and always take a step back to critique what we do in view of anticipated goals. This way, it is possible to achieve the academic rigor and contribute to solving real problems concurrently.

Doing the research, a way of learning to make change

Doing the field research was a great learning experience for me. To start with, I was part of the innovations competence development programme that aimed at influencing change in the University by targeting change in individual lecturers. Engaging in this process as an action researcher, I learnt two important things that have had profound impact on my career; facilitation and documentation. Through these, I have discovered my hidden potentials to make change; gained exposure to different ways of thinking about development and academics; acquired skills for engaging in research and consultancy to influence change; enhanced abilities to relate theory and practice; and more important, learning to learn – *i.e.* learning from every experience through reflection. I will only highlight a few incidences related to these issues.

By practicing facilitation skills in different fora, some people recognised my abilities to guide processes. This earned me several invitations to facilitate meetings, some of very high calibre. I will give only two examples in this respect. First was the invitation to facilitate a three-day retreat on micro-restructuring of Makerere University and harmonisation of operations between top management, establishment and administration committee, and planning and development committee. This was amidst contradictions of a new policy, the Tertiary Institutions Act and the University Act. As a mere lecturer in the same university, this was an enormous challenge but it was also an opportunity to engage with my employers to find a solution to a real challenge of our institution. At the end of it, I was more encouraged by the high level of participants' satisfaction. To express this satisfaction, the University Planner who hired me for the job said; "what I am going to pay you is not worth the job you have done". Little did he know that I was already satisfied by the success of the meeting and the complements of appreciation from my superiors. From this experience, I learnt that what matters most in organisational management is what people agree to do together and not necessarily what the laws stipulate. The challenge in such situations is how to come to a consensus to do things in a particular way for the good of the organisation.

Second example was the opportunity to facilitate a high level consultative meeting on "Food Fortification for Africa", organised by the New Partnership for Africa's Development (NEPAD). This meeting aimed at harmonizing food fortification initiatives in Africa and exploring opportunities for partnerships and collaboration of the different actors. Again this was a high level of trust in me to be offered such opportunity. Each of these, of course presents challenges but the lessons gained are life-long. With regard to my research, it was because of the facilitation skills that I was invited to participate in the IAR4D initiative, which provided the opportunity to interact more intensively with researchers and academicians to understand the practical challenges of IAR4D.

Through documenting the PM/SS learning process as part of my research, I developed skills for process documentation. As a researcher, the intention was to capture all processes and events for purposes of my data collection and feedback to participants. While doing that, it did not occur to me that this was a skill or service that is required by many organisations. Good process documentation creates transparency and is a form of accountability as well as reference material. I have been to many international meetings to document processes especially those that relate to strategic planning and organisational reform processes. Documentation is itself a discipline required in all organisations but it has to be developed.

Often we are not aware of how much potential we have to do things. Much of our potential is obscured by 'clouds', which are beliefs about ourselves – what we believe we are and/or can be. Even a PhD does not clear those 'clouds', in fact it might be another 'cloud'. The only way to clear the 'clouds' to see more of our potential is to "learn to learn". Learning to learn requires being aware of our ignorance – realising that there is much more to learn than we know, acknowledging that our worldviews are limited, accepting that we can learn from everybody, and believing in our capability to do much more than we are now able to.

Writing the thesis: the lonely journey

You never know how difficult a thesis can be until you start writing one. It is probably the loneliest and most frustrating part of the PhD process. Lonely because only you fully understands and can best interpret your data. As is often with young researchers, you well know what your data means but you have to write it in such a way that other people understand it the way you do. Aside from the data and its analysis, the art of writing becomes critical. Peers and supervisors can advise but the bottom line is that you have to learn to do it yourself. It is at this stage that frustration and despair sets in. I have heard many of my peers say, "If I had known all that it takes, I would not have done it". But it is a point of "no return" considering the investment made so far in terms of time and resources, it is worth the perseverance. It is a process that demands a lot of social support and encouragement from peers, supervisors and family.

The pressure to get it done make you feel that you must spend all the time reading literature, doing data analysis and writing. From experience, what I have found most critical is the planning of the thesis. Spending time to think through your work to find patterns that make logical flow and having a strategy to accomplish the task saves a lot of time and frustrations in the long run. A strategy is necessary. You have to know where to start in order to make a break through. Otherwise, iteration though unavoidable can turn out to be frustrating if it does not lead to progress. Navigating your way through definitely requires a lot of self-discipline and having a flexible work regime. Time spent to rest and relax is as valuable as time spent working. There is no panacea; every individual has to get a formula that works for them.

Influence of my worldview on the research

I am aware that my world view and my own learning experiences inevitably influenced the research and the other way round is also true. No researcher can claim that their research is independent of their way of thinking. In essence it is just a matter of honesty and disclosure but even then it is difficult to know how much one's worldview influences their research. Firstly, my conviction that universities should play a dual role of academics and development is different from those who think the two cannot be performed without severely compromising the identity of the university. The design and implementation of this research is situated in my opinions, which may seem obvious to the reader.

Secondly, my own learning experience makes me believe that it is possible to change the mindsets shaped by our disciplinary training and type of education we have had. It is possible to learn new things that have never been in our mainstream professions – real fundamental change is possible. This undoubtedly influences my position of critique or analysis of issues. Alternative view point would probably lead to different conclusions.

Thirdly, my involvement as an active participant in two of the case studies in many ways influenced the interpretation of data and probably the data itself. For many of the things I write about, I have a real-life personal experience. My analysis is not that of an outsider, or an "independent", it is grounded in context and experience. While interviewing my colleagues who participated in the innovation competence development programme, I did my best to restrain from giving my own experiences to avoid biases in their stories but I am still not aware how much could have slipped unconsciously.

Fourthly, I could have been overzealous with the view that universities and research and extension organisations are responsible for the current woeful state of agriculture and small scale farmers in the largely poor sub-Saharan Africa. It would not be fair to put the blame squarely on them; there are many players in this arena. In addition, I recognise the limitations and constraints that are beyond their control to make their desired positive contributions. My intention however is to create awareness that they have contributed to the status quo. Hopefully they can then reflect and find ways to improve their service delivery to benefit society.

Conclusion

In conclusion, I put it that a PhD is not enough, neither is it an end in itself. The bigger challenge is to demonstrate the difference it makes in the lives of other people. Failure to do that, one would be happier without it. The public in general invests so much in a PhD and it is only fair that they get returns to that investment.

Appendix 2: Instrument for self-assessment on impact of the PM/SS programme

B1-B12 are individual profiles that PM/SS programme can influence. This instrument aims at assessing the profoundness of the profiles (before and after) as perceived by participants of the PM/SS programme. You are kindly requested to take a bit of your valuable time to objectively score yourself on a scale of 1 to 10 for these criteria where 1 is the least score and 10 the highest score.

Indicator of successful personal mastery	Score before PM/SS programme	Score after PM/SS programme	Triggers of change	How change manifested
B1: Uses professional networks and alliances for exchange of information and experiences and to pursue common interests				
Actively links to relevant peers and builds professional relationships based on mutual exchange and benefit	1-2-3-4-5-6-7-8-9-10	1-2-3-4-5-6-7-8-9-10		
Sees opportunities and synergies in linking different people and sources for partnerships for joint ventures and synergies	1-2-3-4-5-6-7-8-9-10	1-2-3-4-5-6-7-8-9-10		
Shares experiences with peers and feeds the networks with information	1-2-3-4-5-6-7-8-9-10	1-2-3-4-5-6-7-8-9-10		
Continuously seeks to enlarge the network	1-2-3-4-5-6-7-8-9-10	1-2-3-4-5-6-7-8-9-10		
B2: Promotes team development and consensus building in teams				
Brings together people to work on common interests and enhances collaboration rather than competition	1-2-3-4-5-6-7-8-9-10	1-2-3-4-5-6-7-8-9-10		
Volunteers to do extra work for the sake of improving group performance towards the common interests without taking away from the group the responsibility and ownership	1-2-3-4-5-6-7-8-9-10	1-2-3-4-5-6-7-8-9-10		
Integrates him/herself into teams in a subtle way	1-2-3-4-5-6-7-8-9-10	1-2-3-4-5-6-7-8-9-10		
Is reliable and only makes promises he/she can keep	1-2-3-4-5-6-7-8-9-10	1-2-3-4-5-6-7-8-9-10		
Trusts the other team members and focuses on their strengths rather than on their weaknesses	1-2-3-4-5-6-7-8-9-10	1-2-3-4-5-6-7-8-9-10		

Learning to make change

Recognises and accommodates differences in personalities, interests and speed	1-2-3-4-5-6-7-8-9-10	1-2-3-4-5-6-7-8-9-10			
Sees other team members as partners rather than competitors	1-2-3-4-5-6-7-8-9-10	1-2-3-4-5-6-7-8-9-10			
Gives and accepts feed back	1-2-3-4-5-6-7-8-9-10	1-2-3-4-5-6-7-8-9-10			
Uses appropriate tools to foster team development and performance	1-2-3-4-5-6-7-8-9-10	1-2-3-4-5-6-7-8-9-10			
Recognises the successes of others without bias, envy and jealousy	1-2-3-4-5-6-7-8-9-10	1-2-3-4-5-6-7-8-9-10			

B3: Initiates and facilitates group processes of joint reflection, strategy and vision development and decision making

Stands confidently in front of groups and applies appropriate tools to manage group work and group dynamics	1-2-3-4-5-6-7-8-9-10	1-2-3-4-5-6-7-8-9-10		
Listens considerately and rapidly identifies the points participants put forward	1-2-3-4-5-6-7-8-9-10	1-2-3-4-5-6-7-8-9-10		

B4: Manages and minimizes conflicts

Accommodates other colleagues' interests and speed	1-2-3-4-5-6-7-8-9-10	1-2-3-4-5-6-7-8-9-10		
Listens actively and respectfully and responds without hurting the feelings of those concerned.	1-2-3-4-5-6-7-8-9-10	1-2-3-4-5-6-7-8-9-10		
Clearly analyses and communicates own and other parties' interests and respectfully negotiates solutions	1-2-3-4-5-6-7-8-9-10	1-2-3-4-5-6-7-8-9-10		
Looks for common ground and goals and win-win solutions rather than emphasising irrelevant differences	1-2-3-4-5-6-7-8-9-10	1-2-3-4-5-6-7-8-9-10		
Reacts quickly when conflicts arise and brings out ill-feelings in an acceptable form	1-2-3-4-5-6-7-8-9-10	1-2-3-4-5-6-7-8-9-10		
Focuses on and brings the interaction down to negotiation of interests rather than positions in discussions and arguments	1-2-3-4-5-6-7-8-9-10	1-2-3-4-5-6-7-8-9-10		

B5: Actively seeks to develop him/herself professionally and personally

Knows him/herself, his / her identity and recognises own behavioural patterns and tries to work on them in order to live up to own vision and values in human interaction	1-2-3-4-5-6-7-8-9-10	1-2-3-4-5-6-7-8-9-10		

Continuously tries to increase the space / freedom within he/she can act through enhanced self-awareness and working against the constraints imposed by oneself or the environment (the 'clouds')	1-2-3-4-5-6-7-8-9-10	1-2-3-4-5-6-7-8-9-10		
Builds a reputation based on demonstrated competence and experiences	1-2-3-4-5-6-7-8-9-10	1-2-3-4-5-6-7-8-9-10		
Demonstrates professional ethics and integrity	1-2-3-4-5-6-7-8-9-10	1-2-3-4-5-6-7-8-9-10		
Is curious and interested to explore and learn new things and does not assume to know it all	1-2-3-4-5-6-7-8-9-10	1-2-3-4-5-6-7-8-9-10		
Considers expectations of students and others "clients" and actively seeks ways to satisfy them (utilising visual aids, interactive teaching etc	1-2-3-4-5-6-7-8-9-10	1-2-3-4-5-6-7-8-9-10		
Considers new ideas even if divergent from own perception	1-2-3-4-5-6-7-8-9-10	1-2-3-4-5-6-7-8-9-10		
Pro-actively seeks and develops opportunities for advancing in an authentic (e.g. business, career, consultancy – marketing oneself)	1-2-3-4-5-6-7-8-9-10	1-2-3-4-5-6-7-8-9-10		
Actively makes reference to core values in negotiation (openness, transparency, respect etc.)	1-2-3-4-5-6-7-8-9-10	1-2-3-4-5-6-7-8-9-10		
Puts himself or herself into the shoes of others, recognises, considers and appreciates differences	1-2-3-4-5-6-7-8-9-10	1-2-3-4-5-6-7-8-9-10		
Evaluates and improves his or her own strengths and weaknesses with regard to others and to relevant professional standards	1-2-3-4-5-6-7-8-9-10	1-2-3-4-5-6-7-8-9-10		
Initiates and regularly uses an organised support from colleagues (Peer learning, individual coaching)	1-2-3-4-5-6-7-8-9-10	1-2-3-4-5-6-7-8-9-10		
Concentrates fully on issues at hand and deeply analyses them without getting paralysed	1-2-3-4-5-6-7-8-9-10	1-2-3-4-5-6-7-8-9-10		
B6: Tries out new things with courage and without fear of failure				
Develops new ideas and dares to try them out	1-2-3-4-5-6-7-8-9-10	1-2-3-4-5-6-7-8-9-10		
Evaluates risks in an informed way	1-2-3-4-5-6-7-8-9-10	1-2-3-4-5-6-7-8-9-10		
Takes risks when there is a good chance of success	1-2-3-4-5-6-7-8-9-10	1-2-3-4-5-6-7-8-9-10		
Dares to make mistakes	1-2-3-4-5-6-7-8-9-10	1-2-3-4-5-6-7-8-9-10		
Learns from failures (does not repeat the same mistakes)	1-2-3-4-5-6-7-8-9-10	1-2-3-4-5-6-7-8-9-10		

Quickly sees opportunities rather than problems and makes use of opportunities arising	1-2-3-4-5-6-7-8-9-10	1-2-3-4-5-6-7-8-9-10		
Has a plan B (alternative plans) – diversifies risks	1-2-3-4-5-6-7-8-9-10	1-2-3-4-5-6-7-8-9-10		
Dares to do unconventional things and challenge conventional wisdom even	1-2-3-4-5-6-7-8-9-10	1-2-3-4-5-6-7-8-9-10		
Is not afraid of the judgement others have about him / her, without being arrogant	1-2-3-4-5-6-7-8-9-10	1-2-3-4-5-6-7-8-9-10		

B7: Deals with unforeseen situations in a positive and solution-oriented way

Remains relaxed and fearless in unforeseen situations and is confident to manage them	1-2-3-4-5-6-7-8-9-10	1-2-3-4-5-6-7-8-9-10		
Quickly adapts to changes in the system and the environment adequately and with optimism	1-2-3-4-5-6-7-8-9-10	1-2-3-4-5-6-7-8-9-10		
Sees opportunities and positive elements even in frustrating situations (does not get deeply discouraged or paralysed by fear)	1-2-3-4-5-6-7-8-9-10	1-2-3-4-5-6-7-8-9-10		
Stands out difficulties with perseverance	1-2-3-4-5-6-7-8-9-10	1-2-3-4-5-6-7-8-9-10		
Has a wide variety of methods and tools to work with people and can adapt them in any contexts	1-2-3-4-5-6-7-8-9-10	1-2-3-4-5-6-7-8-9-10		

B8: Shares information in a free and transparent and accountable manner

Counters manipulative efforts in the system through sharing information and creating awareness	1-2-3-4-5-6-7-8-9-10	1-2-3-4-5-6-7-8-9-10		
Informs colleagues and subordinates about relevant issues and events in the system and beyond	1-2-3-4-5-6-7-8-9-10	1-2-3-4-5-6-7-8-9-10		
Communicates timely and clearly using respectful communication techniques	1-2-3-4-5-6-7-8-9-10	1-2-3-4-5-6-7-8-9-10		

B9: Gives and receives feedback as a tool to develop him/herself and others personally

Accepts and uses constructive criticism for self-development	1-2-3-4-5-6-7-8-9-10	1-2-3-4-5-6-7-8-9-10		
Incorporates feedback from students and colleagues (for better lecturing)	1-2-3-4-5-6-7-8-9-10	1-2-3-4-5-6-7-8-9-10		
Pro-actively encourages other to give honest feedback	1-2-3-4-5-6-7-8-9-10	1-2-3-4-5-6-7-8-9-10		

Promotes a culture of feedback in his/her environment and uses appropriate tools (e.g. Johari Window)	1-2-3-4-5-6-7-8-9-10	1-2-3-4-5-6-7-8-9-10	

B10: Develops and Pursues clear vision and values in his/her professional environment

Shares the vision with others in a transparent manner and influence them to engage in a shared vision	1-2-3-4-5-6-7-8-9-10	1-2-3-4-5-6-7-8-9-10
Builds his/her decisions on the vision and articulated values in a consistent and authentic way	1-2-3-4-5-6-7-8-9-10	1-2-3-4-5-6-7-8-9-10
Influences and supports colleagues within the organisation to develop and follow a clear vision	1-2-3-4-5-6-7-8-9-10	1-2-3-4-5-6-7-8-9-10

B11: Assumes leadership roles (formal and informal) to enhance individual, team and organisational performance

Brings together people to work on common interests	1-2-3-4-5-6-7-8-9-10	1-2-3-4-5-6-7-8-9-10
Recognise own potentials and increases sphere of influence without creating resistance	1-2-3-4-5-6-7-8-9-10	1-2-3-4-5-6-7-8-9-10
Installs core values in co-operation and actively calls for their practical application in teams and in relationships with other colleagues, partners and stakeholders	1-2-3-4-5-6-7-8-9-10	1-2-3-4-5-6-7-8-9-10
Integrates and supports efforts and initiatives of other colleagues within his/her subsystem or the larger system	1-2-3-4-5-6-7-8-9-10	1-2-3-4-5-6-7-8-9-10
Delegates tasks, opportunities and power to colleagues according to clear performance criteria	1-2-3-4-5-6-7-8-9-10	1-2-3-4-5-6-7-8-9-10
Rigorously follows up on initiatives and processes he/she pursues	1-2-3-4-5-6-7-8-9-10	1-2-3-4-5-6-7-8-9-10
Effectively organises the use of human and financial resources around performance criteria in order to pursue common interests	1-2-3-4-5-6-7-8-9-10	1-2-3-4-5-6-7-8-9-10
Recognises differences in personalities and adequately reacts to individual strategies of dealing with stress	1-2-3-4-5-6-7-8-9-10	1-2-3-4-5-6-7-8-9-10
Takes time to listen and to comfort team members and other colleagues in times of high group or individual stress	1-2-3-4-5-6-7-8-9-10	1-2-3-4-5-6-7-8-9-10
Remains calm and self-controlled even under stressful situation	1-2-3-4-5-6-7-8-9-10	1-2-3-4-5-6-7-8-9-10

Manages closeness and distance to colleagues and subordinates in a way which allows friendship and good relationships while maintaining respect and authority	1-2-3-4-5-6-7-8-9-10	1-2-3-4-5-6-7-8-9-10		
Supports others to develop their potentials by encouraging them to try out new things and backing them up when they take risks	1-2-3-4-5-6-7-8-9-10	1-2-3-4-5-6-7-8-9-10		
B12: Pursues a balanced life style				
Consumes a balanced diet and takes drugs in a reflected way (alcohol, nicotine etc.)	1-2-3-4-5-6-7-8-9-10	1-2-3-4-5-6-7-8-9-10		
Recognises and addresses his/her spiritual needs adequately	1-2-3-4-5-6-7-8-9-10	1-2-3-4-5-6-7-8-9-10		
Identifies causes of reactions of weakness, pains and illness of his/her body and adapts daily habits to it (e.g. reduce consumption of coffee, give the body some exercise, more sleep, yoga)	1-2-3-4-5-6-7-8-9-10	1-2-3-4-5-6-7-8-9-10		
Accepts his/her emotional, spiritual, physical and mental needs and actively looks for a balanced way to satisfy them	1-2-3-4-5-6-7-8-9-10	1-2-3-4-5-6-7-8-9-10		
In moments of stress and depression, directs his/her inner eye to the positive resources at his(her disposal (memories of success and strength, periods of high performance and appreciation, people who really love him/her)	1-2-3-4-5-6-7-8-9-10	1-2-3-4-5-6-7-8-9-10		

References

Abdalla, Y.A., Egesa, K.A. (2004) "Trade and Growth in Agriculture: A Case Study of Uganda's Export Potential within the Evolving Multilateral Trading Regime", Bank of Uganda Working Paper WP/05/01.

Adams, C., Adams, W.A. (1999) "The Whole Systems Approach^{SM}: Using the Entire Organization to Transform and Run your Business", in Holman, P., Devane, T., eds., *The Change Handbook: Group Methods for Shaping the Future,* San Francisco: Berret-Koehler Publishers, Inc., pp. 139-155.

ADC/IDEA (2000) "ADC Commercialisation Bulletin No. 1".

Allen, M. (1988) *The Goals of Universities*, SRHE and Open University Press.

Altbach, P.G., (1998). "Comparative Perspectives on Higher Education for the Twenty-first Century", *Higher Education Policy* 11: 247-356, Elsevier Science Ltd.

Alvesson, M., Sköldberg, K. (2000) *Reflexive Methodology: New Vistas for Qualitative Research*, SAGE Publications.

Archibald, S., Richards, P. (2002) "Conversion to Human Rights? Popular Debate about War and Justice in Rural Central Sierra Leone", *Africa* 72(3), 339-367.

Asiimwe, D., Ezati, E., Mugisha, F, Muhangi, D., Onweg, T., Nnsabagasani. (2001) "Decentralisation and Human Resources Demand Assessment from the Perspective of the Districts", Makerere University.

Bagnall-Oakeley, H., Ocilaje, M., Oumo, F., Nangoti, N., Oruko, L., Rees, D., (2004) "Mapping and Understanding Farmers' Indigenous Agricultural Knowledge and Information Systems and the Implications for Contracted Research and Extension Systems", *Uganda Journal of Agricultural Sciences* 9: 119-125.

Bahiigwa, G., Rigby, D., Woodhouse, P. (2005) "Right Target, Wrong Mechanism? Agricultural Modernization and Poverty Reduction in Uganda", *World Development* 33(3): 481-496.

Banathy, B.H. (1995) "There is No More Important Task than Transforming Education by Design", *Journal of systems practice and action research* 8(3): 259-262, Plenum Publishing Corporation.

Banathy, B.H. (1999) "Systems Thinking in Higher Education: Learning Comes to Focus", *Systems Research and Behavioral Sciences* 16: 133-145, John Wiley and Sons Ltd.

Bank of Uganda (2004) "Annual Reports for the Period 1984 – 2003", Uganda.

Barnett, R. (1994) *The Limits of Competence: Knowledge, Higher Education and Society,* Bristol: The Society for Research into Higher Education (SRHE) and Open University Press.

Barnett, R. (2000) "Reconfiguring the University", in Scott, P., ed., *Higher Education Re-formed*, Falmer Press, pp.141-129.

Baumgartner, L.M. (2001) "An Update on Transformational Learning", *New Directions for Adult and Continuing Education* 89: 15-24, Jossey-Bass Publishers.

Bellah, R. (2005) "Durkheim and ritual", In J. C. Alexander & P. Smith, eds., *The Cambridge Companion to Durkheim*, Cambridge: Cambridge University Press.

Bernard, H.R. (1988) *Research Methods in Cultural Anthropology,* Sage Publications.

Bhorat, H. (2005) "Poverty, Inequality and Labour Markets in Africa: A Descriptive Overview", Development Policy Research Unit – Working Paper 05/92, University of Cape Town.

Blandy, R., Dawkins, P., Gannicott, K., Kain, P., Kasper, W., Kriegler, R. (1985). *Structured Chaos: The Process of Productivity Advance,* Melbourne: Oxford University Press.

Boyatzis, E.R., Cowen, S.S., Kolb, A.D. (1995) "Introduction: Taking the Path Toward Learning", in Boyatzis, E.R., Cowen, S.S., Kolb, A.D. and Associates, eds., *Innovation in Professional Education: Steps on a Journey from Teaching to Learning,* Jossy-Bass Publishers, pp. 1-11.

Brewer, G.D. (1999) "The Challenges of Interdisciplinarity", *Policy Sciences* 32: 327-337.

Bronckbank, A., McGill, I. (1998) *Facilitating Reflective Learning in Higher Education,* Society for Research into Higher Education and Open University Press.

Brown, M.S. (1999) "A systemic Perspective on Higher Education in the United Kingdom", *Systems Research and Behavioral Science* 16: 157-169, John Wiley and Sons Ltd.

Bua, A., Okorio, J., Kataama, D., Mutabazi, S., Okwadi, J. (2004) "Study on the Process of Technology Development and Uptake in the National Agricultural Advisory Services (NAADS)", Preliminary Report.

Byamungu, G.T.M. (2002) "The Polity of the Syllabus: Pattern Shifting the African Postcolonial Episteme", in Imunde, H.L., ed., *Reflections on Education in Africa,* Loccumer Protokolle, pp.15-24.

Cambron-McCabe, N., Dutton, J. (2000) "Wheels of Learning", in Senge, P., Cambron-McCabe, N., Lucas, T., Smith, B., Dutton, J., Kleiner, A. *A Fifth Discipline: Schools that Learn,* New York: Doubleday, pp. 93-98.

Carnegie Forum on Education and the Economy (1986) "A Nation Prepared: Teachers for the 21st Century", San Diego, California.

Carney, D. (2003) *Sustainable Livelihoods Approaches: Progress and Possibilities for Change,* Department for International Development (DFID), UK.

Chambers Dictionary (1995), London.

Checkland, P. (1981). *Systems Thinking, Systems Practice.* Chichester: John Wiley.

Chiang, A.H. (2005) "The University as a Learning Organisation: A Case Study of Teamwork and Team Learning in a Private University in Taiwan", *Proceedings of HERDSA Annual Conference,* Sydney, 3-6 July, pp. 101-109.

Clegg, S. (2003). "Problematising Ourselves: Continuing Professional Development in Higher Education", *International Journal for Academic Development* 8(1/2): 37-50. Routledge, Taylor and Francis Ltd.

Coleman, J.S. (1984) "Universities in the New States of Africa and Asia", in Hetland, A., eds., *Universities and National Development: A Report of the Nordic Association for the Study of Education in Developing Countries,* Stockholm: Almqvist & Wiksell International, pp. 85-104.

Conley, T., Udry, C. (2001) "Social Learning Through Networks: The Adoption of New Agricultural Technologies in Ghana", *American Journal of Agricultural Economics* 83(3): 668-673.

Corcoran, P.B., Wals, A.E.J., eds. (2004). *Higher Education and the Challenge of Sustainability: Problematics, Promise and Practice.* Dordrecht: Kluwer Academic Publishers

Cowen, S.S. (1995) "Lessons Learnt: Guiding Strategic Change in Higher Education", in Boyatzis, E.R., Cowen, S.S., Kolb, A.D., and Associates, *Innovation in Professional Education: Steps on a Journey from Teaching to Learning,* Jossey-Bass Publishers, pp. 15-31.

Cranton, P. (1996) *Professional Development as Transformative Learning,* San Francisco: Jossey-Bass.

Cranton, P. (2001) *Becoming an Authentic Teacher in Higher Education*, Professional Practices in Adult Education and Human Resource Development Series, Kreiger Publishing Company.

Cranton, P. (2002) "Teaching for Transformation", *New Directions for Adult and Continuing Education* 93: 63-71, Wiley Periodicals, Inc.

Cranton, P., King, K.P. (2003) "Transformative Learning as a Professional Development Goal", *New directions for Adult and Continuing Education* 98: 31-37, Wiley Periodicals, Inc.

Creswell, J.W. (1994) *Research Design: Qualitative and Quantitative Approaches,* Thousand Oaks, CA: Sage.

Creswell, J.W. (1998) *Qualitative Inquiry and Research Design: Choosing Among Five Traditions,* Thousand Oaks, CA: Sage.

Cullen, J. (1999) "Socially Constructed Learning: A Commentary on the Concept of Learning Organisation", *The Learning Organisation* 6(1): 45-52, MCB University press.

Delanty, G. (1997) *Social Science: Beyond Constructivism and Realism*, Open University Press.

Dewey, J. (1922) *Human Nature and Conduct: An Introduction to Social Psychology, London*: Allen & Unwin.

Dillon, J., Wals, A.E.J. (2006) "On the Dangers of Blurring Methods, Methodologies and Ideologies in Environmental Education Research", *Environmental Education Research*, in Press.

Dorward, A., Kydd, A., Morrison, J., Urey, I. (2004). "A Policy Agenda for Pro-poor Agricultural Growth", *World Development* 32(1): 73-89.

Douglas, M. (1986) *How Institutions Think* Syracuse, NY: Syracuse University Press.

Douthwaite, B., Ekboir, J.M., Twomlow, S., Keatinge, J.D.H. (2004) "The Concept of Integrated Natural Resource Management (INRM) and its Implications for Developing Evaluation Methods", in Shiferaw, B., Freeman, H.A., Swinton, S.M., eds., *Natural Resource Management in Agriculture: Methods for Assessing Economic and Environmental Impacts*, CAB International, pp. 321-340.

Dreyfus, A., Wals, A.E.J. (2000) "Anchor Points for Integrating Sustainability in Higher Agricultural Education", in Van de Bor, W., Holen, P., Wals, A.E.J., Filho, L.W., *Integrating Concepts of Sustainability into Education for Agriculture and Rural Development,* Environmental Education, Communication and Sustainability, vol. 6, pp.73-91, Peter Lang.

Dumbutshena, T.S. (2002) "Colonial Education and the Imperial Purpose – A Historical Perspective: The Anglophone African Experience", in Imunde, H.L., ed., *Reflections on Education in Africa*, Loccumer Protokolle, pp.35-33.

Edquist, C., (ed.) (1997) *Systems of Innovation Approaches: Their Emergence and Characteristics*, London: Cassel Academic.

Eger, M. (1992) "Hermeneutics and Science Education: An Introduction", *Science and Education* 1: 337-348, Kluwer Academic Publishers.

Eilu, G., Turamye, B. (2004) "Baseline Survey on Integration of Natural Resources Management in NAADS Activities", Consultancy Report by the Environmental Conservation Trust of Uganda.

Ellis, F., Biggs, S. (2001) "Evolving Themes in Rural Development 1950s-2000s", *Development Policy Review* 19(4): 437-448.

Epstein, R.M., Hundert, E.M. (2002) "Defining and Assessing Professional Competence". *Journal of American Medical Association* 287(2): 226-235, American Medical Association.

Eshuis, J., Stuiver, M (2005) 'Learning in Context Through Conflict and Alignment: Farmers and Scientists in Search of Sustainable Agriculture", *Agriculture and Human Values* 22: 137-148.

Fafchamps, M., Minten, B. (2002) "Returns to Social Network Capital Among Traders", *Oxford Economic Papers 54*, Oxford University Press, pp 173-206.

FAO and World Bank (2000) *Agricultural Knowledge and Information Systems for Rural Development (AKIS/RD): Strategic Vision and Guiding Principles*, Food and Agricultural Organisation of the United Nations and The World Bank.

Farrington, J., Carney, D., Ashley, C., Turton, C. (1999) *Sustainable Livelihoods in Practice: Early Applications of Concepts in Rural Areas*, ODI Natural Resource Perspectives Number 42, Overseas Development Institute, UK.

Forster, A., Hewson, L. (1998) "Universities Learning: The Lure of the Net, in Latchem, C., Lockwood, F., eds., *Staff Development in Open and Flexible Learning*, London: Routledge, pp. 221-231.

Franklin, P., Hodgkinson, M., Stewart, J. (1998) "Towards Universities as Learning Organisations", *The Learning Organisation* 5(5): 228-238, MCB University Press.

Friis-Hansen, Kisauzi, D. (2004) "Evolution of Extension-farmer Relationship in Uganda", *Proceedings of Workshop on Extension and Rural Development: A Convergence of Views on International Approaches*, Washington D.C.12-15 November, 2002,

Galbraith, P.L. (1999) "Universities as Learning Organisations – or Not?", *Proceedings of 17th International Conference of the System Dynamics Society and 5th Australian and New Zealand Systems Conference*, Wellington, July.

Galli, R., Teubal, M. (1998) "Paradigmatic Shifts in National Innovation Systems", in Edquist, C., ed., *Systems of Innovation. Technologies, Institutions and Organisations*, London and Washington: Pinter, pp. 342—370.

Garrant, B. (1997) "The Power of Action Learning", in Pedler, M., ed., *Action Learning in Practice*, Third Edition, Gower Publishing Ltd., pp. 15-29.

Geelan, D.R. (1997) "Epistemological Anarchy and the Many Forms of Constructivism", *Science and Education* 6: 15-28, Kluwer Academic Publishers.

Gibb, A.A. (2000) "SME Policy, Academic Research and the Growth of Ignorance, Mythical Concepts, Myths, Assumptions, Rituals and Confusion", *International Small Business Journal* 18(3): 13-35, SAGE Social Science Collections.

Glasersfeld, von E. (1995) *The Radical Constructivism: A Way of Knowing and Learning*, The Falmer Press.

Goldschmid, M.L., (1998) "Strengthening Traditional Academic Values and Increasing Efficiency and Quality in Higher Education: Is it Feasible?", in Massey, T.B., ed., *Proceedings of the 23rd International Conference on Improving University Teaching, Dublin City University*, Dublin Ireland, Vol. 1 (CPD no 238).

Goldschmid, M.L., (1999) "Creating a New University: a Way of Transforming Higher Education?", A Paper Presented at the Annual International Conference, HERDSA Melbourne, 12-15 July 1999.

Government of Uganda (GoU) (1992). "Uganda Government White Paper on Implementation of the Recommendations of the Report of the Education Policy Review Commission", Government of the Republic of Uganda.

Government of Uganda (GoU) (2001) "The National Agricultural Advisory Services Act, 2001", Acts Supplement No. 9, The Uganda Gazette No. 33, Volume XCIV.

Grabove, V. (1997) "The Many Facets of Transformative Learning Theory and Practice", *New Directions for Adult and Continuing Education* 74: 89-96, Jossey-Bass Publishers.

Guiton, P. (1999) "Professional Reflective Practice and Lifelong Learning", in Harry, K., ed., *Higher Education Through Open and Distance Learning: World Review of Distance Education and Open Learning,* Volume 1, Routledge, pp. 48-56.

Hagmann (2000) "Vision-based Assessment: A Methodology to Mainstream Pilot Initiatives in Organisations", www.picoteam.org

Hagmann, J. (2002) "Competence Development in Soft Skills/Personal Mastery", Report on a Consultancy Mission to Design a Learning Programme at Makerere University, Uganda. Rockefeller Foundation (Unpublished).

Hagmann, J. (2005) "LearningWheel - Creating Common Frameworks for Joint Learning, Action and Knowledge Management: AGREN Newsletter No 52, July 2005, http://www.odi.org.uk/agren

Hagmann, J., Almekinders, C., with Bukenya, C., Guevara, F., Hailemichael, A., Isubikalu, P., Kamau, G., Kamanga, B., Kibwika, P., Limnarankul, B., Matiri, F., Mutimukuru, T., Ngwenya, H., Opondo, C., Zhang, L., Breitschuh, U. (2003) "Developing 'Soft Skill' in Higher Education", *PLA Notes*, No. 48, pp 21-25.

Hagmann, J., Chuma, E., Connolly, M., Murwira, K. (1997) *Propelling Change from the Bottom-up: Institutional Reform in Zimbabwe,* IIED Gatekeeper Series No. 71, International Institute for Environment and Development, UK, 19 pp.

Hall, A., Bockett, G., Taylor, S., Sivamahan, M. V. K., Clark, N. (2001). "Why Research Partnerships Really Matter: Innovation Theory, Institutional Arrangements and Implications for Developing New Technology for the Poor", *World Development* 29(5): 783–798.

Hansen, H.B. (2002) "The Colonial State's Policy Towards Foreign Missions in Uganda", in Hansen, H.B.; Twaddle, M. (Eds.), *Christian Missionaries and the State in the Third World,* James Currey Ltd., Ohio University Press, pp. 157-175.

Harri-Augstein, S., Webb, I.M. (1995) *Learning to Change: A Resource for Trainers, Managers and Learners Based on Self-Organised Learning,* McGraw-Hill International (UK) Limited.

Harvey, L., Knight, P.T. (1996) *Transforming Higher Education,* The Society for Research into Higher Education and Open University Press.

Heron, J., Reason, P. (2001) "The Practice or Co-operative Inquiry: Research 'with' Rather than 'on' People", in Reason, P., Bradbury, H., eds., *Handbook of Action Research: Participative Inquiry and Practice*, Sage Publications, pp. 179-188.

Heymann, F., Wals, A. (2002) "Cultivating Conflict and Pluralism Through Dialogical Deconstruction", in Leeuwis, C., Pyburn, R., eds., *Wheelbarrows Full of Frogs: Social Learning in Rural Resource Management*, Royal Van Gorcum, Assen, pp. 25-47.

Hobart, M. (1993) "Introduction: The growth of Ignorance", in Hobert, M., ed., *An Anthropological critique of development: The Growth of Ignorance*, Routledge, pp. 1-30.

I@mak.com (2001) "Application Guidelines for Funds from I@mak.com: Makerere University Capacity Building Programme for Decentralisation", Makerere University.

ICRA-NATURA (2003) "Mobilising Partnerships for Capacity Building in Integrated Agricultural Research for Development (IAR4D)", Documentation of a Workshop Held at the International Agricultural Centre (IAC), Wageningen, The Netherlands, 27-29 November, 2003.

Ison, R. L. (1990) *Teaching Threatens Sustainable Agriculture*, IIED Gatekeeper Series No. SA21, International Institute for Environment Development, Sustainable Agriculture Programme, London, 20 pp.

Ison, R.L. (1999) "Applying Systems Thinking to Higher Education", *Systems Research and Behavioral Science* 16: 107-112, John Wiley and Sons Ltd.

Ison, R.L. (2001) *Systems Practice at the United Kingdom's Open University*, http: //scholar.google. com/scholar?as_q=Systems+practice+at+the+United+Kingdom%27s+open+university

Jaeger, A.J. (2003) "Job Competence and the Curriculum: An Inquiry into Emotional Intelligence in Graduate Professional Education", *Research in Higher Education* 44 (6): 615-639. Human Science Press, Inc.

Johnson-Bailey, J., Alfred, M.V. (2006) "Transformational Teaching and the Practices of Black Women Adult Educators," *New Directions for Adult and Continuing Education* 109: 49-58, Wiley Periodicals, Inc.

Juma, C., (2005) *We Need to Reinvent the African University*, available from http: //www.scidev.net/ content/opinions/eng/we-need-to-reinvent-the-african-university.cfm

Kanter, M.R. (1995) "Mastering Change", in Chawla, S., Renesch, J., eds., *Learning Organizations: Developing Cultures for Tomorrow's Workplace,* Portland: Productivity Press, pp. 71-84.

Kasozi, A.B.K. (2003) *University Education in Uganda: Challenges and Opportunities for Reform*, Fountain publishers.

Kegan, R. (2000) "What Form Transforms: A Constructive-developmental Approach to Transformative Learning", in Mezirow, J. and Associates, eds., *Learning as Transformation: Critical Perspectives on a Theory in Progress*, Jossey-Bass, pp. 35-69.

Kibwika, P., Tibezinda, J.P. (1998) "Participation of Youth in Agriculture in Iganga District, Uganda." *MUARIK Bulletin* 1: 1-5.

King, C., Jiggins, J. (2002) "A Systematic Model and Theory for Facilitating Social Learning", in Leeuwis, C., Pyburn, R., eds., *Wheelbarrows Full of Frogs: Social Learning in Rural Resource Management*, Royal Van Gorcum, Assen, pp. 25-47.

Kline, S.J., Rosenberg, N. (1986) "An Overview of Innovation", in Landau, R., Rosenberg, N., eds., *The Positive Sum Strategy: Harnessing Technology for Economic Growth*, Washington: National Academic Press, pp. 275-305.

Knapper, C.K., Cropley, A.J. (1985) *Lifelong Learning and Higher Education,* New Hampshire: Croom Helm.

Kovac, V., Ledic, J, Rafajac, B. (2003) "Academic Staff Participation in University Governance: Internal Responses to External Quality Demands", *Tertiary Education and Management* 9: 215-232, Kluwer Academic Publishers.

Kreutzer, P.D. (1995) "FASTBreak^{TM}: A Facilitation Approach to Systems Thinking Breakthroughs", in Chawla, S., Renesch, J., eds., *Learning Organizations: Developing Cultures for Tomorrow's Workplace,* Portland: Productivity Press, pp. 229-242.

Kyeyune, R. (2002) "Colonial Education and the Imperial Purpose – A Historical Perspective: The Anglophone African Experience", in Imunde, H.L., ed., *Reflections on Education in Africa*, Loccumer Protokolle, pp.35-49.

Latour, B., Woolgar, S. (1986) *Laboratory Life: The Construction of Scientific Facts*, Princeton University Press.

Laurillard, D. (1999) "A Conversational Framework for Individual Learning Applied to the Learning Organisation and the Learning Society", *Systems Research and Behavioral Science* 16: 113-122, John Wiley and Sons Ltd.

Levin, M., Greenwood, D. (2001) "Pragmatic Action Research and the Struggle to Transform Universities into Learning Communities", in Reason, P., Bradbury, H., eds., *Handbook of Action Research*, London: Sage Publications, pp. 103-113.

Light, G., Cox, R. (2001) *Learning and Teaching in Higher Education: The Reflective Professional*, SAGE Publications.

Liles, R.T., Mustian, R.D. (2004) "Core Competences: A Systems Approach for Training and Organisational Development in Extension", *The Journal of Agricultural Education and Extension* 10(2): 77-82.

Lippitt, L.L. (1999) "Preferred futuring™: The Power to Change Whole Systems of any Size", in Holman, P., Devane, T., eds., *The Change Handbook: Group Methods for Shaping the Future,* San Francisco: Berret-Koehler Publishers, Inc., pp. 159-174.

Lundvall, B.A., Johnson, B., Andersen, E.S, Daalum, B. (2002) "National Systems of Production, Innovation and Competence Building", *Research Policy* 31: 213-131, Elsevier

Lysons, A. (1999) "Strategic Renewal and Development Implications of Organizational Effectiveness Research in Higher Education in Australia", *Tertiary Education Management* 5: 49-64, Kluwer Academic Publishers.

Macpherson, M. (1964) *They Built for the Future: A Chronicle of Makerere University College 1922-1962*, Cambridge University Press.

Maiteny, P.T., Ison, R.L. (2000) "Appreciating Systems: Critical Reflections on the Changing Nature of Systems as a Discipline in a Systems-learning Society", *Journal of Systems Practice and Action Research* 13(4): 559-586, Plenum Publishing Corporation.

Makerere University (2003) *Annual Report 2003*, Makerere University.

May, T. (1997) *Social Research: Issues, Methods and Process*, Second Edition, Open University Press.

Mazrui, A.A. (2003) "Towards Re-Africanizing African Universities: Who Killed intellectualism in the Post Colonial Era?" *Alternatives: Turkish Journal of International Relations*, 2(3&4): 135-163.

McGill, I., Beaty, L. (1995) *Action Learning: A Guide for Professional, Management and Educational Development*, Second edition, London: Kogan Page.

McKernan, J. (1991) *Curriculum Action Research: A Handbook of Methods and Resources for the Reflective Practitioner*, New York: St. Martin's Press.

McNiff, J., Lomax, P., Whitehead, J. (2003) *You and Your Action Research Project*, 2nd Edition, London: RoutledgeFalmer.

Memorandum of Understanding (MoU) (2003) "Learning Together for Change in Integrated Agricultural Research for Development in Uganda: A Memorandum of Understanding between the National Agricultural Research Organisation (NARO) of Uganda, Makerere University (MAK) and the International Centre for Development Oriented Research in Agriculture (ICRA)"

Mettrick, H. (1993) *Development Oriented Research in Agriculture: An ICRA Textbook*, ICRA.

Mezirow, J. (1991) *Transformative Dimensions of Adult Learning*. San Francisco: Jossey-Bass.

Mezirow, J. (1997) "Transformative Learning: Theory to Practice", *New Directions for Adult and Continuing Education* 74: 5-12, Jossy-Bass Publishers.

Mezirow, J. (2000) "Learning to Think Like an Adult: Core Concepts of Transformation Theory", in Mezirow, J. and Associates, eds., *Learning as Transformation: Critical Perspectives on a Theory in Progress*, Jossey-Bass, pp. 3-33.

Mezirow, J. (2003) "Transformative Learning as Discourse", *Journal of Transformative Education* 1(1): 58-63, Sage Publications.

Mezirow, J., and Associates. (2000) *Learning as Transformation*, San Francisco: Jossey-Bass.

Ministry of Agriculture, Animal Industry and Fisheries (MAAIF), (2003) *The National Agricultural Research Policy*, Government of Uganda.

Moran, L., Myringer, B. (1999) "Flexible Learning and University Change", in Harry, K., ed., *Higher Education Through Open and Distance Learning: World Review of Distance Education and Open Learning*, vol. 1, Routledge, pp. 57-71.

Mosse, D. (2005) *Cultivating Development: An Ethnography of Aid Practice*, Pluto, London

Mowery, D.C.; Sampat, B.N. (2004) "Universities in National Innovation Systems," in Fagerberg, J., Mowery, D.C. and Nelson, R.R.,eds., *Handbook of Innovation*, Oxford, UK: Oxford University Press.

Moyo, E., Hagmann, J. (2000) 'Facilitating Competence Development to put Learning Process Approaches into Practice in Rural Extension, in FAO: *Human Resources in Agricultural and Rural Development*, Rome: FAO, pp. 143-157, online at http://www.fao.org/DOCREP/X003/X7925M/X7925M14.htm

Mubangizi, N., Mangheni, M.N., Garforth, C.J. (2004) "Information Sources and Constraints Under National Agricultural Advisory Services Programme, of Service Providers in Uganda", *Uganda Journal of Agricultural Sciences* 9: 257-264.

Mulder, M. (2001) "Competence Development – Some Background Thoughts", *The Journal of Agricultural Education and Extension* 7(4): 147-158.

Murwira, K., Hagmann, J., Chuma, E. (2001) "Mainstreaming Participatory Approaches to SWC in Zimbabwe", in Reij, C., Waters-Bayer, A., eds., *Farmer Innovation in Africa: A Source of Inspiration for Agricultural Development*, Earthscan Publications Ltd.

NAADS (2000). "National Agricultural Advisory Services Programme (NAADS): Master Document, Ministry of Agriculture, Animal Industry and Fisheries (MAAIF), Uganda.

NARO (2003) "*NARO's* "Realigned Strategy and Plan 2003-2005 and Beyond", From a Commodity Based Organisation Towards an Integrated Agricultural Research Service Provider for Development (unpublished).

Nienke, M.B, Tizikara, C. (2002) "Agricultural Science and Technology Indicators: Uganda", *ASTI Country Brief*, No.1.

Nyerere, J.K. (1971) "The Role of an African University", *The Journal of Modern African Studies*, 9(1): 107-114.

Obaa, B., Mutimba, J., Semana, A.R. (2005) "Prioritizing Farmers' Extension Needs in a Publicly-funded Contract System: A Case Study from Mukono District, Uganda", *Agren*, paper No. 147.

Opio-Odong, J.M.A. (1992) *Designs on the Land: Agricultural Research in Uganda, 1890-1990,* African Centre for Technology Studies: ACTS Press.

Opio-Odong, J.M.A. (1993) *Higher Education and research in Uganda,* African Centre for Technology Studies: ACTS Press.

Orsmond, P., Stiles, M. (2002) "University Teaching: A Challenge to Staff Development", *Innovations in Education and Training International* 39(4): 253-255. Taylor and Francis Ltd.

Oxfam-GB and FOWODE (2004) "Obusobozi: Enhancing the Entitlements of Subsistence Farmers in Uganda", A Discussion Paper on the Impact of PMA/NAADS on Female Subsistence Farmers, Kampala (Unpublished).

Page, S., Hewitt, A. (2001) *World Commodity Prices: Still a Problem for Developing Countries?* London: Overseas Development Institute.

Park, P. (2001) "Knowledge and Participatory Research", in Reason, P., Bradbury, H., eds., *Handbook of Action Research: Participative Inquiry and Practice*, Sage Publications, pp. 81-90.

Patel, K.B., Maina, M., Hagmann, J., Woomer, P.L. (2001) "Curriculum Development and Transformation in Rural Development and Natural Resource Management" Documentation of a Strategy Workshop Conducted at the Rockefeller Foundation's Bellagio Center in Italy, 12-16 November, 2001 (Unpublished).

Pawson, R., Tilley, N. (1997) *Realistic Evaluation*. London: Sage.

PEAP (2004*)* "Poverty Eradication Action Plan 2004/5-2007/8", Ministry of Finance, Planning and Economic Development, Government of Uganda.

Pedler, M. (1997) "What Do We Mean by Action Learning? A Story and Three Interpretations", in: Pedler, M., ed., *Action Learning in Practice,* Third Edition, Gower Publishing Ltd., pp. 61-75.

Pedler, M., Aspinwall, K. (1996) *'Perfect plc?': The Purpose and Practice of Organisational Learning*, Maidenhead: McGraw-Hill.

Phillips, D. C. (2000) "An Opinionated Account of the Constructivist Landscape", in Phillips, D.C., ed., *Constructivism in Education: Opinions and Second Opinions on Controversial Issues,* Ninety-ninth Yearbook of the National Society for the Study of Education, University of Chicago Press, pp. 1-16.

PMA (2000) "Plan for Modernisation of Agriculture: Government Strategy and operational Framework for Eradicating Poverty", Ministry of Agriculture, Animal Industry and Fisheries (MAAIF) and Ministry of Finance, Planning and Economic Development (MFPED), Uganda.

Punch, K.F. (2000) *Developing Effective Research Proposals,* Sage Publications.

Purseglove, J.W. (1972) *Tropical Crops: Monocotyledons*, Longman Group Ltd.

Raven, J. (2001) "The Learning Societies, Learning Organisations, and Learning: Their Implications for Competence, Its Development, and Assessment", in Raven, J., Stephenson, J., eds., *Competence in the Learning Society*. New York: Peter Lang Publishing, Inc.

Reason, P., Bradbury, H. (2001) "Introduction: Inquiry and Participation in Search of a World Worthy of Human Aspiration", in. Reason, P., Bradbury, H., eds., *Handbook of Action Research: Participative Inquiry and Practice*, SAGE Publications, pp. 1-14.

Reij, C., Waters-Bayer, A., eds. (2001) *Farmer Innovations in Africa: A Source of Inspiration for Agricultural Development*, Earthscan Publications Ltd.

Retna, S.K. (2005) "Universities as learning organisations: Putting tutors in the picture", *Proceedings of HERDSA Annual Conference*, Sydney, 3-6 July, pp. 422-429.

Revans, R. (1997) "Action Learning: Its Origins and Nature", in Pedler, M., ed., *Action Learning in Practice,* Third Edition, Gower Publishing Ltd., pp. 3-13.

Richards, P. (1993) "Cultivation: Knowledge or Performance?", in Hobart, M., ed., *An Anthropological Critique of Development: The Growth of Ignorance*, pp. 61-78, London: Routledge,

Richards, P. (1995) "Participatory Rural Appraisal: A Quick and Dirty Critique" *PLA Notes*, Issue No. 24, pp. 13-16.

Richards, P. (2006) "Against Discursive Participation: Authority and Performance in African Rural Technology Development." European Association for Studies of Science and Technology, Lausanne Conference, August 2006, Session: Approaching Participation.

Richmond, B. (1993) "Systems Thinking: Critical Thinking Skills for the 1990s And Beyond", *Systems dynamics review* 9(2): 113-133, John Wiley and Sons Ltd.

Rip, A. (1995) "Introduction of New Technology: Making Use of Recent Insights from Sociology and Economics of Technology", *Technology Analysis and Strategic Management* 7: 417-431.

Röling, N. (2004) "Teaching Interactive Approaches to Natural Resource Management: A Key ingredient in the Development of Sustainability in Higher Education", in Corcoran, P.B., Wals, A.E.J., eds., *Higher Education and the Challenge of Sustainability: Problematics, Promise and Practice*. Dordrecht: Kluwer Academic Publishers, pp. 181-211.

Röling, N.G. (2002) "Beyond the Aggregation of Individual Preferences. Moving from Multiple to Distributed Cognition in Resource Dilemmas", in Leeuwis, C., Pyburn, R., eds., *Wheelbarrows Full of Frogs: Social Learning in Rural Resource Management*, Royal Van Gorcum, Assen, pp. 25-47

Ross, G.M. (1976) *The university: The Anatomy of Academe*, McGraw-Hill Book Company.

Sayer, A. (1992) *Method in Social Science: A Realist Approach*, Second Edition, Routledge.

Seat, E., Lord, S.M. (1999) "Enabling Effective Engineering Teams: A Program for Teaching Interaction Skills," *Journal of Engineering Education* 88(4): 385–390

Segal, L. (1986) *The dream of reality: Heinz von Foerster's constructivism*, New York: Norton.

Senge, P.M. (1990) *The fifth discipline: The Art and Practice of the Learning Organization,* Bantam New York: Doubleday Dell Publishing Inc.

Singh, B. P. (2002) "Nontraditional Crop Production in Africa for Export", in Janick, J., Whipkey, A., eds., *Trends in New Crops and New Uses*, Alexandria VA: ASHS Press, pp. 86-92.

Smith, D. (2003) "Convergence, The University of The Future and The Future of The University", *AI and Society: The Journal of Human-centred Systems and Machine Intelligence* 17: 1-11, Springer-Verlag, London.

Spradley, J.P. (1980) *Participant Observation,* Holt, Rinehart and Winston.

Srikanthan, G., (2000) "Can Universities Learn", *4th International Research Conference on Quality Management*, Sydney, February.

Ssebuwufu, P.J.M. (2005) "Transforming an African University to be Responsive to Stakeholder Needs: My Personal Experience as Vice-Chancellor of Makerere University 1993-2004", Key-note presentation at the RUFORUM strategic planning meeting, Imperial Resort Beach Hotel, Entebbe, March 30 – 1 April 2005.

Ssekamwa, J.C. (2000) *History and development of education in Uganda*, Second edition, Fountain Publishers

Staver, J.R. (1998) "Constructivism: Sound Theory for Explicating the Practice of Science and Science Teaching", *Journal of Research in Science Teaching*, 35(5): 501-520, John Wiley and Sons, Inc.

Sterling, S. (2000) "The Significance of Systems Thinking to Environmental Education, Health Education and Beyond", in Jensen, B.B., Schnack, K., Simovska, V., eds., *Critical Environmental and Health Education: Research Issues and Challenges,* Research Centre for Environmental and Health Education, The Danish University of Education, pp. 251-270.

Sterling, S. (2001) *Sustainable Education: Re-visioning and Change*. Schumacher Briefing No. 6. Green Books Ltd.

Sterling, S. (2004) "Higher Education, Sustainability, and the Role of Systemic Learning", in Corcoran, B.P., Wals, A.E.J., eds., *Higher Education and the Challenge of Sustainability: Problematics, Promise and Practice*, Kluwer Academic Publishers, pp. 49-70.

Stevenson, C.B., Duran, R.L., Barret, K.A., Colarulli, G.C. (2005) "Fostering Faculty Collaboration in Learning Communities: A Development Approach", *Innovative Higher Education* 30(1): 23-36. Springer Science + Business Media, Inc.

Sutz, J., (2005) *The Role of Universities in Knowledge Production*, available from http: //www.scidev. net/dossiers/index

Tamale, I., Namuwoza, C. (2004) "Addressing the Challenge of Providing Technological Optons that Respond to Demands and Market Opportunities for Vanilla in Uganda: The Experience of Taimex (U) Ltd", *Uganda Journal of Agricultural Sciences* 9: 776-770.

Taylor, E.W. (2006) "The Challenge of Teaching for Change", *New Directions for Adult and Continuing Education* 109: 91-95, Wiley Periodicals, Inc., available from www.interscience.wiley.com

Thorpe, R., Taylor, M., Elliott, M. (1997) "Action Learning: in an Academic Context", in Pedler, M., ed., *Action Learning in Practice,* Third Edition, Gower Publishing Ltd., pp. 145-172.

Tiberondwa, A.K. (1998) *Missionary Teachers as Agents of Colonialism in Uganda: A study of their activities in Uganda 1877-1925*, Second Edition, Fountain Publishers

Uganda Government (1992) "Education for National Integration and Development", Government White Paper on Implementation of the Recommendations of the Report of the Education Policy Review Commission entitled, Kampala (Unpublished).

UNESCO (2003) "Synthesis Report on Trends and Developments in Higher Education Since the World Conference on Higher Education (1998-2003)", UNESCO.

Vavakova, B. (1998) "The Social Contract Between Governments, Universities and Society: Has the Old One Failed", *Minerva* 36: 209-228, Kluwer Academic Publishers.

Verschuren, P.J.M. (2003) "Case Study as a Research Strategy; Some Ambiguities and Opportunities", *Intenational Journal of Social Research Methods* 6(2): 121-139, Routledge.

Wals, A.E.J. (1993) "What You Can't Measure Still Exists", in Mrazek, R., ed., *Alternative Paradigms in Environmental Education Research: Monographs in Environmental Education and Environmental Studies*, Vol.VIII, The North American Association for Environmental Education.

Wals, A.E.J., B. Jickling. (2000) "Sustainability in Higher Education: From Doublethink and Newspeak to Critical Thinking and Meaningful Learning", *Higher Education Policy 15*

Wals, A.E.J., Bawden, J. (2000) "Integrated Sustainability into Agricultural Education: Dealing with Complexity, Uncertainty and diverging Worldviews", *Interuniversity Conference for Agricultural and Related Sciences in Europe (ICA)*, AFANet.

Wals, A.E.J., Caporali, F., Pace, P., Slee, B., Sriskandarajah, N., Warren, M. (2004) "Education for Integrated Rural Development: Transformative Learning in a Complex and Uncertain World", *The Journal of Agricultural Education and Extension* 10(2): 89-100.

Webb, G. (1996) *Understanding Staff Development,* Society for Research into Higher Education & Open University Press.

Weil, S. (1999) "Re-creating Universities for Beyond the Stable State: From Dearingesque Systemic Control to Post-Dearing Systemic Learning and Inquiry", *Systems Research and Behavioral Science* 16: 171-190, John Wiley and Sons Ltd.

Wheatley, J.M. (1999) *Leadership and the New Science: Discovering Order in a Chaotic World,* San Francisco: Berret-Koehler Publishers Inc.

Williams, G. (1993) "Total Quality Management in Higher Education: Panacea or Placebo?", *Higher education* 25: 229-237, Kluwer Academic Publishers.

Wood, H.J. (1995) "Restructuring Education: Designing Tomorrow's Workplace", in Chawla, S., Renesch, J., eds., *Learning Organizations: Developing Cultures for Tomorrow's Workplace,* Portland: Productivity Press, pp. 403-416.

Woodhill, J. (2002) "Sustainability, Social Learning and the Democratic Imperative: Lessons from the Australian Landcare Movement", in Leeuwis, C., Pyburn, R., eds., *Wheelbarrows Full of Frogs: Social Learning in Rural Resource Management*, Royal Van Gorcum, Assen, pp. 317-331.

Woodhill, J., A. (2003) "Dialogue and Transboundary Water Resources Management: Towards a Framework for Facilitating Social Learning", in Timmerman, J. G., Langaas, S., eds., *Environmental Information in European Transboundary Water Management,* IWA Publishing.

Woolcock, M. (2002) "Getting the Social Relations Right: Toward an Integrated Theology, Theory, and Strategy of Development Cooperation", Von Hügel Institute Working Paper WP2002-11 (draft), downloaded July 2006 from http://www.st-edmunds.cam.ac.uk/vhi/research/woolco2.pdf

Woolcock, M. (2006) "Higher Education, Policy Schools, and Development Studies: What Should Masters Degree Students be Taught?", *Journal of International Development*, in press, DOI: 10.1002/jid, John Wiley & Sons, Ltd.

Yin, R.K. (1994) "Case Study Research: Design and Methods", Second Edition, *Applied Social Research Methods Series Volume 5,* Sage Publications.

Summary

Background

There is concern that the present education designed for the 19th century and an industrial machinery no longer suits the complex problems of the post-industrial 21st century. Complexity arises out of the fused multi-dimensional characteristics of social and development problems, yet universities continue to address these as if they were well configured to be addressed by existing academic disciplines. Universities, expected to be champions of educational reforms to suit development needs are themselves challenged concerning their relevance. The challenge is even more crucial for African universities especially those in the sub-Saharan region confronted with persistent and unbearable levels of poverty and food insecurity. Can African universities contribute to the reversal of the situation? Through innovations competence development for university staff, this thesis addresses the question of relevance of the African university in the sub-Saharan region to contemporary development challenges. Farming being an important element in the livelihood of the majority of people in the region, the research focuses on agriculture using Makerere University in Uganda as a specific case.

Experiences of the sub-Saharan Africa suggest that a narrow technological focus, as the driver of development is unlikely to eliminate the pervasive poverty and food insecurity. The problem is more than technological, it is has social and political dimensions and therefore calls for innovative and integrated approaches. In addition to providing education and training, the African university is also expected to influence development change in society through research and outreach. To combine its traditional academic role with a developmental role, staff in the African university must be innovative and actively engage in problem solving in community. This represents fundamental reforms in the university – dealing with the basic elements of changing mindsets, and building a new vision and new skills for training and research amongst the academic staff. Without such radical moves, universities in Africa risk becoming – rightly – obsolete in the face of huge challenges posed by poverty and international commitments such as the Millennium Development Goals.

This thesis describes and evaluates an experiment of innovation competence development for transforming learning, research and consultancy in Makerere University with the hope of making it more innovative and able to influence wider processes of change in society. Transformation is examined specifically from the perspective of learning, innovation and change in agriculture. Making change in society requires innovation competences over and above disciplinary expertise and these competences have to be learnt. The learning starts with the university lecturers, hence the title of the thesis *"Learning to make change"*. Competence has been treated as the capability to learn and influence learning. Innovation has been viewed as an adaptation and translation of learning into options for solving real-life problems in a complex and dynamic environment, while change has been seen as the desirable outcome of learning to improvement of life (or better development).

Summary

Objectives and research design

The overall objective of the study was to establish how the innovation competence development programme for university lecturers could be set-up and implemented to increase relevance of Makerere University to national development. Specifically the study aimed at: (1) identifying the main functions of agricultural professionals in enhancing farmer innovations, (2) identifying the key competence challenges for agricultural professionals to engage in an innovation system, (3) describe how an innovation competence development programme for university lecturers could be designed and implemented to respond to challenges of agricultural development, and (4) determine the contribution of the innovation competence development programme to making universities relevant to development. These objectives were pursued with three case studies: The first case study explores farmer learning and innovation among smallholder vanilla farmers in Uganda. From this, functions of university graduates (*i.e.* researchers and extensionists) in enhancing farmer learning and innovation are proposed. The second case study explores challenges faced by research and extension in demand-driven service delivery systems. These are used to identify competences relevant to functions graduates are expected to perform in innovation systems. These two case studies provide a context for the third case study on the innovation competence development at the university. The third case study focuses on an experiment of how these required competences are first developed in the university staff so as to be passed on to the graduates. The experiment based on personal mastery and systemic "soft skills" as foundation for building broader change skills comprising of six thematic areas namely: personal development, team development, facilitation methods and techniques, organisational development, communication and alternative ways of conducting training, research and consultancy. It involved 26 lecturers from three faculties of Agriculture, Veterinary Medicine and Forestry and Nature Conservation over a period of 1½ years.

The research sought to understand phenomena underlying social structural mechanisms influencing action and practice among vanilla farmers, researchers and extensionists and university lecturers. In this view, the research embraced a combination of constructivism and realism as methodology to take the stance that social reality does not exist independent of the social actors, but at the same time seek the possibility of casual explanations of how that reality is shaped by actors. Data were generated for each case study by a triangulation of methods which included: interviewing, workshops, documentary reviews, participant observation and self-assessment. Key findings of the research are highlighted below.

Findings

With market incentives, farmers learn and innovate through their social networks and interactions. Interpersonal relationship is the mechanism that allows free exchange of knowledge and innovations in an informal way. This learning can however be enhanced by research and extension if they engage to learn with farmers to integrate local and scientific knowledge. To the contrary, researchers and extensionists 'shy' away from social learning processes in preference of linear top-down approaches. By their training, researchers and extensionists are modelled to be 'experts' to provide solutions, while social learning takes place in non-hierarchical interaction with farmers. To facilitate social learning as a way of enabling smallholder farmers gain adaptive capacity, agricultural professionals require new skills and attitudes. They should have competences and mindsets to perform functions which include: knowledge and information brokerage, organisational development, facilitating joint learning and multi-stakeholder dialogues, and developing entrepreneurial skills and attitudes.

In an agricultural innovation system context where services are directed by demand and necessity, both the supply (research and extension) and demand (farmers) sides need innovation competences to enable them function harmoniously. The supply side requires competences to facilitate action learning and experimentation; broker information and knowledge between farmer and other stakeholders; develop and empower local organisations; think systemically, develop teams and work in teams; develop and manage partnerships; and facilitate enterprise development. The demand side also should have capacity to self organise, lobby, advocate and negotiate for services, elect visionary and accountable leadership, act with entrepreneurial attitude, and learn by experimenting. Competences of the demand and supply sides appear to be mutually dependent and this thesis recognises that the supply side has the responsibility to facilitate the emergence of requisite competences on the demand side, while the demand side provides all-important feedback. The implication is that such skills have to be integrated in the professional training of all those likely to work with farmers.

For the African university to integrate those competences in its educational system, the academic staff have to reorient their mindsets towards systemic thinking and integration of disciplines, and learn new skills for facilitating interactive learning processes and linking research and consultancy to development. The innovation competence development experiment at Makerere University provides one possible way of doing that through an integrated learning programme for the academic staff. The experiment presents evidence of enhanced staff capabilities in: self-awareness to fully utilise their potentials; influencing change in organisations through feedback; working in teams and promoting peer learning; facilitating interactive learning and collective action processes; overcoming fear to try out new things as reflective practitioners; communication in problem solving situations; and thinking 'out of the box' to influence development impact through action research and process consultancy.

There is a relationship between innovation competences at the farmer, agricultural professionals and university levels, but those at the university have to be at a meta-level to ensure that agricultural professionals and farmers can be linked. To bring the African university into the mainstream of development, it is argued in this thesis that the university focuses on (a) building relationships across the different levels with regard to learning and change as individual and collective action processes, (b) inducing and managing change in social systems, (c) development of and access to tools for making change, (d) achieving solution-oriented thinking and practice, and (e) attaining to a culture of authenticity

However, some of the challenges of developing innovation competences in the African university include ensuring: appropriate reward systems; feedback mechanism between students, lecturers, management and other stakeholders; dealing with student attitudes and stereotypes to support interactive learning and critical thinking; dealing with embedded institutional cultures and practices to promote innovation; and shifting towards integrated curriculum.

Conclusions

The three case studies allow the following conclusion to be drawn, in terms of possible lessons for the African university more generally:

1. Social learning is inevitable in agriculture, but to support this phenomenon, agricultural professionals need new skills and re-orientation of mindsets. It is therefore imperative that the African universities re-orient their programmes to produce graduates capable of enhancing innovation and social change in the community of smallholder farmers. But university lecturers must acquire the necessary competences first.
2. From a policy perspective, the participative and democratic paradigms of development have implicitly imposed new roles, responsibilities and forms of accountability for development professionals but in practice the professionals have not changed. Deliberate efforts are needed to address the competence challenges of such a system, since the current training regimes are not in fact fit-for-purpose_ in a collaborative demand-led world.
3. The competence deficiencies of agricultural professionals reflect the short-comings of their training. Undoubtedly African universities need to redesign their curricula, but before that they have to re-examine their own capacity to provide the type of education that ensures the competences demanded by contemporary African society. The effort requires not only a change in knowledge and skills; the larger task is to transform a 'technical' university into a 'developmental' university, and this demands a shift in attitudes, mindsets, values and responsibilities.
4. African universities on their own are incapable of initiating fundamental reforms in their way of doing things – they need external help to stimulate systemic thinking that is not in the mainstream of conventional academic practice, and to build capabilities to manage change processes.
5. The fundamental reforms needed in the African university are reorientation of mindsets and building capacities for reflective practice to foster personal and organisational development goals. The starting point is to challenge some entrenched beliefs and values, in order to awaken consciousness and desire for personal change towards a preferred future. The incentives for personal change in the African context are benefits that enhance social relations, potential to supplement meagre salaries through worthwhile research and/or consultancy activities and professional or career growth.

About the author

Paul Kibwika was born on 20th September 1965 at Busambira, Iganga District, Uganda. He joined Makerere University in October 1989 where he graduated with a BSc. Agriculture and MSc. Agriculture (Agricultural Extension) in 1993 and 1997 respectively. After his Bachelors degree, he was employed by the Department of Agricultural Extension/Education, Makerere University as Assistant Lecturer and later promoted to Lecturer in 1998 after his Masters degree. In his thirteen year experience in the University, he has taught several undergraduate courses related to Agricultural Extension Education and Rural Development, and engaged in a wide range of research and consultancy in that field.

He coordinated the Continuing Agricultural Education Centre (CAEC), from 1999 till 2002 when he started on a PhD in the Technology of Agrarian Development (TAD) Group of Wageningen University, The Netherlands. CAEC is a unit in the Faculty of Agriculture that provides short-term non-academic demand-led training programmes for professionals, practitioners and farmers. He also coordinated a Student Internship Programme of the Faculty of Agriculture from 1998 till 2002. The Internship programme enables undergraduate students and their supervisors to gain exposure to real-life problem solving situations. On appointment by the Permanent Secretary, Ministry of Education and Sports, he served as External Examiner to Agricultural Colleges in Uganda for six years.

After writing his Masters thesis on Rural Youth in Agriculture in Uganda, he developed a strong research interest on Youth and their livelihoods. More recently, his professional carrier has been more oriented understanding and supporting processes of "Learning and Change". Within this broad theme, he has special interest in Action Learning, Impact Oriented Research, Local Organisations Development, Change Management and Strategic Planning Processes. In pursuance of these thrusts, he has accumulated substantial experience in facilitation and documentation of such processes. Learning and change are likely to be prominent in his academic and professional carrier in the near future.

Printed in the United States
by Baker & Taylor Publisher Services